W. H. HUDSON

A Biography

W. H. HUDSON

A Biography

RUTH TOMALIN

Oxford   New York

OXFORD UNIVERSITY PRESS

1984

Oxford University Press, Walton Street, Oxford OX2 6DP

London Glasgow New York Toronto
Delhi Bombay Calcutta Madras Karachi
Kuala Lumpur Singapore Hong Kong Tokyo
Nairobi Dar es Salaam Cape Town
Melbourne Auckland

and associated companies in
Beirut Berlin Ibadan Mexico City Nicosia

Oxford is a trade mark of Oxford University Press

First published by Faber and Faber Limited, 1982
First published as an Oxford University Press paperback, 1984

British Library Cataloguing in Publication Data
Tomalin, Ruth
W. H. Hudson.—(Oxford paperbacks)
1. Hudson, W. H. 2. Authors, English—Biography
3. Naturalists—Biography
I. Title
828.8'08   PR6015.U23Z/
ISBN 0–19–281421–4

Library of Congress Cataloging in Publication Data
Tomalin, Ruth.
W. H. Hudson. (Oxford paperbacks)
Reprint. Originally published: London: Faber and Faber, 1982.
Bibliography: p. Includes index.
1. Hudson, W. H. (William Henry), 1841–1922—Biography
2. Authors, English—19th century—Biography.
3. Naturalists—England—Biography. I. Title
PR6015.U23Z852 1984   828'.809 [B]   83–22035
ISBN 0–19–281421–4 (pbk.)

Printed in Great Britain by
Richard Clay (The Chaucer Press) Ltd
Bungay, Suffolk

To Nicholas, Gail and Claire

The power, beauty and grace of the wild creature, its perfect harmony in nature, the exquisite correspondence between organism, form, and faculties, and the environment—all this was always present to my mind....

We want to know more about the living thing, even about its common life habits.

W. H. HUDSON, The Book of a Naturalist

Contents

Part III: 1899–1922

Preface and Acknowledgements

W. H. Hudson was told in his mid-teens that he might die at any moment from a heart attack. He lived to be eighty-one, always deeply in love with life, and deeply secretive also about his age: to be thought younger than he was 'helped him to live'. In a book on his boyhood in Argentina, written in his seventies, he gave only one clue to his date of birth, and this was misleading. He was equally reticent about other dates and facts of interest to biographers, and in his last years he burned many personal papers. His first biographer, Morley Roberts, a close friend for over forty years, had to apply to a nephew in Buenos Aires, after Hudson's death, to find out the birth date and other family particulars for his *W. H. Hudson: a Portrait.* He had to guess at the time of Hudson's arrival in England, and guessed wrongly by five years. There was also some mystery about the date on the marriage certificate: at one point Roberts wondered if Hudson and his wife Emily Wingrave had ever been married at all.

I am grateful to A. P. Watt & Son and to Morley Roberts's executors for permission to quote extracts from this valuable discursive memoir, which appeared in 1924. Other writers have since uncovered the main facts of Hudson's life. In 1929 Dr Fernando Pozzo of Quilmes, Buenos Aires, 'the greatest lover and prophet of Hudson in the new world', identified his birthplace there after long search. In the 1930s family letters came to light showing that he landed in England in May 1874. Another landmark came in the 1940s with the discovery of letters from Hudson to the Smithsonian Institution, Washington, and to the Zoological Society of London, shedding light on the 'lost years' of

17

his life as a young man on the pampas. A great deal of research has now been done into his background, family and early life, following that of Professor Herbert Faulkner West of Dartmouth College, Hanover, New Hampshire, and Mr Masao Tsuda of Tokyo, Japanese Ambassador in Argentina from 1958 to 1963.

I am indebted to these researchers, to others also listed in my Bibliography, and in particular to John R. Payne, Associate Librarian at the Humanities Research Center, the University of Texas at Austin, for generous help, and for his definitive *Bibliography* of Hudson's writings, published in 1977; also to his publishers, William Dawson Ltd, for allowing me to read this in proof.

While writing a short Life of Hudson for H. F. & G. Witherbys' Great Naturalists Series (1954) I was fortunate in meeting Alice Lady Rothenstein, who with her husband, the painter Sir William Rothenstein, had known Hudson well for over twenty years; and in receiving from Mrs Helen Thomas, wife of the poet Edward Thomas, an account of her meeting with Hudson two days before his death. I am grateful to Myfanwy Thomas and to *The Times* for permission to quote from a longer account published later. The late Vita Sackville-West was most helpful in sharing with me her own deep knowledge of Hudson.

While working on the present biography it was a great pleasure to hear from Mrs Caroline Merriam Stuart-Smith and Mr Tom Merriam, two of Hudson's North American relatives, now again living in England; also to meet David Garnett, who as a child naturalist had a unique friendship with Hudson, and Mrs Marcella Carver, who knew him in his last years.

I am most grateful to the Royal Society for the Protection of Birds and The Society of Authors as the literary representative of the Estate of W. H. Hudson for allowing me to read and quote from unpublished letters and papers in their archives and from other sources; to Miss Dorothy Rook, their Librarian, and her successor, Mr Ian Dawson, for invaluable help; to the Smithsonian Institution, Washington, Mr Philip S. Hughes, Acting Secretary, Mr William Deiss and Mr William Cox, Archives, for letters between Hudson and Professor Spencer Fullerton Baird, and for biographical material on Professor Baird; to the Humanities Research Center, the University of Texas at Austin, Mr David Farmer, Assistant Director, and Miss Ellen S. Dunlap, Research Librarian, for letters from Hudson to Margaret Ranee of Sarawak; and to the Lockwood Memorial Library, State University of New York at Buffalo, and Mr Kenneth C. Gay, Curator, for letters from Hudson to Edward Garnett.

Grateful thanks also to Mr G. H. Green, MBE, Librarian at Canning House, Belgrave Square, home of the Hispanic and Luso Brazilian Council, and to his staff, for extensive use of the Hudson Collection there. Other librarians who have greatly helped me include Mr R. Fish, the Zoological Society of London; Mrs S. Balson, the Penzance Library, Cornwall; Mr E. S. Deady, Principal Librarian, West Berkshire County Library, Newbury; Mr H. R. H. Harmer, Local Studies Librarian, West Sussex County Library, Chichester; together with the staff of the British Library Reading Room and the Newspaper Library, the Civil Service Department Library, the Customs and Excise Department Library and Records Department, the Guildhall Library, the Science Reference Library, and reference sections of public libraries at Highgate, Hornsey, St Pancras, Swiss Cottage and Victoria, London, and Kingston-upon-Thames, Surrey.

I owe special thanks to Mr Gordon Phillips, Archivist to *The Times*; also to Mr J. D. Herniman, Clerk to the Justices, Chichester; Mrs A. Hopley, Archivist to the British Museum; Mrs J. Pingree, Archivist to Imperial College, London; Miss Lynne Williamson, Research Assistant, the Pitt Rivers Museum, Oxford; the staff of the Public Record Office and of Surrey County Record Office, Kingston-upon-Thames; and Press Officers of British Rail and Royal Mail Lines Ltd.

Requests for specialized information addressed to the British Museum (Natural History) were most kindly dealt with by Mr I. C. J. Galbraith, Head of the Sub-Department of Ornithology, Mr B. T. Clarke of the Department of Zoology and Mr A. F. Stimson of the Reptile Section, the Department of Zoology. Any mistakes which may nevertheless appear are of course my own.

Many publishing records relating to Hudson were lost by enemy action in the Second World War or have otherwise not survived. I am therefore particularly grateful to Mr Piers Raymond and J. M. Dent Ltd, for giving me access to their records, and for permission to quote three extracts from J. M. Dent's correspondence with Hudson; and, for similar help, to Lord Horder and Gerald Duckworth Ltd, the Longman Group and Dr J. A. Edwards, Archivist to the University of Reading.

I am indebted to *The Times Literary Supplement* and the executors of E. H. Lane Poole and Wilfrid James Hemp for the use, in Appendix 3, of two letters published in 1945; and to Miss Daphne

Lawes and Dr James Fairweather Milne for two further letters on the Lawes family, published in the *Hants and Dorset Magazine* in 1952/3; to Miss Daphne Lawes for much additional help. Also, to the following publishers, authors and their representatives for permission to quote extracts from the works named: Chatto & Windus Ltd and Sir John and Mr Michael Rothenstein, co-executors of Sir William Rothenstein, for *Men and Memories, 1872–1938*, edited by Mary Lago; the Hogarth Press Ltd and the author's literary estate for *Letters of Virginia Woolf*, Vol. II, edited by Nigel Nicolson and Joanne Trautmann; the Longman Group for *Grey of Fallodon* by G. M. Trevelyan; *The Times*, A. P. Watt & Son and the executors of David Garnett for a letter published on 1 June 1956.

Grateful thanks to the following for special information, letters, articles and other help: Mr G. Bernard Berry, the authority on Hudson's connections with Wiltshire; Mr and Mrs T. Blackall; Mr Ernest Morley Cock; Jean Cunninghame Graham (Lady Polwarth); Mr S. Peter Dance; Mr Laurence Davies; Dr James Fairweather Milne; Miss Joan Gibbs; Professor Louis J. Halle; Mr Robert Hamilton; Mr Brian Harris; Mrs Margaret Howard; Mr Edward Hussey; Señora Alicia Jurado; Mr John Lavender; Mr Christopher Lovell; Mr C. G. Maby, CBE; Mr Ernest W. Martin; Mrs Margaret Massey-Stewart; Mr Herbert L. Matthews; Mr William J. Meade; Miss Joan Miller; Mr J. Milvey; Mr Thomas C. Moser; Miss Blanche Osborn; Mr Anthony Pearce; Mrs Félice Spurrier; Mr P. Stanley; Dr John Walker; Mr Colin Watson; Miss Ida Weston; Mrs D. Zielinski.

I should like to thank the Rev. O. R. Tennant, Rector of Talaton, Devon, and Priest-in-charge of Clyst Hydon, for kindly making the Clyst Hydon parish registers available; and Miss E. Baker-Clarke, Clerk to Clyst Hydon Parish Council and Secretary to the Church Council, for telling me about the history of the village. I am most grateful also to Mrs Rosemary Clarke of 23 North Parade, Penzance, Cornwall; Mr and Mrs W. L. Griffiths of Jefferies House, Goring-by-sea, Sussex; Mrs Hope Harris of Greyslea, Itchen Abbas, Hampshire; Mr Edward Morant of Roydon Manor, Hampshire, and many others whose local knowledge helped me in tracing Hudson's links with the countryside; and especially to three of my own family who shared many walks in Hudson's footsteps, and to whom this book is dedicated.

Foreword

Hudson, like most field naturalists, began as a hunter and collector, but so young that at first the wild creatures could easily get the better of him.

In one of his earliest memories, aged about five, he was standing alone by a deep moat surrounding his home on the Argentine pampas, a haunt of water-birds, teal and wild duck and snipe. The banks were tunnelled by rats, and men were at work on the rat-holes with a smoking machine. Suddenly an armadillo bolted from its earth, ran to where he stood and began vigorously burying itself in the ground at his feet.

Determined to capture this marvellous prize unaided, he seized the black bone-cased tail and tugged till his arms ached, throwing himself flat on the ground and exerting all his strength. Still the armadillo went on digging, shovelling mould back over his face, dragging him steadily underground. He had to let go or be smothered.

Another day he set out to raid a *carancho*'s nest, choosing a moment when the birds—large and savage carrion hawks—were out of sight, perhaps tearing a live sheep to pieces, out on the plain, with their great hooked beaks. Despite the danger, he longed

to get up there, above the nest, and look down into the great basin-like hollow lined with sheep's wool and see the eggs, bigger than a turkey's eggs, all marbled with deep red, or creamy white splashed with blood-red! For I had seen *carancho* eggs brought in by a gaucho, and I was ambitious to take a clutch from a nest with my own hands.

21

But the birds returned and flew at him with menacing screams. Crashing back to earth, he had to race for cover.

The small child was warned, too, to run for his life when he saw a snake, and later to kill any he found. Out on the pampas there were other hazards: fierce wild cattle and horses, savage guard-dogs, bloodthirsty pigs that might devour a small boy, 'bones and boots included', leaving only blood-soaked rags behind.

But he was too adventurous, and from the first too enthralled by his surroundings, to stay out of harm's way.

Soon the marauding instinct gave way to the quiet watching of the born field naturalist. He was always asking questions: about swallows, for instance. In autumn they flew north with the other migrants, yet on mild sunny days in winter a few swallows would reappear, 'nobody could guess from where'. And about snakes: once he saw a pit viper curled up in an opossum's nest. The venomous snake, the fierce-tempered beast—could they really have been living peaceably together?

Birds from the first were his great love, and snakes he found irresistible. One mysterious black serpent, unlike any other he had heard of, drew him to wait and watch day after day, 'thrilled with terror', in a thicket of weeds where it had its den. A dangerous secret, he knew; but he could not keep away.

This habit of going off by himself instead of playing with other children at first caused his mother deep anxiety. She would follow and see him mooning about in some wild place, staring into vacancy, as it seemed. Then it dawned on her that he was watching 'some living thing, an insect perhaps, but oftener a bird—a pair of little scarlet flycatchers building a nest of lichen on a peach tree, or some such beautiful thing'. This discovery was a huge relief to her. She had feared the child was going queer in the head.

At fifteen he was still watching, and still solitary from choice; but now it was he who began to feel anxiety. At that age, he knew, he should be outgrowing boyhood amusements and getting ready to earn his living; yet he wanted only to go on as he was, to devote his life to nature. No one else, so far as he knew, had this strange obsession. In a world of strenuous pastoral occupations, sheep-rearing, cattle-driving, slaughtering and trading, he was painfully aware of his own idleness and oddity compared with other youths.

But one family friend, a merchant in Buenos Aires, took a kindly interest in him and his bird-watching. On a visit to

London, this good friend picked up a book in a shop, glanced at a page or two and thought it 'just the right thing to get for that bird-loving boy out on the pampas'.

It was the right thing, and it came at the right moment. The book was Gilbert White's *Natural History of Selborne*, a series of letters—field-notes, country lore, questions, speculations—written to fellow naturalists by an English country curate towards the end of the eighteenth century.

What could be more remote from young Hudson's situation? Yet, as he read, he realized that he had far more in common with this long-dead Englishman than with his own brothers, let alone his Spanish neighbours. One letter went straight to the root of his trouble, his isolation:

> It has been my misfortune never to have had any neighbours whose studies have led them towards the pursuit of natural knowledge; so that, for want of a companion to quicken my industry and sharpen my attention, I have made but slender progress in a kind of information to which I have been attached from childhood. (Letter 10.)

From this modest opening the same letter went on to subjects astonishingly familiar. First to the question of wintering swallows: was there real evidence that some would stay behind while the rest migrated? Then the writer described a species of 'water rats' living on the banks of a stream, and spoke of wild ducks and snipe on marshy ground, and a falcon that attacked them.

Another letter said that a female viper was supposed to swallow her young 'on sudden surprises, just as the female opossum does her brood into the pouch under her belly . . .' There were notes on jackdaws nesting in rabbit burrows—as miner birds nested in rodent burrows on the pampas—and owls raiding a dovecot, as a marauding owl had done to the Hudsons' dovecot.

A companion to quicken my industry and sharpen my attention . . . In England, it seemed, there were men like White and his friends who shared his own feeling for nature, his dedicated watching and questioning. The surrounding plain with its marshes, groves and thickets became in secret 'my parish of Selborne', and from that time he thought of England as home, 'the land of my desire'. He had no idea that he would ever see it. But, while still a young man, he crossed the Atlantic and spent the rest of his life here.

. . .

Tuesday, 19 May 1925, was a day of bright sunshine in London, dappling the turf of a tree-shaded enclosure on the north side of

Hyde Park. That morning a crowd gathered beside the railings to see the Prime Minister, Stanley Baldwin, unveil a piece of sculpture inside the enclosure. A carved inscription read: *This sanctuary for birds is dedicated to the memory of William Henry Hudson, writer and field naturalist.* He had died three years earlier.

Great love and care had gone into the planning of the memorial. A monument of white Portland stone stood behind a shallow pool, with a raised base where birds could alight to bathe and drink beside jets of running water. The designers had wished to add a life-sized figure of Hudson himself, 'lying on the grass and watching the birds in the water'. But portrait sculpture was forbidden in the Royal Parks. What the Prime Minister unveiled was the Rima Panel, carved in the stone monument by Jacob Epstein.

Rima was the mysterious girl in Hudson's forest story *Green Mansions*; a symbol of wild nature threatened by man, and perhaps symbolic also of some quality in Hudson, something primitive, innocent and savage, offset from the crowd. The sculptor had to show this allegoric figure in outlines positive enough to be seen sixty or seventy feet away, washed over by moving lights and shadows from foliage and water. To this task he devoted seven months, working in a lonely forest shack, surrounded by trees, mist and silence. The result, *The Times* said, 'is pretty sure to be found one of the most beautiful memorials in the country'.

Experience showed, however, that any imaginative work by Epstein was pretty sure to be violently attacked. Rima brought an uproar 'unequalled', the sculptor wryly noted, 'for venom and spite'. One onlooker claimed that at the moment of unveiling the Prime Minister was so staggered at what he saw that his jaw dropped, and he forgot the usual handshake of congratulation to the sculptor. Letters of protest appeared at once in the press, vilifying the work, with threats and demands for its removal—'Take This Horror Out Of The Park!' was a typical headline—and pictures of the panel in harsh close-up, torn from its harmonious setting. For a whole summer, crowds flocked to the sanctuary, wearing down the grass into hard beaten earth, 'seeking the obscenities that did not exist'. One might almost say that the allegory of Rima was being acted out again in Hyde Park; and during those months, for the first and only time, Hudson's name was a household word. The irony would have appealed to him.

A public memorial in London is a rare distinction, the mark of someone greatly honoured by the great. Hudson had made a deep impression on some of the famous of his time. Yet they saw little of him. In England, as in South America, he spent much of his life in solitary wandering, preferably in the country; watching birds, picking up adders to measure their length, listening to the life stories of humble people, shepherds, field workers and cottage women with long memories. 'Nothing but a common tramp', one Cornishman called him. 'Unsurpassed as an English writer on Nature,' a *Times* obituary said.

But at his death influential men of the day insisted that he had been much more: the chief standard-bearer of a new faith, John Galsworthy declared. H. J. Massingham said he was 'one of the most romantic figures in the world . . . a primitive in habit of mind, yet so modern that he directed the evolution of human thought and revolutionized the relations between man and nature'. He had been, said Massingham, 'virtually the parent and inspiration of a new driving force in the world'.

The 'faith' was not of course new. It had been around for at least a century; but in 1925 the means for mass conversion had not yet appeared. Thirty years on, largely through television, his message would begin at last to come over to a receptive public.

Hudson deeply pitied those who knew only stuffed birds in museums; and he was apt to disparage the scientific work carried on in laboratories and dissecting rooms. He urged that it was the *living* creature that mattered; that the natural lives and habitats of wild creatures must be studied and understood, or they would be lost; and that wildlife and human life were one, making up 'the chain of Nature' threatened by twentieth-century trends. All this has become familiar under various labels—conservation, ecology, survival. 'Earth life' was Hudson's own term for his vision of harmony between birds and man.

Today his constant readers number perhaps, world-wide, a few hundreds. In Britain alone his followers, in name at least, total hundreds of thousands, still increasing yearly. Few of these have ever heard of him.

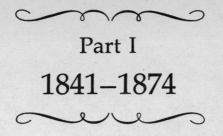

Part I

1841–1874

1

Running Wild

In the 1840s a line of giant ombu trees made a landmark beside a long low farmhouse near the village of Quilmes on the pampas of La Plata, about ten miles away from the growing city of Buenos Aires. On this small estancia or cattle ranch, known as The Twenty-five Ombus, Hudson was born on 4 August 1841. It was St Dominic's Day, and Catholic neighbours wished him to be called Dominic, but his mother chose the names William Henry.

Daniel and Caroline Hudson, his parents, were among the first North American settlers in that part of La Plata. Daniel, the son of a Devon man and an Irish mother, was then in his late thirties, having been born on 1 May 1804 at Marblehead, Massachusetts. His wife, Caroline Augusta Kimble, was a few months younger, born on 10 October 1804 at Berwick, Maine. Her family claimed descent from one of the Pilgrim Fathers, and were said to own one of many Bibles 'brought out in the *Mayflower*'.

As a young married man Daniel had worked in a brewery, and while running along a tier of barrels he had a bad fall, injuring his back. A threat of tuberculosis followed, and the couple decided to go south to the more genial climate of Argentina, where Daniel could recover his health and make a living in the open air, farming sheep and cattle.

They bought The Twenty-five Ombus in April 1837 from Tristan Valdez, a brother-in-law of Juan Manuel Rosas, the Dictator of Buenos Aires. At this time they had two sons, born since their arrival in Argentina: Daniel, aged twenty-one months, and Edwin, three months. A daughter, Caroline Louisa, was born at the estancia in 1839, and William Henry two years later. Within a few years another boy and girl, Albert Merriam and Mary Ellen, completed the family and became the childhood companions of the future naturalist.

The house stood in a vast sea of grass and thistles, with primitive doors and windows open to the air. Born in early spring, William must have heard bird-cries from his first hours. In summer there were haunting smells, of the dust of cattle coming home, of moist earth from the stream—the Conchitas—at the back of the house, the scent of evening primroses and fennel. Before he could walk, set on a rug in the shade, he could watch black and gold woodpeckers on the ombus overhead, the oven-bird building on the roof, and the little brown and yellow tyrant-birds that seemed to sing out like children from the treetops, *Bien-te-veo*, 'I-can-see-you.'

Soon William was following the older children into the branches. The ombu, with its massive roots and spreading trunks, was a natural playground for any child old enough to climb. The young Hudsons took one of the grove for their own tree-house, carrying up planks to form bridges from one branch to another, and amusing themselves overhead during the noon siesta while their elders slept.

At night, they were told, the grove was haunted by the pitiful ghost of a negro slave, beaten to death there fifty years before; a pale, luminous shape that roamed about the trees. William never saw it. His most vivid memory of this early time was the evening return of the herds, hundreds of cattle bellowing and sending up clouds of dust, while gaucho herdsmen galloped and shouted, urging them on. It was a world of horsemen—'a man without a horse was a man without legs'—and children began to ride as soon as possible. A gaucho infant, too small to jump on a pony's back, would plant one foot on its knee and scramble up that way. William's first lessons were given by his elder brothers on the back of an amiable sheep-dog. One day, to see how well he could stick on, they dashed away calling to the dog, which bounded after them. The novice was thrown and broke a leg.

Just before his fifth birthday the family removed to a larger estancia forty miles away, known as The Acacias (though The Twenty-five Ombus remained their property). William remembered the bustle of departure at sunrise on a bright June day, midwinter in that region; the loading of the wagon, rattling chains, stamping horses and a great struggle to ford the stream at the back of the house. Then followed a long day's journey across undulating plains gleaming with winter floods; the drowsy arrival after dark, and the excitement of waking next day in a strange new home.

The house was another long low brick building, thatched with rushes. Behind it lay a homestead of eight or nine acres, with gardens, orchards and plantation; the whole ringed by a fosse about twelve feet deep and twenty or thirty feet wide, dug in earlier times when Indian raids were common, and still useful to keep cattle off cultivated ground.

A tree-loving owner, long before, had planted many white acacias, from which the place took its name, and had enclosed the gardens with shady Lombardy poplars and made an orchard of peach trees, still flourishing and bearing heavy crops. There were mulberry walks where birds and children could feast in summer; quinces, willows, paradise trees and trees of heaven, besides a modern orchard with pear, apple, plum and cherry trees.

When the Hudsons took possession, however, the place was a paradise of vermin. The derelict house and outbuildings, kitchen, bakery, dairy and barns, were in an appalling state of dirt and disorder, overrun by rats, fleas, centipedes, snakes and huge hairy spiders. Beyond the barns lay rubbish yards with heaps of evil-smelling offal from slaughtered animals. Carrion hawks ranged overhead, and at sunset hordes of enormous rats swarmed out to feed, sometimes invading the house and running over the children's beds. If a child screamed for help it was laughed at as 'a poor little coward'.

There were other night terrors. Children in Victorian England lay awake and trembled, fancying that a tiger, puma or python might be crouching on the canopy or under the bed. A child on the pampas had more reason to tremble. No puma, William was told, would attack him. But there were snakes actually living under his bedroom floor, and he could not trust them to stay there: 'It was dark in the room, and to my excited imagination the serpents were no longer under the floor, but out, gliding hither and thither over it, with uplifted heads, in a kind of mystic dance; and I often shivered to think what my bare foot might touch if I were to thrust a leg out. . .'

Sixty years later, Hudson was urging that English country children, future farm workers, should be educated by first-hand experience and not only from books. His own education as a nature writer was certainly first-hand.

The front rooms of the house, facing the road, formed a store in which the country people traded their own produce—wool, hides, horsehair, tallow and cheeses—and bought their groceries, household goods, tobacco, clothes, saddlery, even coffins. With this valuable business, as well as the flocks and herds, there seemed every hope of prosperity. But not for Daniel Hudson. His son would remember him, with mingled affection and exasperation, as a man of 'shining defects'. Trusting as a child in his business dealings, never doubting the good faith of others, he was intent neither on getting rich nor outdoing his fellow men. 'Things being what they are, this inevitably led to his ruin.' In those important early years, language must have added immensely to his problems. Probably he and Caroline knew no Spanish before reaching Argentina, though their children would grow up bilingual.

While Daniel tackled the sheep and cattle, the store and the swindlers, Caroline set about making a civilized home in this rough setting. Blessed with health and energy, a happy outgoing nature and serene religious faith, she was clearly able to shoulder this immense task without feeling overburdened. Besides running the home and bringing up her family, she would welcome any chance traveller as a guest; and found time also to help anyone in trouble, to drive many miles on visits to friends, and later to teach the younger children.

William's earliest memory showed her sitting out of doors, a book on her lap, the sunset lighting up her face, smiling at the children as she watched their evening games. But such moments of leisure must have been brief. All the pioneer spirit of her ancestors would be needed, in a country where Nature gave lavishly with one hand and dealt destruction with the other.

Giant thistles fattened the stock and produced mountains of dry fuel, but spoiled the taste of milk and butter, and threatened the homestead with disastrous fires. Hot summers supplied Caroline's kitchen with peaches, melons, pumpkins and every kind of vegetable; but months of searing drought would follow, ending in storms, terrifying lightning, floods and hailstones that killed animals, ravaged the fruit trees and cut the garden crops to pieces.

A boy of six could be sent out to gather unlimited wildfowl eggs, a boy of ten could shoot wild duck and other game for the pot, and one ostrich egg would make an omelette for the whole family. But the first word a baby must learn was *ku-ku*—'dangerous'—a warning cry as it was snatched away from a venomous insect or spider. And, when the older ones were late in coming home, their mother would have a string of dangers to remember: wild beasts, snakes, treacherous swamps, all the hazards of climbing, bathing and riding; besides any mischief that might have befallen them in running wild among gaucho boys. William was once nearly drowned when a boy knocked him off a rock into deep water. Both parents believed, however, 'that children were best left to themselves, that the more liberty they had the better it was for them'. So William, as he grew up, would find himself leading three separate lives: the active round of games, lessons, quarrels, jokes and ambitious schemes in a circle of six high-spirited brothers and sisters; the life of a young native learning to survive in a 'savage wilderness'; and, most important, the secret life that began on his first days in the new home.

The first urgent task was to make the house habitable, to lay new floors and replace the rotten thatch, crawling with vermin, by a sound wooden roof. While this was going on the young ones were encouraged to keep as far away as possible, to explore the grounds and run wild among the trees which to their unaccustomed eyes seemed like a great forest. Soon William was going off alone day after day to the wintry plantation; loitering quietly, watching the sky through leafless branches, learning each tree by touch and smell before he knew its name; breathing the scent of bark, moss and rank weeds, then of new grass and early violets discovered among the roots of a poplar.

Even in winter the trees were teeming with bird-life. Glossy purple troupials, known as cow-birds, swarmed like dark foliage on the boughs. Shrill screams would herald the visit of a flock of green parrots, migrants from Patagonia—a name that was to haunt William for a quarter of a century. On sunny days there would be the mysterious visiting swallows. On still, warm winter mornings huge bird-voices filled the air: cries of the great rail and crested screamer in lagoons three miles away. Then on misty mornings in July came the first spring notes of soaring pipits, and the drumming and cries of spur-wing lapwings in their mating dances out on the plain.

In August the old peaches flowered, and thousands of small yellow finches burst into song in the branches. Nothing in a long life would compare with this: the clouds of rose-pink blossom, blue skies, bittersweet scent, and the chorus of long pure trills, streaming across the ear like a vision of straight bright rain to the eye. That whole year brought a succession of new experiences. When the blossom was gone he watched the trees coming into leaf, crushing the young poplar leaflets to smell their balsam tang, and then hearing for the first time the sound of poplar groves in summer foliage, 'like the wash of the sea on a wide shore'.

One day a flock of small green parrakeets came screeching into the orchard, stripping the twigs for perches, scattering showers of petals with their sharp little beaks. William was filled with delight at their coming, fury at their careless depredations, grief at their departure.

Strange and beautiful birds were arriving every day. Soon there were nests everywhere. Tyrant-birds came south from tropical forests, flashing in black and scarlet among the new green leaves. A pair of scissor-tail tyrants built at the top of the highest tree, a red willow. William was never tired of watching the cock bird battling in mid-air, fending off raids from carrion hawks and chasing them with angry shrieks 'like the whetting of a scythe'. Little gold siskins built in the poplars, finches in the orchard, doves all over the plantation. Cow-birds, not cuckoos, were the parasites here; and, while still at the meddling age, he would search out and remove their eggs from the nests, in pity for the small foster-parents and their young.

No one felt as he did about birds; but they were not persecuted. His father tolerated even the *caranchos*, which preyed on poultry, young lambs and sucking pigs. To the Spanish country people the smaller harmless species were 'God's birds' and were protected. Many of the names William learned were vivid and affectionate. *Bien-te-veo* imitated the call of one tyrant-bird—named 'tyrant' from its marked aggressiveness. A little bird that built its nest from many sticks and twigs was the 'firewood-gatherer', and the painted snipe was *dormilon*, 'sleepy-head', from its reluctance to fly when disturbed. One of the rails was 'little ass' because of its braying call; another 'crazy widow', from its mourning plumage and long melancholy screams. 'Throat-cut' was a starling with a scarlet throat. The oven-bird's nest was shaped like a clay oven. When it nested on the house-tops it was the 'housekeeper', and elsewhere 'John-of-the-mud-puddles'. The oven was begun in winter, when rain softened the mud, and building went on at a leisurely pace until spring. A pious little bird, the gauchos said: the nest took so long because it would not work on Sundays or saints' days.

Early summer was a time of brilliant colour, before drought baked the earth and turned all vegetation brown. When the white acacias flowered, swarms of glittering humming-birds arrived to suck the honey, hovering in the bright air like tiny emerald bees and sometimes darting in and out of the house.

Butterflies drifted in clouds—red, black, yellow and white— over fields of blue alfalfa. In the garden there were blue morning-glories, jasmine, scarlet four-o'clock bushes. But William preferred the weedy thickets and waste places where no one went but himself, the haunts of snakes, opossums, foxes and large black weasels: jungles of sow-thistle, thorn-apple, viper's bugloss, also loved by the humming-birds; the dried-up moat where snipe came in summer; a mulberry clump near by, where bats hung in dense shade. Another favourite place was a thicket of wild fennel where he spent hours on blazing summer days, watching the scissor-tail battles overhead, nibbling bits of the feathery herb and sniffing its pungent scent, 'perhaps thinking, perhaps of nothing', in a childish summer dream.

Such places were dangerous. There was always the risk of treading on a snake, perhaps a deadly pit-viper, or the fearful blue and crimson serpent 'regarded by everyone as exceedingly venomous and most dangerous on account of its irascible temper and habit of coming at you and hissing loudly, its head and neck raised, and striking at your legs'. At the age of five, William had not yet found out that this was all bluff on the snake's part; yet he half-longed to see one, or at least to find a sloughed skin, 'silvery bright, soft as satin to the touch', and carry it home in the hope of giving someone else a fright.

The snakes under the bedroom floor, a harmless species, had been left in peace: another example of Daniel Hudson's tolerance. On these summer nights one could hear them 'gliding ghost-like about their subterranean apartments' and holding long, eerie conversations, 'a kind of low mysterious chorus, death-watch and flutter and hiss'.

The chorus died away in autumn as the snake colony grew torpid. Then, listening on still nights, the child heard different sounds that stirred him to the heart: ringing cries in the darkness, and the beat of wings passing over, high in the air. Swans, wild geese, flamingoes, whistling duck and ibis, whimbrels and rails, swallows and martins, the migrant flocks streamed away north- ward under the stars. They seemed to him like the thistledown that was first loosed from its husk by a soft breeze, then blown lightly from one resting-place to another by wandering currents, and at last whirled away on the surge of a rising gale.

For weeks the sky was filled with them. Then it was winter again, and at night there were only hooting owls and the inter-mittent cries of crested screamers high above the plain: 'counting the hours,' the gauchos said, like watchmen in the city. Then in late winter the toads would begin their mating chorus in marshy ground close to the house. Here, in the flooded water-courses, swarms of great amphibians preyed on smaller toads, and chanted in a raging chorus that ranged through every key.

This year the signs of spring were familiar and eagerly awaited: violets, fruit blossom, the notes of the returning plover, the call of the cuckoo in late September. William was becoming a practised climber, ready to venture forty or fifty feet up into the poplars, as they swayed in a hot November wind, to look down at the siskins' cup-shaped nest and small pearly eggs; even to brave the vicious spines of the black acacias by the moat, to see the Guira cuckoo's eggs, 'purest turquoise flecked with snowy white'. From the top of a red willow he could gaze out over the plain and see other plantations, the distant gleam of a river, and birds soaring above and around him in the air, making him long for wings. Especially he envied the crested screamers, 'a bird as big or bigger than a goose, and heavy almost as I myself', yet able to lift itself from the ground, circle to an immense height and remain there for hours, floating in circles, pouring out wild resonant cries. He was seeing something not explained in his own lifetime, the bird's use of air currents or thermals.

For the past year he had lived like a forest bird, shut in by trees and tall weeds. Now he was ready for a wider range.

One day in early spring, soon after his sixth birthday, his elder brothers took him for his first long walk across the plain. It was a tiring expedition for a small child, struggling through waist-high grass and skirting wide thistle patches; but he had his reward. Reaching a flooded marsh two miles away, he found a new and marvellous scene—a great concourse of water-birds, wild duck, swans, ibises, herons, roseate spoonbills. Most striking were three tall graceful birds, white and rose-coloured. As he watched, one of the three raised its long neck and shook out wings of a glorious crimson.

'The cloud of shining wings, the heart-enlivening wild cries, the joy unspeakable': much of his early life would be spent in scenes like this, and he would often see flamingoes again; but the first shock of delight could never be repeated.

Within a few decades, as the draining and fencing of the pampas began, many of these habitats—reed-beds, lagoons and flowery meres—would be lost for ever. So Hudson's experience at six recalls that of another child naturalist, Edmund Gosse, his friend in later years. Gosse, in some of the saddest pages ever written, described the English seashore of the mid-nineteenth century as he saw it first on a spring day in early childhood: a ring of living beauty and unbroken silence, the rock-pools and sea-gardens teeming with fragile, radiant forms of life, 'undisturbed since the creation of the world'.

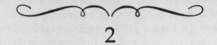

2

Riding Out

Before venturing on that first long walk, William had to be assured that there was no herd of half-wild cattle in that direction. The thought of these beasts terrified him, with good reason, since they would often attack anyone caught on foot in the open. Soon afterwards, however, William became a horseman. The Hudson children learned to ride on Zango, an old cavalry horse left to end his days in their father's care: he lived on for nine years as a family pet, much mourned when he was killed in a violent hailstorm. At six William had his own pony and was 'well able to ride bare-backed at a fast gallop without falling off'. The pampas stock pony was trained to twist and turn at full speed to head off runaway beasts, or to dodge round thistles and rodent burrows: the rider must learn to 'go' with his mount whatever it did. For the next twenty-seven years much of William's life was to be spent on horseback.

From his pony's back he could look out across miles of wind-swept plain where 'the crystal blue dome of the sky' rested on a level green expanse; no fence in sight, and no trees but a few scattered plantations like the Hudsons' own. Much of the plain was covered with coarse tussocky grass, three or four feet high, or with patches of thistle and cardoon, European artichoke run wild. Other parts were broken up into rough warrens by the *vizcacha*, 'a big rodent the size of a hare, a mighty burrower in the earth'. There were also smooth areas closely grazed by the sheep, and moist, low-lying 'meadows' where thousands of little yellow blossoms shone like English celandines in early spring. Not only were these *mácachina* flowers delightful to look at, and the first of

38

the year: they were also good to eat, with an acid taste, and grew from an equally tasty little bulb the size of a hazel-nut, pearly white and sweet as sugar, very tempting to a child with a knife.

A short ride from home William found water-meadows thick with wild flowers. There he would dismount and lead the pony by the bridle, walking knee-deep in the grass, pausing at every step to stoop down and look at the scarlet verbenas, irises, small scented lilies, yellow, white and red; and others like yellow dog-roses, too fragile when picked to survive the homeward ride.

These rambles were taken in the early morning or late afternoon, when myriads of spiders' webs silvered the turf like dew, so that the rising or sinking sun cast a wide beam as though shining across water. Like water too the bright air shivered and dazzled in waves above the plain, from early spring through the parched months when the sluggish rivers failed in the marshes. In this desert mirage, distant estancias were changed into blue islands, and the thirsty cattle seemed to graze knee-deep in lapping floods.

The summer grass was full of strange noises—whistling alarm calls of deer, the wild outcry of *vizcachas*, metallic hammer-notes of ibis, pipe of grasshoppers, flitter of dragon-flies. Also there were powerful smells, from wild pigs, skunks, troops of yellow deer bounding into cover as William rode past. By a bird-haunted stream, a mile or so from home, he rediscovered the exhilarating smell of moist riverside earth, a reminder of his first home, with many other new scents, 'herby, fishy, flowery and even birdy, particularly that peculiar musky odour given out on hot days by large flocks of glossy ibis'.

That was the great summer of his childhood, perhaps the happiest of his life.

> I rejoiced in colours, scents, sounds, in taste and touch: the blue of the sky, the verdure of the earth, the sparkle of sunlight on water, the taste of milk, of fruit, of honey, the smell of dry or moist soil, of wind and rain, of herbs and flowers; the mere feel of a blade of grass made me happy; and there were certain sounds and perfumes, and above all certain colours in flowers, and in the plumage and eggs of birds, such as the purple polished shell of the tinamou's egg, which intoxicated me with delight.

In summer the whole plain might become a jungle of giant thistles, ten feet high, set with spines like daggers. For the freedom-loving gaucho it was misery to be shut in on all sides, his low-roofed house deprived of any view and menaced by lurking robbers; while on horseback he had to keep to narrow tracks where his bare feet, shod only with spurs, were raked by the long thorns. But for children a 'thistle year' had special pleasures.

The huge purple crowns would ripen to puffs of thistledown that floated like bubbles when the air was still. On windy days the gossamer stuff whirled about in blizzards; by moonlight it gleamed with a ghostly air. Riding at night, it was exciting to urge a nervous pony breast-high through white drifts that billowed up all around, eerie and soundless. When the jungles withered to rusty brown, there was always the chance of a fire. The gauchos smoked incessantly, and probably set fire to the hated barriers on purpose, in spite of the risk. A wisp of smoke in the distance would send every man or boy on horseback to the danger spot. If a flock were grazing nearby, a few sheep would be killed and dragged to and fro at a gallop in the path of the flames, making a wide flat swathe where the blaze might be stamped out or smothered with horse-rugs.

Everyone waited impatiently for the coming of the pampero, the south-west gale that would sweep away the dead thistles or flatten them to the earth. Then at last one could gallop again over level ground, hearing the crackle of hollow stems underfoot 'like the bones of perished foes'.

In a normal season, thistles and wild artichokes grew in isolated patches, giving cover to deer, ostriches and smaller birds. William found that, if he rode up to a doe and fawn, they would stand quite still and gaze at him. Then, as though at a signal, the fawn would dash away and hide, while the doe bounded off the other way; slowly at first, pretending to limp, and then faster and faster, shaking off pursuit.

The rhea, the great noble-looking pampas ostrich, reacted to his approach in a more subtle way. Once, sent to turn the sheep homeward, he found himself close to a flock of rheas; unexpectedly, for their colouring blended with the grey of the artichoke bushes. The birds let him come quite near and sit watching as they cropped the clover. If a horseman were to appear on the horizon, he knew, they would make off at high speed. The small boy on his pony was ignored. But what would happen, he wondered, if he were to ride straight at one of these disdainful creatures?

What happened was astonishing. As the pony trotted near, the bird still showed no sign of alarm; but suddenly it was no longer there. It had turned and doubled back, at a quaint dancing trot, eluding him with ease. Looking back, he saw it feeding quietly a dozen yards away. Again and again the same thing happened. With this graceful trick, he realized, it had learned to outwit the huntsman swinging his lasso, the deadly weighted bolas that, skilfully thrown, would wind itself round the victim and bring it down. But this cool evasive action left the rider defeated. By the time a galloping horse could be reined in and turned, the quarry would be far away, its dim plumage 'fading mysteriously out of sight in the landscape'.

The game of 'hunt the ostrich' was to become a favourite with William and his younger brother when they played with gaucho boys: the only game they played on foot. William, the fastest and most nimble, would be chosen first as the ostrich, to run and dodge until he was captured. To the gaucho, ostrich-hunting was not only a challenge but a lucrative trade, the birds being taken for medicine as well as food or feathers. Long before medical science discovered pepsin, the Spanish settlers had learned from the Indians to use ostrich stomach, dried and powdered, as a cure for digestive troubles.

To children the bird's weird swallowing habits were highly entertaining. At the end of their game the quarry would be 'cut up' and the players would go through the 'gizzard' pretending to find all kinds of objects; last of all a silver coin to be won in a free fight. No doubt this search, and the subsequent fights, were part of the real hunts. A tame ostrich at a neighbouring house was never allowed indoors because of its habit of swallowing coins, spoons, thimbles and other treasures. On visits there, the younger Hudsons would entice it away to the orchard and amuse themselves by giving it half a dozen peaches at once, so as to watch the sequence of large round bulges working slowly down the long neck.

Visits to another ranch, nine miles away, were also keenly enjoyed by William. A grove by the house was the home and nesting-place of the little green parrakeets that visited his own orchard. 'O why, I thought, many and many a time, did not these dear green people come over to us and have their happy village in our trees!'

These kindly feelings were not returned. A visit to the parrakeet colony sounds unnerving. As William came into the grove, the shrill chatter would stop abruptly, and in the ominous hush he would feel the hostile glitter of hundreds of small beady eyes.

Then there would be uproar, the whole colony rising up together to hover and shriek over his head until he had to retreat.

The large migrant parrots from the south also resented his interest. Now, when they left the home plantation, he could ride after them and watch as they swooped down to feed on wild pumpkin seeds, smashing the shells with their formidable beaks. If he rode too near they also would mob him with angry screams.

William himself was wild and shy with strangers. Venturing on to other people's land, he was at first terrified by the noisy dogs that rushed out to inspect him, and even more wary of their owners. But the lure of birds and nests was stronger than shyness. Soon he became a familiar sight in plantations all over the district, and in time he was persuaded to talk to the people he met, finding them as a rule most friendly, even to a child of 'an alien and heretic race'.

These groves and orchards had been planted by colonists who, in the early years, carried on the Spanish way of life, making gardens, producing herbs and salads, growing corn for bread, olives for oil and grapes for wine. Such customs were, however, discouraged by the mother country, anxious to keep the monopoly of traditional money-making crops; and this attitude was reinforced by a gradual changeover from agriculture to a pastoral and hunting life. The first colonists of La Plata had landed in 1535 with seventy-two horses, and cattle were soon introduced. Like the artichoke and fennel, horses and cattle had flourished and run wild. By the eighteenth century, vast herds were roaming the pampas. The cattle were hunted for tallow and hides, and the tough meat later exported as dried beef to feed slaves in Brazil and the West Indies. Meanwhile the orchards and vines went untended; neglected gardens were overrun by poultry and animals. Now only a few herb patches remained, with the ancient European remedies, parsley, rue, sage, tansy, horehound. The country people lived chiefly on roast or boiled meat flavoured with onions, garlic and spices—cummin seed and cinnamon—bought at the store. Their everyday drink was maté, green tea made from the leaves of the Paraguayan ilex tree, with imported wine or rum at festivals. Those who still had orchards feasted when the crop was ripe, and went without fruit for the rest of the year.

The Hudsons managed differently. Caroline, a clever and thrifty housekeeper, varied the meat and game with splendid North American dishes: hot maizemeal cakes with syrup for breakfast, as well as cold roast duck, plovers' eggs, broiled pigeon and mutton cutlets; sweet corn, potatoes, salad and other vegetables at dinner, followed by pumpkin pies, peach pies or puddings. Hot bread, scones and jam appeared at tea; cold meat and pickled peaches for supper. Casks of green peaches were laid down every summer in spiced vinegar, and ripe fruit of all kinds made into jam to last the year round. Not into wine, apparently. Though the house verandah was covered with grape-vines, it would seem that the family drank only tea or coffee at home, no doubt because of Caroline's New England religious principles. But though devout she was wonderfully tolerant, and when she gave a wedding breakfast for Catholic neighbours there was wine 'in plenty': this of course had a Biblical precedent.

Daniel Hudson took a special pride in his potato crop. The finest specimens were weighed, scrubbed and set on show on the mantelpiece; an English village custom, perhaps brought from Devonshire by his own father. These potatoes were a delicacy, 'beautifully white and mealy', cooked in their skins, seasoned and eaten with butter. To William the English boarding-house version would later come as a shock.

All this intrigued the Spanish neighbours. Don Ventura Gutierres, tasting pickled peaches for the first time at the Hudsons' table, declared that next year he would lay in gallons of vinegar and cloves by the handful, and command his wife and four daughters to follow Caroline's recipe. William and his brothers hid their laughter, knowing that the wife and daughters would not bestir themselves: their kitchen was a place for gossip and flirtation, always full of young men sipping maté and making themselves agreeable.

One old dame, Doña Pascuala, catching sight of William in her plantation, would question him closely about his family and their customs. He in turn was intrigued by her 'thousand-wrinkled face', brown as her cigar, and by her fun-loving eyes and dictatorial ways. She once came in triumph to his mother, after a long spell of storm and flood, to announce that the rain would not last much longer. She had hung her image of St Anthony, her patron saint, head down in the well, 'to find out how *he* liked it'; and there he should stay till the weather improved.

Riding about the plain, William fell in with other children on horseback, and visited their homes. Already 'a field naturalist of six with considerable experience of wild birds', he was learning that men and women could be equally captivating. Seventy years

43

on, he could describe many of them in vivid detail from these childhood memories.

Don Anastacio Buenavida, 'an exquisite' with a grand manner, wore ringlets and splendid gaucho costume, embroidered blouse, yellow kilt, lace drawers. His ruined estate was overrun by his poor relations; also by herds of feral pigs, equally useless—evil-smelling red beasts to whom he was devoted. Another neighbour, Don Gregorio, had a passion for piebald horses. An English friend, George Royd, dreamed of making his fortune from sheep's-milk cheeses; but his Spanish workers were outraged at being ordered to milk such creatures. '"Why not milk the cats?" they scornfully demanded.'

Don Evaristo Penalva, an aristocrat and patriarch, with six wives and many children, was esteemed for his learning and medical skill: should the latter fail, Don Evaristo knew his letters and could write down the last will and testament. He had a remarkable cure for shingles, a common and dangerous malady. Often the sufferer's waist would become encircled by the painful rash; and if the ends of the circle joined up, it was said, he would die. Don Evaristo would take pen and ink and write in this space, on the patient's skin, the benediction beginning 'In the name of the Father'. Then a live toad would be brought from the marsh, and he would gently rub it over the toad-like blistered area. 'The toad, enraged by such treatment, would swell itself up almost to bursting and exude a milky secretion from its warty skin. That was all, and the patient got well!'

Learned physicians, Hudson later commented, might laugh at this cure; but once they had laughed at the idea of using powdered ostrich stomach for digestive troubles.

The young Hudsons too found a good deal to laugh at, though they had to behave themselves in company: 'our father knew that we were only too liable to explode in the presence of an honoured guest, and nothing vexed him more.' Both parents were warmly hospitable to chance travellers as well as friends; the more uncouth and eccentric, the kinder their welcome. Meanwhile the children would sit entranced, not daring to exchange glances, drinking in the visitor's oddities so as to imitate him afterwards.

An elderly English neighbour, Mrs Blake, taking refuge at The Acacias from her husband's drunken bouts, would be pressed by the young ones to sing in her wailing, cracked falsetto her favourite air, 'Home, sweet Home'. But poor Mrs Blake was to be remembered in quite another light. One day when William was eight the Hudsons and some friends were walking in the orchard when they came across a long green snake. Though it was harmless, someone at once took a stick to kill it, as usual; but Mrs Blake caught his arm, took up the snake in her hands and released it in the grass. To the 'loud expressions of horror and amazement' that followed, she returned simply, 'Why should you kill it?'

Why indeed? 'My young mind was troubled at the question, and there was no answer.' But a seed was sown. As he grew bigger, William had begun to follow local custom, killing any snake he found and beating it to pulp. From now on he found himself looking at snakes as he looked at birds, flowers and spiders, noticing their beauty and their way of life. It was a long step forward; and in old age, recalling Mrs Blake, he made amends: 'her voice in the choir invisible sounds sweet enough.'

Then came another memorable incident. One blazing December day, loitering in a barren weedy place, he heard a rustle and saw a great snake six feet long, coal-black and shining like quicksilver, flowing past him into cover. 'At last it vanished, and turning I fled from the ground, thinking that never again would I venture into or near that frightfully dangerous spot in spite of its fascination.' But he went back again and again, until once more he saw it glide past and pour itself into a hole under the weeds. Now he began to wait and watch outside its den. One day, wandering off to look at a cluster of bats in a tree, he felt a pressure on his foot, looked down and saw the great reptile crawling slowly across his instep. Yet, after the first thrill of horror, he felt no fear, knowing he was safe so long as he kept still.

He never saw it again. Later he heard of melanism, and realized that it had been a freak specimen of a snake found in another part of the district. He then recalled that one rather like it had once crawled on to his little sister's rug, and Daniel had killed it. Possibly the two had been mates, the last survivors of a colony in the plantation.

At that time, everyone said what a lucky escape little Mary Ellen had had: fortunately, like Miss Muffet, she had merely been frightened away. And William kept his secret: 'that last encounter had left in me the sense of a mysterious being able to inflict death with a sudden blow, but harmless and even friendly and beneficent towards those who regarded it with kindly and reverent feelings in place of hatred.'

Up till now his response to nature had been one of mere

childish pleasure. When he found a green expanse of turf covered with scarlet verbenas he would throw himself off the pony and lie on the ground, feasting on their brilliant colour. It was purely animal happiness, like that of a colt turned out to grass or a cat basking on a catmint bush. His feeling for the black snake was part of a new emotion, primitive and intense, 'the sense and apprehension of an intelligence like our own but more powerful in all visible things'. Later he would call this animism. As a boy of course he had no words for it. One particular wild flower could call up this sense of the supernatural; certain trees evoked it powerfully, especially by moonlight; sometimes the great flaring pampas sunset seemed more than he could bear. Nor could he speak of the feeling to anyone else. It remained as secret as the early longing for wings, the mysterious serpent in the weeds, the first experience of falling in love. This too came at the age of eight.

Two little girls of his own age were met with on his rides. Either, perhaps both, may have been this 'she'. Adelina was the favourite daughter of an English neighbour, blue-eyed and golden-haired, 'to us the most beautiful being in the world'. Gold hair especially charmed him all his life. Anjelita had a different appeal. She was a wild, aloof little creature, white-skinned, dark-haired, touchingly serious and unchildlike, flying about the plain on horseback, on errands for her family: a small drudge, unacknowledged by her mother, yet with the natural dignity of her race:

> To my small-boy's eyes she was a beautiful being with a cloud on her, and I wished it had been in my power to say something to make her laugh and forget, though but for a minute, the many cares and anxieties which made her so grave. Nothing proper to say ever came to me, and if it had come it would no doubt have remained unspoken. Boys are always inarticulate where their deepest feelings are concerned.

And older men may be reticent: this was always true of Hudson. But at eighty he would repeat from memory the long plaintive ballad *Annabel Lee:*

> I was a child and she was a child
> In this kingdom by the sea . . .

The Silver Sea—that romantic name for the muddy red waters of the Plata river—had been familiar to William since the age of six, when his delightful rambles on horseback were interrupted by a visit with his mother to friends in Buenos Aires. It was not his first visit; as an infant he had been christened there at the First Methodist Episcopal American Church. But it was his first experience of city life, and filled with vivid new impressions.

As usual, he wandered about alone; his brother Albert was not yet five, too young for long walks. This made it all more memorable: the narrow streets where he was quickly lost; the loud-voiced policeman, armed with a sword, from whom he fled in alarm; the river front where he spent hours watching the ships unloading; the fishermen and water-carts, and an eccentric sportsman who tried to kill small birds with pebbles. One day, stealing up a stairway to the gallery of a church, he heard an orchestra for the first time. To the child from the plain, knowing no instrument but a guitar, it was a miracle, and the beginning of a lifelong passion for music.

Even in the city he found birds to watch; caged parrakeets and cardinals in the bird-market, flights of sparrows and finches feeding on the beach. A crowd of men splendidly dressed, talking together outside a church, made him think of a flock of military starlings, a black or dark-plumaged bird with a scarlet breast. Also he saw for the first time the *serenos*, the night-watchmen from whom the crested screamer got its nickname, and heard their long-drawn cries in the darkness as they told the hours: 'eleven of the clock and all serene.' A favourite spot was the shore where washerwomen, the *lavanderas*, flocked together 'to wash all the dirty linen of Buenos Aires in public', gabbling and laughing like 'a great concourse of gulls, ibises, godwits, geese . . .' But this happy din would change to shrieks and curses when rich young idlers baited the women by walking over the fine garments spread out to dry. Another pastime of the same young men was to set on the frail old *serenos* by night and steal their staves and lanterns.

The innocent onlooker was shocked by these rough sports, and by the brutal-looking beggars in the streets; criminals drafted into the army, then 'thrown out to live like carrion hawks on what they could pick up'. This was the darker side of life under the Dictator Rosas. Yet it was thrilling to see the Dictator's 'court jester' marching past, dressed up in the scarlet uniform of a general—'one of the Dictator's little jokes'—with his bodyguard of soldiers; ready, as children were warned, to cut down anyone rash enough to laugh at the spectacle.

In these years William was developing exceptional gifts; imagination, compassion, a keen sense of beauty, a dawning ability to question common attitudes. Not all his development, however, was on such unusual lines. Like country boys everywhere, his chief ambition was to be allowed as soon as possible to carry a gun and shoot wild birds.

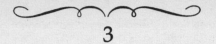

3

Wars and Alliances

William was not allowed to shoot until he was ten. This ban was imposed, not by his parents, but by his elder brother Edwin, who had appointed himself the family armourer and had taken charge of all the guns and weapons in the house. Meanwhile William had to be content with following Edwin to retrieve the birds and hold his pony when he went out to shoot game for the table.

This remarkable boy had a great influence on William. Five years older, clever, impatient, extremely high-handed, he could never be a companion like Albert. The two smaller boys stood together against his tyranny, but they were flattered when he came with them on egg-hunting, fishing or bathing expeditions, or pressed them into helping in more imaginative schemes.

One of these was inspired by the night chorus of huge and venomous toad-like amphibians in the winter marsh. Edwin proposed that they should be killed off in a lake battle, the attackers using a cattle trough as their war canoe and home-made javelins for weapons. But it was not a happy idea. The canoe capsized time after time, and, though they killed seventy or eighty toads, the slaughter itself was sickening to William: 'I was too young for it, and again and again, when thrusting one of the creatures through with my javelin, I experienced a horrible disgust and shrinking ...' They ended the day soaked and exhausted, with feverish colds and nightmares. And, like Parson Woodforde after a similar foray, they found their efforts wasted: 'when we went burning and shivering to bed we could not sleep; and hark! the grand nightly chorus was going on just as usual. No, in spite of the great slaughter we had not exterminated the

49

enemy; on the contrary, they appeared to be rejoicing over a great victory . . .'

Keen as he was to copy Edwin and become a sportsman, William was apt to have qualms. He had learned to make and throw a bolas, and thought he would use it to kill plover for the table. After following the flocks for several days, and knocking down only one bird, he was hailed by a gaucho from a nearby house: 'Why do you come here, English boy, frightening and chasing away God's little birds?' This seemed unwarranted from a ruffian 'who like most of his kind would tell lies, gamble, fight, steal and do other naughty things without a qualm'—and he was astonished to hear plover called 'God's little birds' as though they were 'wrens or humming-birds or the darling little many-coloured kinglet of the bulrush beds. But I was ashamed too and gave up the chase.'

Evidently the Hudson boys learned ideas of 'English fair play' from their father; and, like Daniel, found them a handicap. When they took part at local race-meetings they rarely won: 'the native boys were too clever on horseback for us, and had all sorts of tricks to prevent us from winning, even when our ponies were better than theirs.'

The two younger ones also joined in rough games and sham fights, using long canes or poplar boughs for lances. One day a boy stole up on William from behind, without warning, and knocked him off his pony with a vicious blow that skinned his face from forehead to chin. Stunned and bleeding, and crying with rage, William's first impulse was to go straight to the boy's parents and have him punished. On the way, however, he met an old shepherd who advised him to keep quiet and pay out the other boy himself, if he must, 'and then you will be quits'. Much the same advice as Tom Brown was given at Rugby some fifteen years before; but the sequel would be unfamiliar to schoolboys in England for another hundred years or so. For the gaucho boy, knocked off his pony in turn, drew a knife and flew at William, who had to retreat 'rather hastily'. But his father, called to judge between them, laughed and said they had already settled the matter themselves, and the next time they met they were friends.

Looking back after more than sixty years, Hudson said he had often wondered if he had done right: should he have followed the Christian principle and turned the other cheek? But his young friends would hardly have understood courage of that kind. Nor would Edwin, whose good opinion meant so much to him.

Edwin was a natural fighter, keen to excel as a fencer and boxer and to be a good shot. He was also determined to make himself handy with the knife, the gaucho weapon, so as to defend himself if attacked. For practice, he persuaded his reluctant young brothers to attack him with butchers' knives, while he used his own knife as guard, trying at the same time to disarm them. Despite his blithe assurances, this experiment ended as one might expect; William received a deep cut on the arm that left a permanent scar. But the affair had one good result. Proud of Edwin's rare praise at his courage, he managed to keep the wound out of sight; and Edwin showed his gratitude by becoming more friendly and less tyrannical.

Still, he would not give way over the shooting; but soon after William's tenth birthday this ambition was realized. A family friend gave him a set of architectural drawings which Edwin coveted. A bargain was struck. The pictures were handed over, and William at last had his own gun, a silver-mounted fowling-piece, two inches taller than himself, but light enough for him to carry. He was shown how to load it, with powder, shot and percussion cap, wadded and rammed down with an ancient ramrod; and passed a brief test, bringing down a pigeon on his first attempt. He was now turned loose as a wildfowler: Edwin wasted no more time on instruction. Soon he was wriggling over the marsh to shoot his first duck, and then riding far afield after blue-winged teal, pintails, widgeon, geese and swans that wintered on the plain:

> but we could shoot for the table all the year round, for no sooner was it the ducks' pairing and breeding season than another bird-population from their breeding-grounds in the arctic and sub-arctic regions came on the scene—plover, sandpiper, godwit, curlew, whimbrel—a host of northern species that made the summer-dried pampas their winter abode.

Daniel Hudson himself did not care to shoot; but cold roast duck was his favourite breakfast dish, and this, with other game, the boys were expected to provide. Their father hated killing birds. William only once saw him do so, in a sudden flash of temper, when he came upon an owl that had been raiding his dovecote, and struck it down with an iron bar.

Kindness, honesty, tolerance, these were three of Daniel's chief characteristics. Another was unshakeable physical courage, amounting at times to recklessness. In a violent thunderstorm, he would stand on a dizzy look-out point at the top of the barn, spy-glass in hand, coolly searching the plain for missing horses. The family watched in terror, 'expecting every moment to see him struck by lightning and hurled to the earth below'. He seemed to lack a normal sense of self-preservation.

During the civil war of 1852, when the Dictator Rosas was overthrown, Daniel's coolness put the whole family in danger. It also saved their lives. The soldiers of the defeated army were in retreat, killing and looting as they went. In spite of neighbours' warnings, the Hudson house remained without means of defence, the doors and windows open as usual. Daniel only laughed at the idea of attack, saying casually, 'Oh, they won't hurt us.' His only precaution was to have the horses driven into the plantation out of sight. When a troop of men appeared, shouting for horses, he met them courteously and said he had none to give them. Threatened with a drawn sword, he remained perfectly calm, 'smiling as if the little practical joke had greatly amused him'.

The soldiers could not see beyond the shady verandah into the house. Daniel's manner convinced them that he must have a strong guard behind him, covering them with rifles. In fact there were only women and children, tensely watching; and one other man, a visitor, who sat with drawn sword, 'trembling and white as a corpse', until the danger was over.

To the younger ones at least their father's conduct must have seemed admirable. It was chillingly underlined by what happened next. The visit ended with a sudden dash for freedom by one of the troop, an officer whom the soldiers had disarmed: they meant to murder him. The rest galloped after him. The wretched young man fled to the house of an elderly magistrate, his mother's cousin, imploring protection. But the old man, weeping with horror at what he was doing, gave him up to save his own family.

Next morning, when the soldiers were gone, a shepherd boy invited William to go and see something interesting out on the plain. Expecting to be shown a bird's nest, he was led to a great bloodstain on the grass, where the prisoner's throat had been cut.

In those dark times in the Argentine Republic, when, during half a century of civil strife which followed on casting off the Spanish 'yoke', as it was called, the people of the plains had developed an amazing ferocity, they loved to kill a man not with a bullet but in a manner to make them know and feel that they were really and truly killing.

When Hudson wrote this in old age he added, 'As a child these dreadful deeds did not impress me': a remarkable tribute to the courage and stability of his parents.

But when lawless troops again threatened the district the brothers were no longer children, and Edwin set out to prepare the defence of the house. The eldest, Daniel, was away in the besieged city of Buenos Aires. An army was advancing from the south to raise the siege, sacking and burning houses and driving off cattle, according to alarming rumour. The three boys at home were determined to make a good fight, and they cleaned up a strange collection of weapons, ancient muskets, horse-pistols and fowling-pieces. Edwin set the young ones to melt down all the old lead they could find and make bullets in bullet-moulds of different sizes. The three were laughed at, but allowed to carry on with their preparations, and Edwin kept them at it, turning out rows and shining pyramids of bullets. 'Let them mock now,' he told his helpers. 'By and by, when it comes to choosing between having our throats cut and defending ourselves, they will probably be glad the bullets were made.' And after so much labour they could hardly escape a pang of disappointment when the advancing horde was routed a short way off, without one of their bullets being fired.

In this time of hoarding powder and shot, Edwin did not restrict his own shooting, but took care that William should not be wasteful. Once, after a long crawl through the marsh, he got within twenty-five yards of a flock of rosy-billed ducks, and fired a single shot, expecting to take home a heap of birds. But not one fell. Edwin had drawn out the shot for his own use.

All this frank delight in shooting might seem out of character, especially as William, from his earliest years, had loathed the sight of animals being slaughtered; brutal sport as well as necessity to the gaucho. But, compared with that butchery, the act of firing a gun and seeing a bird fall was too impersonal to seem like killing. To shoot for food, or to gather wildfowl eggs, was a kind of bread-winning, part of the business of growing up and taking part in the life around him.

At thirteen, thanks to a favourite horse, William once distinguished himself at a dangerous gaucho sport of another kind. Thirty or forty men were catching and branding cattle, and several of them began trying to knock down the angry beasts as they were set free from the lasso.

At length a bull was released, and, smarting from the fiery torture, lowered his horns and rushed away eluding three horsemen in succession. At this moment my horse—possibly interpreting a casual touch of my hand on his neck, or some movement of my body, as a wish to join the sport—suddenly sprang forward and charged on the flying bull like a thunderbolt, striking him full in the middle of his body, and hurling him with a tremendous shock to earth. The stricken beast rolled violently over, while my horse stood still as a stone watching him. Strange to say, I was not unseated, but, turning round, galloped back, greeted by a shout of applause from the spectators—the only sound of that description I have ever had the privilege of listening to. They little knew that my horse had accomplished the perilous feat without his rider's guidance.

But the old love of nature was as strong as ever; and from such gatherings he would escape to long days of bird-watching and nest-hunting. One lake, covered in spring with sheets of *camaloté*—brilliant yellow flowers like mimulus—was the breeding-place of grebes and shy painted snipe. Other lagoons had dense reed-beds, where William and Albert would urge their ponies through deep water, among towering bulrushes, to find the nests of small birds woven in the stems, and larger species—egrets, herons, cormorants—nesting in the sedges. A distant lagoon was the habitat of large water-snails, which attracted many birds to feed. Here the brothers found the nests of marsh hawks, black and red jacanas with great golden wings, and long-legged stilts; besides storks, ibises, and roseate spoonbills.

Here too was a nesting colony of three or four hundred marsh troupials, the bird William loved most. He knew them already from their visits to the home plantation, where they would settle on a tree and sing in unison with a ringing sound like countless little bells. Their deep nests, woven of dry sedges, hung two or three together in a forest of water-plants with purple flowers and glossy black berries. The troupials too were purple, with bright chestnut caps; their eggs were white or pale blue, spotted with black. The whole scene, nests and eggs, plants like miniature palm trees, and small bright birds trilling and flying, was one of enchanting beauty.

Yet in another mood William would hunt partridges with the gaucho boys, using snares on long canes; and join them in riding down burrowing owls for sport, little grey and white birds with 'pretty dove-like voices' that hooted round the house at night. Sometimes, outside the nesting season, he and Albert would find thousands of coots clustering together on the shores of a lake. Then they would whip up their ponies and charge, to see the panic-stricken flocks take to wing, raising clouds of spray as they skimmed out over the water.

> The moving sun-shapes on the spray,
> The sparkle where the brook was flowing,
> These were the things we wished would stay;
> But they were going.

So he feared; in his early teens he had begun to dread the future. He wanted to remain just as he was, free to ride and wander or to lie on the grass listening to the sounds of wind and reeds and water-birds, 'hidden rails and coots and courlans conversing together in strange human-like tones . . .'

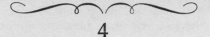

4

Finding a Future

One of the Hudsons' oddities, in the eyes of Spanish neighbours, was their wish to educate their children. Was it really true, old Doña Pascuala used to ask six-year-old William, 'that all of us, even the girls, when big enough were going to be taught to read the almanac?'

His response must have been glum. By then he had already suffered a year in the schoolroom, hating indoors, bored by lessons, bullied by the schoolmaster. Mr Trigg was a middle-aged Englishman who detested the young but had taken to teaching as the easiest way to support himself. He had been wandering about on horseback finding employment here and there in English families. When he came to The Acacias, both he and the Hudson parents felt themselves in luck. He found a well-run house where there were books to read and intelligent people to talk to; even more gratifying, an audience who could appreciate his aptitude for story-telling and impersonation. He had been an actor for a time in England, and was certainly gifted in this direction. One day a 'quaint old Scotch dame' came to call, announcing herself as a neighbour from a distant farm. As usual the children gathered round the tea-table, hoping for entertainment; but it was their turn to be made game of. They actually sat for an hour gazing at the odd visitor and enjoying her scandalous gossip, without detecting Mr Trigg.

Like so many Victorians he found Dickens's novels a splendid outlet for his talents. In the evenings he would give long dramatic readings, acting each character in turn. But in the schoolroom he was a different man, bored and irritable, despised by the older

56

boys and hated by the younger. Forbidden to punish his pupils by striking them, he would pinch their ears cruelly until they almost bled. Their parents of course knew nothing of this, and for several years Mr Trigg kept up the role of agreeable guest and genial entertainer. But at length he took to spending weekends away, drinking rum with other exiles; returning on Monday morning sober, but 'with inflamed eyes and the temper of the devil'. The end was now in sight. One morning, 'tried beyond endurance', he snatched up his horse-whip and began to lash out at the children. Hearing the uproar their mother was quickly on the scene, and Mr Trigg's reign was over.

For a time the younger ones were taught by Caroline, who was anxious for their spiritual and mental welfare in a country of such 'strange moral atmosphere, where lawless acts were common'. Daniel and Edwin had already outgrown the schoolroom and had begun to study on their own. Edwin, then in his early teens, had a strong bent for mathematics and was delighted to hear presently that a new master was coming, qualified to help him. But the promised coaching did not take place. The newcomer, Father O'Keefe, under a placid, amiable, absent-minded manner, was an ambitious churchman. As later appeared, he had merely taken the post because it suited his plans to spend a year away from the city. 'Reculer pour mieux sauter' was a horseman's tactic which his pupils would have understood: but he made no confidences and had as little contact with them as possible, exacting almost nothing in the way of work, and always ready to let them off for the afternoon while he himself went fishing. Edwin soon reported in disgust that he 'knew as little of the infinitesimal calculus as a gaucho or a wild Indian', and was only fit to teach infants their ABC.

Even under Mr Trigg, William had got further than this. He had learned to read, and enjoyed some of the story books that came his way. 'The Discontented Squirrel' was one little fable read and re-read when he was seven, because the squirrel, like himself, longed to follow the birds on their autumn migration, that theme of life-long interest to him. But most books were still merely 'lessons, and therefore repellent'.

He was nine when Edwin decided to start a family newspaper and ordered him to contribute some bird-notes. He set about this with enthusiasm, trying for the first time to put thoughts and facts into writing. Had the scheme prospered it would have been invaluable to him: 'even if it had lasted but a few weeks it would have given me the habit of recording my observations, and that is a habit without which the keenest observation and the most faithful memory are not sufficient for the field naturalist.' But Edwin began to levy contributions from pocket-money for running expenses, and, when Albert rebelled, threatened to hold him up to public scorn in an editorial. This threat he made so convincing that the frightened child tracked down and destroyed the first copy of the paper. Edwin, told by their parents that he was in the wrong, threw up the scheme in disgust and never mentioned it again. So William lost, as he said, 'a great part of the result of six years of life with wild nature, since it was not until six years after my little brother's rebellious act that I discovered the necessity of making a note of every interesting thing I witnessed'.

Meanwhile, one more attempt was made to provide a tutor. A brilliant young man arrived on the scene; 'a linguist, a musician, he had literary tastes, and was well read in science, and above all he was a first-rate mathematician.' He was also the only genuine teacher of the three. Besides coaching and befriending Edwin, he took on the younger ones and, by his keenness and scorn of such 'ignorant young barbarians', actually began to spur William into interest and effort.

How did such a paragon come to take this modest post? Friends who passed him on to the good-natured Hudsons explained that he had been 'a bit wild' and needed a stay in a quiet country home to steady him. But the stay was brief, and his story a familiar one. Soon he began riding off to drink at other estancias and to come back raving: 'a very little alcohol would drive him mad.' All attempts to help him failed; and, with his going, schooldays ended for William. He would go on learning for the rest of his life, and his last book would be by far his most ambitious; but from now on he was his own master.

The English school in Buenos Aires had a bad name as a crowded, unhealthy house, and no money could be spared to send the boys further away. Their parents probably supposed that their lives would lie in farming on the pampas, and that formal education would not be greatly missed. As it turned out, only the eldest, Daniel, became a farmer. Edwin always refused to accept this view of his future. He set himself to follow his mathematical bent, despite delays and difficulties in getting books and instruments, and all the problems of trying to study alone. Devoting himself to work, he gave up outdoor sports, shooting and fencing, his role as family story-teller, and all reading for amusement; until, by sheer determination, he had his way and left to continue his education abroad, and to qualify as a land surveyor.

Though deeply impressed by his brother's conduct, William had no idea as yet of following his example. For the next few years he was still happy and carefree, helping sometimes with the sheep and cattle, exploring the marshes, prolonging his childhood in the company of his young brother.

The first great event of his life, the removal to The Acacias, had taken place just before his fifth birthday. Ten years later came a second turning-point, preceded by a narrow escape from death.

Buenos Aires, with its crowded streets and markets, so fascinating to the country youth, had long lost its 'good airs' and become a place of pestilence. There was no drainage system. Drinking water was carted from the river and sold in muddy buckets, or taken from rainwater cisterns alive with mosquito larvae: 'you always had one or two to half a dozen scarlet wrigglers in a tumblerful, and you drank your water quite calmly, wrigglers and all.' The city was flanked by atrocious killing-grounds where herds of cattle and sheep were slaughtered daily under the hot sun. Blood and dust mingled to form a thick crust over the whole area, and thousands of skulls made a macabre kind of fencing for nearby orchards. 'Travellers approaching or leaving the capital by the great south road, which skirted the killing-grounds, would hold their noses and ride a mile or so at a furious gallop until they got out of the abominable stench.'

The city was soon to become for a time notorious, from outbreaks of typhus, cholera and yellow fever, as the most unhealthy in the world. Before these outbreaks, when he was fourteen, William spent several weeks' holiday there. At first he enjoyed visiting his favourite haunts, the bird-market, the cliff gardens and orange groves, and the river front where he could fish from the rocks for 'little silvery king-fishes'. But soon all was spoiled by a deadly sense of lassitude. He thought this was caused by the change from riding to walking on city pavements; but the feeling persisted. Setting out at last for home, and breathing the pure air of the plain, he seemed to recover. The sense of relief lasted throughout the ride and his first days at home; then he collapsed with typhus.

In that isolated place, far from medical help, he would have

died but for his mother's skill. The fever left him gaunt and
wasted, unable to stand or speak. It was feared that, even if he
recovered, he would be dumb for life; but after another fortnight
his speech came back. Slowly, after months of weakness, he
regained his strength, marvelling to find himself alive. The first
time he was able to walk out of the house, the effects of spring sun
and wind, bird-song and the smell of earth and grass, were so
poignant that he fainted. Then one morning his brothers and
sisters took him by surprise with birthday presents and congratu-
lations.

> Fifteen years old! This was indeed the most memorable day of my
> life, for on that evening I began to think about myself, and my
> thoughts were strange and unhappy thoughts to me—what I was,
> what I was in the world for, what I wanted, what destiny was
> going to make of me! Or was it for me to do just what I wished, to
> shape my own destiny, as my elder brothers had done? It was the
> first time such questions had come to me, and I was startled at
> them. . . . What, then, did I want?—what did I ask to have?

The answer was just as startling, since it was one he dared not
accept:

> I want only to keep what I have; to rise each morning and look out
> on the sky and the grassy dew-wet earth from day to day, from
> year to year. To watch each June and July for spring . . . To listen in
> a trance of delight to the wild notes of the golden plover coming
> once more to the great plain, flying, flying south, flock succeeding
> flock the whole day long . . . To climb trees and put my hand down
> in the deep hot nest of the Bien-te-veo and feel the hot eggs . . . To
> ride at noon on the hottest days, when the whole earth is a-glitter
> with illusory water, and see the cattle and horses in thousands . . .
> to visit some haunt of large birds at that still hour and see storks,
> ibises, grey herons, egrets of a dazzling whiteness, and rose-
> coloured spoonbills and flamingoes, standing in the shallow water
> in which their motionless forms are reflected . . .

Unable any longer to put off thinking of the future, he could see
no link between this desire for freedom and 'earth life', and the
need to earn his living. Even when the link was forged it was to
remain pitifully tenuous. Forty years later he was writing, 'Better,
I say, to live as I do on rather less than £100 a year and be
free . . .'

A hundred a year, earned in observing and describing wildlife!
It is not everyone who, looking back in middle age, can feel he
would win the approval and envy of his fifteen-year-old self; but

to young Hudson this would have seemed a pinnacle of success and happiness.

At his age, he had seen Daniel and Edwin giving up boyhood pastimes for 'the dull business of life', one on the farm, the other in hard study. But he had neither Daniel's physical strength nor Edwin's talent and self-confidence, nor, so far as he could see, any aptitude that he could turn to account. Like Hardy and also like Richard Jefferies, another sensitive and isolated farm boy, he was keenly aware of others' criticism. Jefferies's father would refer with disgust to 'our Dick poking about in them hedges'. Nothing Hudson wrote suggests that, in the family circle, he himself met with anything but kindness and consideration; but one neighbour would assert in after years that 'young Hudson did very little work because he spent much of the day lying on his face studying the bird-life.' No doubt this view was typical: indeed, it was his own, and self-criticism increased his sense of isolation.

In all his fifteen years, and in the fifteen years that followed, surrounded as he was by some of the most beautiful birds, animals, snakes and insects in the world, he never met another soul to whom he could speak of his love of nature. His mother was closest to him in this respect; too close perhaps, for she understood his feelings too well to question or intrude, and theirs remained a secret bond. Perhaps the nearest they came to communication was when, as a child, William had brought home her favourite wild flowers from his spring rides. His younger sister, Mary Ellen, loved animals, and would befriend motherless lambs and other forlorn creatures. But he needed a friend in the world of men, a fellow naturalist, known and respected like his elder brothers, whose alliance would have assured him of a place in the future. In real life no such friend appeared. Instead, he found Gilbert White and the poets.

For days after the memorable birthday he remained 'in a troubled state of mind, ashamed of my ignorance, my indolence, my disinclination to any kind of mental work . . .' These painful youthful thoughts led to a compromise. He would go on with his bird-watching, his walks and rides, since he could not give them up; but also he would start on a course of serious reading.

Up to now he had read little, and, after the brief attempt for Edwin's newspaper, had written nothing. When he did open a book it had been in search of something about nature. Among the books on the family shelves—three or four hundred old volumes, theology, history, biography, travel, philosophy—he had found only three that appealed to him: a general *Natural History* and two small books on birds. There was also an eighteenth-century *Geography* from which he had filched a print of Stonehenge, which he imagined standing high as the heavens on a plain as vast as the pampas. He had also come across a landscape painting of some pampas scene, and had thought for a time of becoming a painter himself; and although he gave up this idea he was always to keep an interest in painting—not only as a picture lover but 'as a practising artist'—and a fondness for the company of professional artists.

He began his new regime with Rollin's *Ancient History*, attracted by its illustrations and large clear type, easier reading for a novice than many books of the period. It was a happy choice. 'Rollin, the good old priest, opened a new wonderful world to me, and instead of the tedious task I had feared the reading would prove, it was as delightful as it had formerly been to listen to my brother's endless histories of imaginary heroes . . .' Obviously he had reached that moment when the adolescent suddenly stops resisting education, develops an appetite for learning and feels ready to tackle almost any subject. Gibbon, however, was still outside his range. After a brief trial, *The Decline and Fall of the Roman Empire* was set aside for a history of Christianity in sixteen or eighteen volumes. 'Fascinating reading' he found these lives of the Fathers of the Church, especially that of Augustine. They sent him to another, *Leland on Revelation*, 'which told me much I was curious to know about the mythologies and systems of philosophy of the ancients—the innumerable false cults which had flourished in a darkened world before the dawn of the true religion'.

As this indicates, he had not yet begun to question the faith learned from his mother. From Leland he must also have learned for the first time how ancient were the roots of his secret 'animism', the strongest factor of his emotional life:

> I used to steal out of the house alone when the moon was at its full to stand, silent and motionless, near some group of large trees, gazing at the dusky green foliage silvered by the beams; and at such times the sense of mystery would grow until a sensation of delight would change to fear, and the fear increase until it was no longer to be borne, and I would hastily escape to recover the sense of reality and safety indoors, where there was light and company . . .

Panic terror was succeeded by renewed fascination:

> On the very next night I would steal out again and go to the spot
> where the effect was strongest, which was usually among the large
> locust or white acacia trees which gave the name of Las Acacias to
> our place. The loose feathery foliage on moonlight nights had a
> peculiar hoary aspect that made this tree seem more intensely alive
> than others, more conscious of my presence and watchful of me.

This attitude to certain trees, the sense that something living
and growing might have a soul and powers of its own, he was to
find still existing in remote English places. 'Not such survivals as
the apple-tree folk-songs and ceremonies of the west, which have
long become meaningless, but something living, which has a
meaning for the mind, a survival such as our anthropologists go
to the end of the earth to seek among barbarous and savage
tribes.'

Already his thoughts were turned to England. White's *The
Natural History and Antiquities of Selborne* had come into his life,
pointing the way to a career as a field naturalist. He read and
re-read it many times, until, like Mary Russell Mitford, he knew
much of it by heart and could 'form a friendship with the fields
and coppices, as well as with the birds, mice and squirrels who
inhabit them'. Nothing so good of its kind had come his way
before. He began to keep his own diary, recording the sights and
sounds and weather for each day. The book was to have another
important outcome. One cannot doubt that White's letters were
the model for his own initial work, the foundation of his career as
a writer: his letters to the Zoological Society of London.

But the time for these was still a dozen years ahead. His
apprenticeship had only just begun. And, for all its importance to
him, something was lacking in *Selborne*. Enthusiast as he was,
White had his feet firmly planted on the earth. His accounts of
'the life and conversation of animals' lacked the spiritual quality
in Hudson's feeling for nature—'the feeling of which I was becoming more and more conscious, which was a mystery to me
...' That quality he now discovered in poetry. But there was little
of this on the old bookshelves, except for scanty quotations scattered through the prose works. A few of these, however, were
rewarding; such as the description of nest-building by an obscure
Sussex poet, James Hurdis (1763–1801):

> No tool had he that wrought, no knife to cut,
> No rail to fix, no bodkin to insert,

> No glue to join: his little beak was all:
> And yet how neatly finished! What nice hand,
> With every implement and means of art,
> And twenty years' apprenticeship to boot,
> Could make me such another?

The only book of verse was by Shenstone (1714–63) who wrote in the pastoral tradition of Corydon and Phyllis, 'bright Roxana tripping o'er the green', and shepherds 'so chearful and gay, Whose flocks never carelessly roam', or suffer from maggots or predators. Hudson, brought up among sheep and shepherds, found this artificial stuff exasperating. But now came a lucky find. On another visit to Buenos Aires, in a dusty secondhand book-shop, he unearthed a copy of Thomson's *The Seasons*.

This, the first book in English that he ever bought for himself, was also the first to express his own sense of exhilaration in the natural world, based on country knowledge as down-to-earth as Gilbert White's. James Thomson (1700–48) looked forward to Crabbe and Wordsworth, to social realism and scientific observation, heightened by romantic feeling. His shepherd, still a central figure of the landscape, was a real countryman, 'merry-hearted' or pensive not only from dalliance but from the state of the weather and the well-being of his flock; just as the moon was no longer a goddess to be apostrophized but a 'spotted Disk' with real wonders to be seen through a telescope,

> Where Mountains rise, umbrageous Dales descend,
> And Oceans roll, as optic Tube descries.

As with *Selborne*, despite the difference of region the poem was full of familiar things, like the showers of thistledown floating on the autumn breeze, 'wide o'er the thistly Lawn'. The scale is merely smaller, the telescope reversed; and the description of the poet's feelings as a child in winter must have brought a sense of delighted recognition:

> Pleas'd have I, in my chearful Morn of Life,
> When nurs'd by careless Solitude I liv'd
> And sung of Nature with unceasing Joy,
> Pleas'd have I wander'd thro' your rough Domain ...
> Heard the Winds roar, and the big Torrent burst
> Or seen the deep fermenting Tempest brew'd
> In the grim Evening Sky. Thus pass'd the Time
> Till thro' the lucid Chambers of the South
> Look'd out the joyous Spring, look'd out, and smil'd ...

Above all *The Seasons* was full of splendid passages on bird life, seen with the eye of love and the precision of a naturalist, as in the account of mating behaviour:

> First, wide around
> With distant Awe, in airy Rings they rove,
> Endeavouring by a thousand Tricks to catch
> The cunning, conscious, half-averted Glance
> Of their regardless Charmer. Should she seem
> Softening the least Approvance to bestow,
> Their Colours burnish, and by Hope inspir'd
> They brisk advance; then, on a sudden struck,
> Retire disorder'd; then again approach;
> In fond rotation spread the spotted Wing,
> And shiver every feather with desire . . .

Not till the day of the nature film would such close observation be outclassed. Even more striking was the description of bird flocks in migration from the far north of Scotland:

> Who can recount what Transmigrations there
> Are annual made? What Nations come and go?
> And how the living Clouds on Clouds arise?
> Infinite Wings! till all the plume-dark Air
> And rude resounding Shore are one wild Cry . . .

Hudson might have written it himself; and no doubt his own poems began with Hurdis and Thomson, as the field-notes began with White.

Returning to the same shop, he had a second stroke of luck, finding a copy of *The Farmer's Boy* by the Suffolk peasant poet Robert Bloomfield (1766–1823). This poem gave him something he had not found elsewhere—a detailed and factual account of the English labourer's seasonal round 'with a sense of continuity in human and animal life in its relations to nature'. As he read, he felt himself living with the farmer's boy 'from morn till eve . . . in woods and green and ploughed fields and deep lanes—with him and his fellow-toilers, and the animals, domestic and wild, regarding their life and actions from day to day through all the vicissitudes of the year'.

With him from morn till eve: was Hudson thinking of his Devonshire grandfather, also a country boy at the end of the eighteenth century?

'A Shepherd's Boy . . . he seeks no better name', ran Bloomfield's epigraph. Starting work at the age of ten, he had learned every aspect of the shepherd's trade; and all about ploughing, sowing, scaring birds and being scared himself on dark nights on his way to the lambing fold. Again, Hudson found much that was familiar; such as the vivid description of lambs at play, followed by the misery of seeing them butchered. All the hard grind of the field worker's life was there, set off by moments of happiness; as when the shepherd boy

> Claims a full share of that sweet praise bestow'd
> By gazing neighbours, when along the road
> Or village green, his curly-coated throng
> Suspends the chorus of the spinners' song

—a picture that takes one back another 200 years, to 'the spinsters and the knitters in the sun' of Shakespeare's day.

Hudson would reach England too late for cottage industries, except for a few odd survivals. But he was in time to catch and record a last glimpse of that older England, from the memories of country people; among them an aged woman who used Shakespeare's name, dive-dapper, for the moorhen; and a shepherd who in boyhood had cut the nine-men's-morris in the turf and learned the old country songs from his father.

There were other links between Bloomfield and Hudson, still hidden in the future. At fifteen, too frail for a lifetime of farm work, the poet went to London, learned a trade (as a shoemaker), began to read—Thomson's *Seasons* 'particularly delighted him'—and then to write. Staying on in London, he educated himself, married, worked hard at his trade in a garret and wrote of country things. He never forgot the world he had lost.

5

Facing Death

With health apparently restored, fresh hopes and interests, and so much unexpected pleasure from his reading, Hudson must have felt his prospects brighter than at any time since he set out a year or two earlier for that unlucky holiday.

Continuing his studies, he found a more recent work, Carlyle's *French Revolution*; and after that high drama Gibbon's prose may have seemed refreshingly sober. He tackled it again, and was deep in the *Decline and Fall* when another blow fell, this time involving the whole family.

It appeared that his father, from characteristic 'child-like trust in his fellow men', had neglected in taking over the derelict ranch and homestead of The Acacias to safeguard his possession by deed. The place, restored by his efforts and capital, should have remained the family home, to be passed on in due course to the younger Daniel. But now a counter-claim was made and legally upheld. The property passed into other hands, and the unfortunate Hudsons had to go back to live in poverty at their one remaining possession, The Twenty-five Ombus.

Here Daniel again ran a small store, worked the ranch and engaged in various trading enterprises, helped by his sons. William went on reading in his spare time, 'so taken up with the affairs of the universe, seen and unseen, that I did not feel the change in our position and comforts too greatly. I took my share in the rough work, and was much out of doors on horseback looking after the animals, and was not unhappy'—though sometimes dreamy and unhandy, liable when deep in thought to lose his rein or even drop his knife: something unthinkable to the gaucho.

Since his illness he had grown rapidly, remaining very thin, and perhaps the fever had left him more delicate than anyone suspected. Doctors said later that he had 'outgrown his strength'; and clearly he drove himself too hard. One winter day he undertook to bring a herd of cattle single-handed from a distant ranch. Exposed for hours to wind and rain, he was soon drenched, exhausted and numb with cold as he struggled with the restive beasts. His long boots filled up with rain till they were 'slopping over at the knees', and for the second half of the day he could not feel his feet and legs. An attack of rheumatic fever followed, and his heart was so severely affected that the doctors in Buenos Aires thought his case hopeless. He was told that he might fall dead at any moment.

This dreadful verdict threw over his next years, 'to others the fullest, richest and happiest in life', a shadow so deep that afterwards he could hardly bear to recall them. No sooner had he begun to find himself than everything had to be given up, 'all thoughts of a career, all bright dreams of the future, which recent readings had put into my mind'. Yet, bitter as it was, this was not the hardest part of his mental suffering. Far worse was the fear of death, or rather the thought of being cut off so soon from the world of birds and animals.

Probably few people can recall the exact moment when they first realized that they would die. Hudson could do so with painful clarity. Soon after the arrival of Trigg, the histrionic schoolmaster, an old dog had died, a much-loved family pet, and the children had watched his burial. As they stood silently around the grave, Mr Trigg saw his chance to play on their feelings. With a solemn air he told them, 'That's the end. Every dog has his day and so has every man; and the end is the same for both. We die like old Caesar, and are put into the ground and have the earth shovelled over us.'

No performance of his ever made more impression. Five-year-old William had had the idea—no doubt from early religious teaching—that only wicked people died, while the rest would live for ever. The sudden revelation threw him into a state of horror. His mother, appealed to after days of misery, tried to explain the idea of spiritual survival, and for a time he was reassured. But he had received a lasting shock, and the grim facts of death were kept in his mind by crime, accident and fatal illness, as well as by the slaughter of farm animals, 'an awful object-lesson' repeated every day.

Now the first terror came back, plunging him into a search for religious truth. Edwin, he knew, had thrown off all belief in his early teens; but he had been in perfect health, 'that state when we regard ourselves as practically immortal'. In his agony of mind, William compared his own state to that of a prisoner in the hands of Argentine soldiers, bound and helpless, taunted with knives as he awaited death. He turned for help to sombre volumes of theology: what hope did they hold out of life after death? But he soon realized that everyone must try to answer that question for himself. The books could only tell him to have faith.

The 'old vexed question'—how to reconcile the cruelty of nature with 'the idea of a beneficent Being who designed it all'—had already troubled the young field naturalist; when, for instance, he discovered that wasps paralysed their prey and left it imprisoned, to be eaten alive by their new-hatched young. But sometimes now, after weeks of prayer and mental conflict, there would come an interval of peace, when he felt he had been 'lifted or translated into a purely spiritual atmosphere and was in communion and one with the unseen world'. Then doubt would return, as he remembered some tale or read some fresh passage dismissing belief in survival as a delusion.

He knew that his mother watched his struggle with deep anxiety, though their habit of reticence prevailed, and she could only speak now and then of the help and support her own faith had been to her in the hardships and reverses of life. But he was soon to lose her sympathy and care, with all that it meant to him. Two months after his eighteenth birthday, on 4 October 1859, she died after a brief illness. Her last words showed her distress at leaving him to contend alone with his broken health and troubled spirit.

Unknown to him, his experience reproduced in microcosm the great crisis of faith in the outer world, springing from scientific advances of which so far also he knew nothing. Doctrinally, he was back in the seventeenth century, reading in Baxter's *Saints' Everlasting Rest* (1650) of the torments of the damned, everlasting fire and thirst, 'the shrieks and cries of their companions', and worse; and telling himself that even this would be better than extinction: 'in that dreadful place I should be alive and not dead, and have my memories of earth.' Meanwhile mankind was being deprived, as one comment put it, of that hope of everlasting damnation. Throughout the century the ancient split between science and religion had intensified as new light was shed on the geological history of the world. At this moment—November 1859—the conflict was brought into the open by the chief scientific event of the century, the appearance of Darwin's work *On the Origin of Species by Means of Natural Selection*, summarizing a great mass of facts on evolution to which the educated could no longer turn a deaf ear.

Orthodox Christianity held that 'in six days the Lord made heaven and earth, the sea and all that in them is', as recorded in Genesis and summarized in Exodus. Aspin's *Chronology*, published in 1812, followed that of Archbishop Ussher in the seventeenth century, and began: '4004 Creation of the World ... on Sunday the 23d of October. Adam and Eve created in the evening of the sixth day, or Friday, October 28, and placed in Paradise.' Since 1701 the date 4004 had been printed in the Bible. To accept the concept of man as part of the animal world, and not as a unique creation in God's image, was to repudiate the word of God and to abandon the Christian faith, and with it all hope of an after-life, whether in heaven or hell. So it seemed to many of Darwin's readers, and to William among them when the book came his way.

It was Edwin, home on a visit after five years' absence, who gave him a copy. Edwin, now a genial young man in his twenties, had grown more tolerant in manner, but his character had not changed. Soon, with all his old confidence and authority, he was drawing out his young brother, uncovering his views on life and expressing surprise that he still kept to the religion of their childhood. 'How, he demanded, did I reconcile these ancient fabulous notions with the doctrine of evolution?'

Like thousands of others, at the first reading, William's reaction to the *Origin of Species* was one of flat rejection. 'I could not endure to part with a philosophy of life ... which could not logically be held, if Darwin were right, and without which life would not be worth having.' When Edwin asked what he thought of the book he flashed out, 'It's false!'—adding more carefully that 'it had not hurt me in the least, since Darwin had to my mind succeeded in disproving his own theory with his argument from artificial selection. He himself confessed that no new species had ever been produced in that way.'

That, Edwin pointed out, 'was the easy criticism that anyone who came to the reading in a hostile spirit would make'. But he was obviously surprised and impressed that this uneducated youth should understand and criticize such a work. Darwin himself at a later reading found the closely printed pages 'tough reading'. In fact the book, written before science adopted its own specialist language, is immensely readable, exoteric in approach, simple in language, the points illustrated (as in the Gospels) by reference to everyday things of the countryside, familiar to Darwin's fellow countrymen; and to William from Gilbert White and the poets. Where an example is worlds away from Victorian England the great naturalist still gives it with the same unassuming air, as though any reader might bear him out: 'We see the value set on animals even by the barbarians of Terra del Fuego, by their killing and devouring their old women, in times of dearth, as of less value than their dogs.' This simplicity of course is deceptive, and Edwin was right to be impressed. Mrs Humphry Ward in her novel *Robert Elsmere* (1888)—later read by Hudson 'with great labour'—would point out that it was one thing to know about Darwin's theory from hearsay and take it half for granted; but 'to drive the mind through all the details of the evidence, to force one's self to understand the whole hypothesis and the grounds for it, is a very different matter.' William's grasp of the work shows how remarkably his mental powers had developed, with little guidance but his own thought and observation of nature.

Edwin sensibly advised him to read the book again 'in the right way for you to read it—as a naturalist'. Having done so, he told himself that he would think no more on the subject: 'I was sick of thinking' (a mood of exhaustion shared by Darwin when he wrote, 'At last I fell asleep on the grass and awoke with a chorus of birds singing around me, and squirrels running up the trees, and some woodpeckers laughing ... and I did not care one penny how any of the beasts and birds had been formed.') But all the while William's subconscious mind went on revolving the question; and in time he was ready to admit that he had become an evolutionist, and now found it strange that the great truth of man's relationship to other forms of life should not have been recognized earlier.

Yet he felt he had come out of the contest a loser. Much as he longed to do so, he could not, like many other Christians—including his brother Albert in later years—retain his faith and reconcile scientific truth with belief in man's immortal soul.

But, in compensation, the shadow of early death had lifted. The doctors had been wrong. The condemned man, as he said, was reprieved, allowed out on bail and eventually pardoned: 'barring accidents, I could count on thirty, forty, even fifty years with their summers and autumns and winters.' For a long time he was still to suffer agonizing heart attacks, sometimes collapsing with palpitations and lying almost insensible, hardly able to move, out on the pampa in the rain, until he recovered and could crawl painfully home. One such attack was brought on by the excitement of duck-shooting. But, finding by desperate experiment that walking and riding at least made him no worse, he continued to spend much of his time in the open air, and gradually resumed all his old pursuits: although, when he was called up at eighteen for service with the National Guard, his state was so precarious that his Captain—a friendly man, fond of birds—became worried enough to wish that he would drop dead and get it over. At twenty, no doubt from so much close study of ancient print, he was threatened for a time with blindness and forced to give up reading. This too sent him out of doors. Now began the wandering life that he was to lead for the rest of his time in South America.

6

Hunting Birds

Disaster had saved him, and would do so again, though he might never realize it. Given health and full strength, his sense of duty must have thrust him into some career that would have hindered and perhaps destroyed him as a great naturalist and writer. Illness had prevented this. Now convalescence set him free to travel in lonely places, where he was 'healed for a long life and prepared for duties none knew of, not even himself'. So Morley Roberts wrote in his memoir after Hudson's death. The comment is perceptive, but not the whole truth. Fresh facts later came to light which show that for him the 1860s and early 1870s were not only years of travel, learning and recuperation, but also of practical field work, splendid reporting and swift professional recognition as an authority on birds. It was a brilliant and hopeful start, based on wide knowledge, youthful keenness and delight in his subject, and this must have done much to make up to him for the dark time he had endured since he was fifteen; though perhaps at one point his keenness went too far for his future good.

Hudson ended the account of his early life in *Far Away and Long Ago* with no more than half a dozen lines to indicate what followed. From now on, he wrote, he was often away from home for days or weeks, 'sometimes staying with old gaucho friends and former neighbours at their ranchos, attending cattle markings and partings, dances, and other gatherings'. Later journeys took him all over Argentina, to Brazil, Uruguay and the Rio Negro. The flavour of these travels may be found in his books. Like Richard Lamb, hero of his novel *The Purple Land*, he would seek 'permission to unsaddle' in some wayside home at sunset, spending the evening in a communal kitchen crowded with old and young, cats and dogs, livestock and strange pets. In one of these kitchens, like a vast barn thatched with reeds,

> the hearth, placed in the centre of the floor, was a clay platform, fenced around with cows' shank-bones, half buried and standing upright. Some trivets and iron kettles were scattered about, and from the centre beam, supporting the roof, a chain and hook were suspended to which a vast iron pot was fastened. One more article, a spit about six feet long for roasting meat, completed the list of cooking utensils. There were no chairs, tables, knives or forks; everyone carried his own knife, and at meal-time the boiled meat was emptied into a great tin dish, whilst the roast was eaten from the spit, each one laying hold with his fingers and cutting his slice.

As Darwin had found thirty years earlier, bread was a rarity, 'and as for a potato, one might as well have asked for a plum-pudding'. Seats were logs of wood or horse skulls. The traveller slept on the floor, on a pile of hides or a sheepskin; unless he were kept awake by the bloodthirsty *vinchuca*, a winged insect with a bite like a red-hot needle. At daybreak the household would be up, the men smoking and sipping maté by the hearth, then riding away to gather up the herds. If the guest's horse were tired, he could count on the loan of another to finish his journey: 'Just turn him loose at night . . . no matter how far you take him, he will soon find his way back here.'

An Englishman, Hudson said, has little idea of making himself agreeable in company—'that is why he does not learn to perform on musical instruments.' Probably, in those evening gatherings, he left the guitar solos, and the singing of ballads on 'love and the prowess of horses', to more extrovert characters; but he had a natural gift for getting on with strangers. His Spanish looks must have been an asset. A photograph taken in his mid-twenties shows a young man of striking appearance, with dark curling hair and beard, keen eyes, an air of vitality and sensitive pride. Already he may have shown that quality of strangeness that later set him apart, yet drew others to him. No doubt he paid for hospitality by his good looks and good manners, and the novelty of his presence; by answering questions; showing courtesy to the women, and discreet admiration—or sometimes less discreet, if any of Lamb's adventures were his own; by talking to children, and amusing them with stories; above all, by hearing with genuine interest the life histories of men and women starving for a listener. These were ways he never lost, springing from natural warmth and sympathy as well as the quick ear of the naturalist and writer for anything worth noting; though offset at other times by his love of solitude, and, as he grew older, by increasing wariness of bores.

In wilder country he would live out of doors for months at a time, shooting his own food and cooking on a fire of bones and thistle stalks. When other game was wanting he could enjoy rhea and armadillo, 'the two gamiest-flavoured animals on the pampas'; but some experiments were a failure. 'The burrowing parrot ... is very bitter tasted, and yet feeds on the same seeds as the partridge and wild pigeon; the glossy ibis eats the same food as the most delicious flavoured snipes, and yet when cooked its fat emits a sickening smell that renders it unfit for human food.' At night he slept among fireflies and cicadas, wrapped in his poncho; hearing the moan of the wind in tall reeds and its whistle in dry grasses; the resonant notes of tuco-tucos underground, like gnomes hammering away at little anvils; the hooting of owls, the screams of rare wild dogs and eerie cries of marsh birds. In treeless country a horse could be secured by inserting a bone at the end of its tether, burying the bone and sleeping across it; if anything frightened the horse, it would rouse him by jerking at the rope. Often he was in danger: from hostile Indians, cattle more dangerous than beasts of prey, great birds with powerful talons, quiet waters hiding quagmires 'deep enough for a giant's grave'. One night—as he found on waking—he shared his poncho with a venomous snake. The gaucho too could be risky company:

> when passing a river, if he could avoid it, no man rode into the water first, especially if he wore silver spurs or reins, for it might chance that he received a knife-thrust in the back from a too admiring friend, or perhaps merely because the sudden lust to kill, so frequent amongst dwellers of the plains, rose in the heart of the man following immediately behind.

He met with many accidents—'from guns and pistols and bad or stupid men, and horses—vicious or false-footed—and cows with sharp horns, and water and fire and trees and knives and flints and carts'. But this was the earth life he had set his heart on; the kind of freedom that Richard Jefferies dreamed of when he chafed at 'the pettiness of house-life, tables and chairs' and wrote, 'I want to be always in company with the sun and sea, and earth.'

These, and the stars by night, are my natural companions.' They were also Hudson's. Riding at night, he would lie back on his horse, gaze up at the glittering sky and feel himself soaring through space, the soft beat of hooves on the grass sounding like the rush of wings. It was the nearest he came to flying.

At first, on venturing out of doors again, he was troubled with the old self-reproach, feeling that his love of nature was still a hindrance to him, 'a turning aside from the difficult way I had been striving to keep'. Then came a new revelation. Some time in his earlier twenties, evidently through friends in Buenos Aires, he discovered the trade of the scientific bird-collector, and the demand for bird-skins and other specimens. He sent some specimens to the Director of the Natural History Museum in Buenos Aires, Dr German Burmeister, who advised him on his next step. At last he had found a link between bird-watching and a career. He would become a field-worker in the natural sciences.

He was twenty-four years old when, on 27 December 1865, the United States consul in Buenos Aires, Hinton Rowan Helper, wrote on his behalf to Spencer Fullerton Baird, Assistant Secretary in the Department of Natural History at the Smithsonian Institution in Washington, and one of the great ornithologists of the century. Baird, born in 1823, had been a field naturalist, explorer and collector from his earliest years, and might have preferred to remain an outdoor man; but his dream was to create a great natural history museum, and at twenty-seven, with this in view, he had joined the Smithsonian Institution. Seven years later, in 1857, the United States National Museum was established, largely through his efforts, and with his own immense collections as its nucleus. He was now supervising Government explorations and surveys in North and South America, selecting the collectors and describing their work in the Smithsonian Annual Reports.

Mr Helper's letter explained that Professor German Burmeister, the museum director, had introduced to him

> a Mr Wm. H. Hudson, of Conchitas, Partido de Quilmes, in this Republic—a sort of amateur ornithologist, who would like to be employed in collecting birds ... Mr Hudson has been recommended to me as quite capable in what he professes. I have asked him for his terms; but he says he has never made any collections except as a matter of mere interest to himself; and does not, therefore, know how to charge for his services.

In view of this diffidence, the writer suggested that Mr Hudson should be paid 'so much for such and such birds', and offered to help the two parties come to an arrangement.

Baird, in his reply two months later, observed that he could not find Conchitas on any map, but that little was known of the birds of Argentina, and it would therefore give him much pleasure to see Mr Hudson's collections and help him in disposing of them. Small, inconspicuous birds, he added, were of the greatest scientific interest; and various prices were suggested.

Six months later, on 5 September 1866, Hudson sat down at The Twenty-five Ombus and carefully copied in excellent, clear handwriting, on a page cut from his notebook, the letter he had composed to Professor Baird. This (except for a few lines on swallows, quoted from his diary entry for 18 March 1865) is the earliest of his writings to survive:

Dear Sir,

Mr Helper kindly favored me with a copy of your letter to him, in reference to my collecting birds. I hoped then, to have had, before September, two or three hundred specimans, but I have been disappointed: winter birds, which I tried to collect, were so very scarse this season, that several times I have ridden leagues without being able to obtain, or even see, a single speciman. Most of the birds I now send are those that remain with us all the year, and are all probably well known to naturalists: it is too early yet for summer birds, and as I will not collect any more for two or three weeks I think it best to send the few I have got.

I am not confident that they will reach you in a good state of preservation, as I have no experience in this kind of work; however, they are not many to lose, if they should be lost, and by the time your answer reaches me, I hope to have many more ready to send. I will also try to obtain some ostrich eggs, and a box of snail shells, of which I believe there are only four species in this country.

As you have not required the names of the birds, I have only thought it nessisary to mark the sex of each one, on the margin of the paper in which it is wraped; but if you desire it, in future, I can give, with each species, a concise account of its habits. As to the locality in which they were killed, I shot them within eight leagues [twenty-four miles] of Buenos Ayres City.

You remark that the birds best to get are the small inconspicuous ones, as they are better for scientific purposes. By diligently searching through the swampy forests along the rivers, I can obtain many birds of this description. There are here many species of the *certhia* an extensive genus of small and homely birds. And it is reasonable to expect, that in a country so little explored by naturalists as this, many species may be found unknown to science.

You must know from the physical conditions of this country—the Province of Buenos Ayres—that it possesses a very scanty Fauna. Wide as is its extent, it is but one vast, level and almost treeless plain, affording no shelter to bird or beast from the cold South winds of winter or the scorching North winds that blow incessantly in summer: while the yearly droughts banish all the aquatic birds to great distances. But it is not only that there are few species, that makes the work of a mere taxadermist unprofitable, but these are often so widly seperated that vast tracts must be traversed to obtain them all. Though I am not a person of means, it is not from want of other employment I desire to collect, but purly from a love of nature. It would, however, be eisier for me to devote all my time to these pursuits, if I was required to collect other natural objects besides birds, as fossils, insects, grasses etc. and this would enable me to make thorough collections of all the birds.
I am, Sir,

respectfully yours
William H. Hudson.

This letter was delivered in person by Mr Helper on a visit to Washington early in 1867, and the bird-skins also arrived safely. But the mails were uncertain—in a later letter, Hudson advised Dr Baird to write by way of England—and had been further disorganized by the outbreak of war between the Argentine Republic and Paraguay in 1865. On 15 March 1867 Professor Baird sent off two copies of his reply, and also a separate letter, by three different routes. All three in fact arrived, together with a payment of $60; and it is good to know that Hudson had the pleasure of reading a response so full of friendly encouragement.

He was quite pleased, the Professor wrote, with the preparation of the specimens, which was decidedly above the average amateur level. Though he could not guarantee that profits from collecting Buenos Aires birds would justify 'the abandoning of any other business', he thought there was sufficient demand to make it tolerably certain that further contributions could be disposed of on the same terms. 'If therefore you will continue to collect, and send the specimens here, I will do my best to secure good prices for the same.' There followed several pages of practical advice on the preparation, labelling and annotating of specimens—giving, for instance, the proper symbols for male, female and young—and on the numbering and invoicing of each collection. Professor Baird was 'particularly desirous' of getting a good rhea specimen. He also offered to help in the sale of fossil animals—good specimens, especially of more or less perfect skeletons or skulls, would always bring a good price—and of crickets, grasshoppers, etc. His letter ended on a note of cordial optimism:

> Hoping to hear frequently from you and to receive from time to time interesting collections of specimens—
>
>> I remain
>> Very truly yours
>> Spencer F. Baird.

The first printed reference to Hudson's work appeared in the Institution's Report for 1866: 'In South America, explorations have been made and collections transmitted by Mr W. H. Hudson, in Buenos Ayres.'

Two writers, R. Gordon Wasson and Edwin Way Teale, who discovered this correspondence in the 1940s, point out that the bird-skins Hudson prepared and sent could be easily picked out: unversed in formal taxidermy, he had folded the legs to project forward instead of backward. Many of his skins are still in the Smithsonian collections; duplicates were transferred to other museums. Evidently, at 90 cents each, they have proved good value; though Hudson, with his father's honest candour, wrote on receiving the first $60, 'of course it is much more than I thought they were worth.'

During 1866 he again served with the National Guard, and at one time he and his brother Daniel spent several months in a fort at Azul. There he watched great flocks of Magellanic geese feeding on grass and clover: 'they are shy and loquacious, and chatter much during the night in frosty weather.' The bird man as well as the temporary soldier had been keeping watch.

Home again, in May 1867 he wrote to tell Professor Baird that he would soon be sending another collection, before again going south to a point 300 miles away where he hoped to secure 'a number of winter birds that seldom come further north'. He was sorry, he added, that he had been unable to get an ostrich: 'since the fall of Rosas [1852] the gauchos have laughed at all decrees forbidding the "corridas" and have consequently almost exterminated them. I know of one gentleman who keeps a number on his estancia in great wire fences, but as he is very wealthy he would not be likely to part with any of them for money.' So the wild flocks he had watched from his first pony twenty years before now belonged to the past.

In June the new collection of 200 specimens was ready; and the box, sent by sea via New York, may have carried with it a secret hope. It was Hudson's dream to discover a new species; and in his accompanying letter he drew Professor Baird's attention to some 'blackbirds'—cow-birds—which he knew from his observations to be a distinct species. This was the peak year of his career as a collector in his home province: was he also to give his name to one of its birds?

He had to wait many months for the answer. Professor Baird's acknowledgement, sent in November, did not arrive. In December the Professor wrote again, sending another $60 'on account of the collections you are making'. No doubt this was welcome; and with it came an invitation to continue collecting so as to complete the group for Buenos Aires and 'adjacent regions'. But there was no mention of the 'blackbirds'. In February 1868 Hudson wrote to say that he had heard nothing of the box sent eight months before, and feared it was lost. On 15 March, on receiving the December letter, he wrote again: 'I was much disappointed at there being no mention made in your letter of the black-birds I said I thought a new species.... Dr Burmeister desires much to know what name you will give the species.' Two months later some information was at last on its way; but this time his hope was not realized. The collections had been sent on loan to experts in London, and Professor Baird could not now precisely recall the specimens to which Hudson referred, but he suggested that this species might be *Molothrus rufoaxillaris*, brought from Paraguay by a Captain Page. This proved to be the case. But two South American birds were later to bear Hudson's name, the first being a tyrant-bird which he found three years later in Patagonia.

In his letter of 10 December 1867 Professor Baird said he was enclosing a photograph of himself, and asked Hudson to do the same. In March, Hudson sent the photograph already described (see p. 74), taken at the studio of 'Meeks y Kelsey, fotografos, Buenos Ayres': and this, together with the letters, was to lie undiscovered in the files at Washington for over seventy years.

The Institution's Report for 1867 noted that 'an important Smithsonian exploration has been made in the Province of Buenos Ayres by Mr W. H. Hudson, who has transmitted large collections of birds, which have been referred to Mr P. L. Sclater and Mr Osbert Salvin, of London, for examination, these gentlemen having been especially occupied in the study of South American birds.' Of 163 collections received in that year, Hudson's was given special mention as among the eight most important. Fourteen of the species sent were not on Dr Burmeister's list, the most complete at the time for that region.

Though Hudson was often away, his home was still with his family at The Twenty-five Ombus; but changes were now at hand. On 14 January 1868, at the age of sixty-three, his father died after a long illness. Hudson's grief was added to the wretchedness he felt at his country's sufferings in the costly war with Paraguay, which continued until 1870. In his letter of 14 February, writing on black-edged paper, he made an oblique allusion to his loss: 'For several months I have not collected birds at all, as I have had other occupations at home, besides we have not been exempt from the afflictions that have come on almost every household in this country.' Already he was making new plans. In March he wrote, 'I shall perhaps leave the Conchitas to settle in some other part of the country before long, and my continuing to collect in future depends on the leisure I will have, I would prefer collecting altogether could I get a living by it.'

The afflictions to which he had referred included a serious cholera epidemic. Professor Baird wrote that he was 'greatly rejoiced' to learn that Hudson had escaped this, and hoped that before leaving Conchitas he would be able to complete the collection for that part of the country, and would continue to collect elsewhere. Earlier in the year he had sent off another $60, together with a suggestion that Hudson might undertake collections of lepidoptera for private buyers in North America, which, he said, promised a reasonable return: 'Professor Burmeister can put you in the way of preparing these orders in the accepted way.'

A further payment of $100 followed in July 1868, and took a year to reach him. Hudson had been promised copies of Dr Sclater's reports on his collections, but these too were long delayed. In November 1868 he wrote that they had probably been destroyed in the Post Office as not properly directed, and asked Professor Baird, if he were sending others, to use an address in Buenos Aires instead of writing to Conchitas. Hudson had obtained several species to complete his list of birds for the province, and had also been working for private bird-collectors, 'gentlemen in this city', but was still despondent about his chance of making a livelihood: 'As the money I get by collecting scarcely pays half my expenses, I shall probably soon be obliged to give it up.' Though to some extent he could live on the country while travelling, costs of guns and ammunition, taxidermy materials and carriage to Washington must have been considerable. However, he hoped for 'more and sufficient orders in Buenos Ayres to pay me, and in that case will continue longer, and perhaps visit Patagonia and the north Provinces.' This was the first mention of Patagonia.

The spring and early summer of 1868 were spent in the marshes of Ensenada de Barragan, a region rich in bird-life; and the next year opened with an exciting prospect.

> Dr Burmeister has been desired by the Government to name a suitable person as collector to accompany an expedition to explore the passes of the Andes. He has named me, but as usual the Argentine Government is to poor to pay a collector, so I shall only have part of the specimens obtained *in payment for the other part.* I have not yet decided to go, but would rather go than be obliged to relinquish collecting altogether . . .

Nothing more was said, in the surviving letters, of this promising adventure. Hudson did not go.

In the same letter, dated 28 January 1869, he wrote that he had another collection ready for Professor Baird, totalling 305 specimens, 'besides a few other curiosities'. But, while the learned men in Washington and London were deriving immense pleasure and professional credit from studying his hard-earned booty, the field worker, 'diligent as I have been', was again hopelessly out of pocket. Proposals for collecting in Paraguay and the northern provinces, 'a richer field for the taxadermist', were as unlikely as the Government expedition to bring him any profit, since expenses there would be double those in his home province: 'It is therefore impossible for me to continue collecting longer for the Smith. Institution on the terms you have proposed.'

In April, returning from a long visit to the southern frontier—where his brother Daniel had a sheep ranch—he found the promised copy of Dr Sclater's report on the earlier collections. In August he wrote telling Professor Baird that, though no letter had come reporting the safe arrival of his latest consignment to Washington, he had learned from the English newspapers that this too had now reached London. He had not been collecting in recent months, he said, but could offer another 100 specimens, and would also like to know whether nests of the oven-bird would be of value? A month later, on 5 September 1869, he was forced to repeat his ultimatum. The resources of Ensenada de Barragan, he wrote, were by no means exhausted, especially as rain and floods had made collecting difficult on his previous expedition. 'I should have been glad to continue in my researches this season if the proceeds were sufficient to pay expenses. But circumstances oblidge me to seek some other occupation, more lucrative if less agreeable.' What this may have been one can only guess: sheep-farming with Daniel seems indicated. This, and previous remarks on his finances, were clearly appeals as urgent as pride would allow, and much now depended on Professor Baird's reply. On 23 October 1869 the Professor wrote, with obvious regret: 'I wish we were able to secure your services for a thorough exploration of the region in your neighbourhood. We are, however, very much cramped for funds, and at present I fear it is out of the question. Perhaps at some future day we may be more fortunate.'

That day never came for Hudson; and there, except for one more letter from him, the correspondence ended.

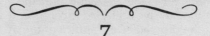

7

Writing to England

The last mention of Hudson's name in the reports of the Smithsonian Institution came in 1869 with the entry: 'Hudson, W. H.
Two boxes birds, Buenos Ayres'. Meanwhile another chapter had
opened in his life.

His collections had been examined in London by the two
experts, Philip Lutley Sclater and Osbert Salvin, both eminent
ornithologists and scientific writers. In February 1868, at a scientific meeting of the Zoological Society of London, they gave the
first account of their studies. They had received 265 skins and had
had great pleasure, they said, in determining the species, 96 in
all. The report, headed 'List of Birds Collected at Conchitas,
Argentine Republic, by Mr William H. Hudson', contained the
encouraging invitation: 'We trust that Mr Hudson will continue
his collections in this interesting locality, and that we may again
have the pleasure of calling the Society's attention to this subject.'
Dr Sclater, who was Secretary to the Zoological Society, himself
wrote to tell Hudson that a copy of the report would be sent to
him.

In his first letter to England, Hudson was able, as it happened,
to settle a disputed point. There was doubt as to whether two of
his specimens were of distinct species (as Darwin had earlier
thought) or male and female of the same species. Hudson had
confused the issue by a slip in labelling these specimens. When
the first report at length reached him, he wrote on 30 April 1869:

> I regret to find that I have made so great a mistake as to mark
> females two of the tree black plumaged Silver-bills—*Lichinops
> perspicillatus*—This was pure carelessness as all the black

84

plumaged birds I have ever opened were males, red, females. I have also watched them pairing and building their nest, and am therefore positive they are sexes, though country people here regard them as different species. There is also another mistake of less importance, the vulgar name of the Scolqux frenata is *patas amarillas* (yellow feet) the Becasina is another bird . . .

It depends upon Dr Baird's answer to my last letter whether I shall continue to collect for him or not. There are not many more birds to be obtained in this district, and the price I am paid (90 cents a specimen) would not pay my expenses, should I extend my researches a distance from home.

By the end of 1869 his hopes in this direction were over; but in the next five years the link with London must have given him fresh hopes as well as increasing pleasure. In the Zoological Society's *Proceedings* for 24 June 1869, Dr Sclater said that the 'vexed question' of the silver-bills might now be considered settled. Two further reports of Hudson's collections followed, the third showing that these totalled 143 species, many almost unknown to European science.

On 5 September 1869 Hudson wrote to Dr Sclater explaining that he had great difficulty in identifying birds by their Latin names, those in the Buenos Aires museum not being labelled. He added this modest suggestion: 'I have from time to time made notes on the habits of the birds, etc., of the Pampas and would like much to know if they would be of any importance to naturalists, perhaps you will kindly favor me with your opinions on this subject.'

Dr Sclater's reply, welcoming this offer, should be remembered with gratitude, as David Dewar points out. It marked the beginning of a correspondence which Sclater edited and published in the *Proceedings* during 1870 and 1871, to be followed by further papers. So the *Selborne* pupil, fourteen years on, emerged as a field naturalist in his own right among the great names of his time, Swinhoe, Père David and Druce; and his work was already known to leading scientists before he was thirty. These first published writings resemble White's in being essays in letter form; and among the virtues which Hudson imitated were the simplicity of approach, the absorption and pleasure in his own information, which mark the *Selborne* letters. At last, after the years of isolation, he was speaking to fellow naturalists; and his powers of expression flowered with each letter, as confidence increased. Also, though he had not taken pains to observe from his mentor the spelling (for instance) of the word 'specimen',

Hudson had learned something far more important: that mistakes should be set right as soon as possible. In his admission of 'pure carelessness' may be heard the voice of Gilbert White telling Thomas Pennant: 'Notwithstanding what I have said in a former letter, no grey crows were ever known to breed on Dartmoor; it was my mistake.' This regard for accuracy was soon to involve him in a bold step, in company even more distinguished than that of Dr Sclater and his confrères.

The first essay, written on 14 December 1869, shows how, even at this early stage, with his uncertain command of language, Hudson's sentences could melt into music when he began to speak of birds. After referring to the ombu trees of the pampas, he described the huge floating islands of the *camaloté*, the water flower of the Parana and its tributaries, which carried new species of seeds, animals, snakes and toads from the north to the swampy thickets bordering the Plata river. By this 'grand highway', he believed, many new species of birds also arrived in the region. He also referred to birds, such as the red-breasted lark, which avoided trees and nested on the ground. Throughout, brief glimpses of his life as a bird-watcher were revealed, as in the description of the ash-coloured cuckoo, *Coccyzus cinereus*:

> Like the common cuckoo it is retiring in its habits, concealing itself in the densest foliage, but it cannot be attracted like the other species, by mimicking its call.
>
> It has a song, which it will sometimes repeat at short intervals for half a day, like the mourning of our little dove, being a succession of long and plaintive notes. It has besides a different note—loud, harsh and sudden, so much resembling the cry of another bird that I was frequently decieved by it . . .

He often spent half a day, he said, in vainly watching for and pursuing another elusive species: 'Once only I succeeded in getting a glimpse of one, at the moment it started screaming from a tree. I was, fortunately, able to secure it, and have it still in my collection.'

Further on appears this poignant description, which, for all the cool detachment of the telling, can hardly have failed to touch the feelings even of this keen collector.

> Another bird of very interesting habits and never seen away from the river wood is the *Icterus pyrrhopterus*. It has a continuous song, sweet, low and varied, with a peculiar ventriloquism in some notes, that give the listener a confused idea that the performer approaches and retires while singing. The first bird of this species I

shot, was but slightly wounded in the wing, and fell into a stream;
to my great surprise it began singing as it floated about on the
surface of the water, and even when I had taken it out, continued
to sing at intervals in my hand...

When he found a pair nesting he returned in a few days 'to secure
the nest and observe them again, but found to my sorrow nest
and birds had disappeared'.

His sorrow, it would seem, was not for the destruction of the
nest, nor for the distress of the parent birds, which he had
observed with professional detachment—'the male and female
fluttered round me manifesting great anxiety'—but for his own
loss of valuable specimens. This attitude, and the whole tone of
the passage, might have seemed incredible to some of those who
in later years were to know him as the ardent protector of birds;
and to know too his prejudice against science in so far as it
consisted in the study of dead objects. Those who came to know
him best, however—men like Morley Roberts and R. B. Cunninghame Graham, who had also lived among primitives, 'scoun-
drels and murderers'—understood that he kept the sense of
reality, of the hard facts of existence, which his early life had
taught him. In boyhood he had worshipped birds and also
enjoyed shooting. Death and suffering were a part of life: so was
hunting for food. Bird-skins were necessary to the study of
ornithology. It was the mindless killing of rare birds for ornament
and fashion, for 'something pretty in a glass case', the 'feathered
woman' and the commercial bird-stuffer who were to arouse his
anger when he came to England, provoking an intense reaction
against the callousness of his youth. He did not then try to hide
his early career—still writing openly, in one of the later books, of
the time 'when I was a sportsman and collector, always killing
things'—but nor did he draw attention to it by republishing these
letters.

At this age his attitude to birds seems to have hardened, as it
had to do if he were to carry on as a collector. Compassion was in
abeyance to ambition, at least on paper, and he cultivated the
sangfroid which later drove him to fury when practised by others.
His notebook for 1870 showed another striking example. One day
he fired at a heron (*Ardetta involucris*) in a reed-bed, and thought
he had killed it, as it disappeared at the report of the gun; but he
could not find it. After long search he was on the point of giving
up 'in disgust and bewilderment' when he saw the bird,
unharmed, only eight inches away in the surrounding reeds: 'the

long tapering neck held stiff, straight and vertically; and the head and beak also pointing up'. He took hold of its head and forced it down, and on being released 'up flew the head, like a steel spring, to its first position. I repeated the experiment many times with the same result, the eyes of the bird appearing all the time rigid and unwinking like those of a creature in a fit. What wonder that it is so difficult, almost impossible, to discover the bird in such an attitude!' How had it happened, he asked himself, that while repeatedly walking around it among the reeds, he had not caught sight of the striped back and broad, dark-coloured sides? He began to walk around it again, and found that the bird turned itself imperceptibly as he did so, 'keeping the edge of the blade-like body before me'.

At this discovery, 'such a degree of delight and admiration possessed me as I have never before experienced . . . much as I have conversed with wild animals in the wilderness. I could not finish admiring, and thought that never had any thing so beautiful fallen in my way before.' Delight and admiration, however, did not hinder him from going on with his experiments.

> For some time I continued . . . pressing down the bird's head and trying to bend him by main force into some other position. . . . I also found, as I walked round him, that, as soon as I got to the opposite side and he could no longer twist himself on his perch, he whirled his body with great rapidity the other way, instantly presenting the same front as before.

Finally Hudson plucked the bird forcibly from the reeds, 'upon which he flew away; but he flew only fifty or sixty yards off, and dropped into the dry grass. Here he again put in practice the same instinct so ably that I groped about for ten or twelve minutes before refinding him.' One wonders if he then thought it necessary to add that specimen to his day's bag.

It is obvious that two Hudsons were at work in this remarkable field study. One was the bird-lover he had always been. The other—the ruthless searcher after facts—had produced a forthright letter to Dr Sclater in the early part of that year (1870). Dealing with the four species of woodpecker found in the province of Buenos Aires, it consisted in the main of an attack on Darwin; and the tone of the letter betrayed a certain glee in aiming at targets so eminent as the *Origin of Species* and its author.

To illustrate his theory that, following changes of habits, natural selection might allow a creature's structure to alter so as to form a new species, Darwin had cited one of the South American woodpeckers, the Carpintero, 'a Woodpecker which never climbs a tree', as having become adapted to life on the pampas 'where not a tree grows'. Hudson himself, in his first letter to Professor Baird, had spoken of the pampas as 'almost treeless'. Now he wrote:

> However close an observer that naturalist may be, it was not possible for him to know much of a species from seeing perhaps one or two individuals, in the course of a rapid ride across the pampas. Certainly if he had truly known the habits of the bird, he would not have attempted to adduce from it an argument in favour of his theory of the Origin of Species, as so great a deviation from the truth in this instance might give the opponents of his book a reason for considering other statements in it erroneous or exaggerated.

Not content with this hit, he went on:

> The perusal of the passage I have quoted from, to one acquainted with the bird referred to, and its habitat, might induce him to believe that the author purposely wrested the truths of Nature to prove his theory; but as his 'Researches', written before the theory of Natural Selection was conceived—abounds in similar misstatements, when treating of this country, it should rather, I think, be attributed to carelessness

—to the same cause, in fact, as the frankly admitted errors of Hudson himself. He then went on to specify the tree-shaded districts of the province, its orchards, groves and the woods along the shores of the Plata, where the Carpintero might be seen 'climbing the trees, resting on his stiff and frayed tail feathers, and boring the bark with his bill as other woodpeckers do'. The letter continued: 'But his favourite resort is to the solitary Ombu, a tree found over a great extent of the plains of Buenos Aires; this tree attains a considerable size'; and then, as though Hudson had lifted his head from the page to gaze out at the hot midsummer plain:

> there is one within fifty paces of the room I am writing in. This very tree was, for many years, a breeding place for several Carpinteros, and still exhibits on its trunk and larger branches, scars of old wounds inflicted by their bills...
>
> Twenty years ago, which is as far back as my recollection extends, it was rather a common bird, but has now become so very rare that for the last four years I have met with only three individuals.

It was a notable tribute to Hudson's growing prestige in the eyes of Dr Sclater that this letter (although somewhat modified) was printed with the rest in the *Proceedings*. Darwin himself, in a subsequent issue, paid him the compliment of writing a long reply, in which he referred to 'Mr Hudson's valuable articles'. Slightly nettled perhaps by that wicked phrase 'a rapid ride across the pampas', Darwin explained that his observations had been made during successive visits to the northern bank of the Plata. While admitting error in saying that the species never climbed a tree, he quoted the naturalist Don Felix de Azara (1746–1811) in support of his own description, and mildly enquired whether the bird might not have different habits in different districts: an argument Hudson himself accepted when he later wrote that Azara's account of the bird referred to its habits in Brazil. To those rash remarks about 'wresting the truths of Nature', Darwin referred with dignity: 'He exonerates me from this charge; but I should be loath to think that there are many naturalists who, without any evidence, would accuse a fellow worker of telling a deliberate falsehood to prove his theory.'

Before this reply appeared, Hudson had followed up his first attack in a letter to Dr Sclater written on 19 May 1870. He quoted a passage, based on Darwin's description, from *Habit and Intelligence* (1869), by Joseph John Murphy:

> Nor can one doubt that our woodpeckers' feet are adapted to climb trees; yet there is a woodpecker inhabiting the Pampas of South America where trees are unknown. The inference is obvious, and I think certain . . . that the woodpeckers of the Pampas are a colony of woodpeckers which have strayed away from their aboriginal forests. . . . In this case the species has become modified by its new habitat.

Hudson's comment ran:

> It will but little affect the theories of Messrs Darwin and Murphy, that one of their numerous statements should be disproved; it is but a leaf plucked from the giant tree in whose shadow they sit—into whose shadow, perhaps, all men must come and sit with them forever—but as to this great question, wether root and branch be sound or rotten, I presume not now to hazard a conjecture. But why should so much stress be laid on this fable of a scansorial bird living on the ground? If it was true, and the bird, transported by some accident to a country destitute of trees, was obliged to feed, roost and breed on the ground, I do not see that it

would lend any great favor to the theories of the above mentioned gentlemen, unless it was proved that it *had become modified* in its structure by its new habitat, an assertion for which Mr Murphy has no authority.

Murphy amended the passage in the second edition of his book (1879). Darwin did the same for the corrected edition of the *Origin of Species* (1888) and again paid generous tribute to 'an excellent observer, Mr Hudson', in a passage on the egg-laying habits of *Molothrus bonariensis*, one of the parasitic cow-birds.

'Mr Hudson', Darwin here commented, 'is a strong disbeliever in evolution.' The above letter certainly suggests that this was still true at the time of writing, close to his twenty-ninth birthday and years after he first read the *Origin of Species*. In later life he said he was a Lamarckian rather than a Darwinian. Some of his hostility towards Darwin, now and later, may be put down to natural impatience with the errors or inexperience of the visitor. Darwin, for instance, had been amused at being told by a gaucho that he was 'too poor to work'. To the Englishman this did not make sense. A native would know that it was the gaucho's pithy way of saying that he had lost his horses, by theft or conscription, and could not afford to replace them. But some at least of Hudson's opposition may have sprung from bitterness at his eventual loss of faith.

At that moment he had another reason for bitterness. A month before, he briefly mentioned, at the end of a letter to Dr Sclater, that a great storm had flooded the friend's house where he stayed when in Buenos Aires, bringing ruin to his friend and to himself the total loss of his collection of bird-skins: 'one hundred species of passerine birds collected in this State, some never before obtained here, and others probably unknown to naturalists'. His brevity underlines what this must have meant to him.

Throughout 1870 he went on summing up a lifetime's bird-watching in his essays, which were read to meetings of the London Zoological Society and reprinted in its reports. The twelve long letters in the series were carefully copied in ink on flimsy paper, the capital letters ornamented with flourishes. He was evidently taking pains to improve his spelling and punctuation. Sometimes a passage would be marred by awkwardness of syntax, as in an account of a swarm of spiders: 'so numerous were they, that they continually baulked each other in their attempts to rise in the air, there being a breeze blowing, as soon as one threw out its web, it would be entangled in that of another. . .' But already his style bore the stamp of the future writer. Letter 9, written at midwinter 1870, opened with a passage on the Glossy Ibis that recalls Thomson's lyrical description of migrating birds in *The Seasons:*

> They have a graceful flight; and when migrating the flocks are seen to succeed each other in rapid succession, each flock being usually composed of from fifty to a hundred individuals, but sometimes of a much greater number. A body of these birds on the wing is a most interesting sight—now soaring high in the air, displaying the deep chestnut hue of their breasts, now descending with a graceful curve towards the earth, as if to exhibit the beautiful metallic green of their upper plumage. The flock is in the mean time continually changing its form or disposition, as if at the command of a leader. One moment it spreads out in a long straight line; suddenly the birds scatter in disorder ... as suddenly they again re-form and proceed in the figure of a phalanx, half-moon or triangle [as though] the birds go through these unnecessary evolutions intelligently to attain greater proficiency in them by practice, or merely to make a display of their aerial accomplishments.

There followed an account of an invasion of mice, in which he quoted Pliny and clearly drew on his own first diary begun when he was fifteen:

> In the year 1856, when the earth swarmed with Mice, ... flocks of the Great Adjutant Stork (*Mycteria americana*) also appeared. Armies of these majestic white birds were seen stalking over the grass on all sides, or at the close of day winging their flight to the distant watercourses in a continuous flock; while the night air resounded to the solemn hooting of the innumerable Owls. ... Pliny, if I remember right, relates that at one season in some part of Asia Minor the Mice increased in an extraordinary manner, but soon appeared 'an army of strangely painted birds' and devoured them all.

The letter went on with this beautiful glimpse of the wide pampas skies:

> It was once a matter of wonder to me that flocks of Swans should almost always appear flying past after a shower, even when none had been visible for a long time before, and when they must have come from great distances. But the simple reason soon occurred to me, that after rain a Swan may be visible at a vastly greater distance than during fair weather, the sun shining on its snow-white plumage against the dark background of a cloud rendering it very conspicuous. The fact of Swans being seen almost always after rain is only a proof that they are almost always passing.

92

Migration continued to fascinate him, as it had done since childhood. In September 1870 he was writing, 'Before many days the cold season will have gone, and with it the birds that annually visit us from the barren tablelands of Patagonia. ... Most anxiously do I wait an opportunity of learning from observation of the ornithology of that country.' A few weeks later he was at sea, bound for the Rio Negro.

There had been anxious financial planning beforehand. In March 1870 he had made a last tentative approach to Professor Baird: 'I have nothing important to communicate, but it is a considerable time since any letter has past between us and I am unwilling that our correspondence should be altogether broken off ...' He would like to know, he said, what a specimen of '*Struthio darwini*' (the lesser rhea, *Pterocnemia pennata*) would be worth in North America; adding, 'I could obtain for you one or two specimens of the Rhea if the trouble and expense of getting and sending them could be paid, perhaps you will let me know how much you could afford to pay for them. I could also send specimens of our mammals.' The letter referred to Dr Sclater's second report—' several copies he has mailed to me have sunk in the fathomless depths of the B.A. Post Office'—gave another address in Buenos Aires for any future communication, and acknowledged the receipt of a second payment of £20, 'but do not know if there is anything more due to me'. It ended: 'I hope, Sir, to have the pleasure of reading other letters from you ...'

Besides the usual collector's expenses, Hudson needed ready money for the sea passage to the Rio Negro and back, for bribes to Indian hunters to help in his search for the rare small rhea, and presumably to make some return to the friendly hosts with whom he stayed and who provided him with horses. Stone Age relics and weapons were to prove a useful harvest, though many were lost in transit—'a severe blow'. Some three or four hundred arrow-heads, found on prehistoric village sites, went eventually to the Pitt Rivers collection in England; a number of these may still be seen in the museum at Oxford. He also mentions finding, on the same sites, fossil bones of animals that had been used as food. However it was financed, this adventure was to remain the most memorable of his life.

He landed on a lonely shore in the midsummer dawn, in December 1870, after a narrow escape from the threat of shipwreck. 'At last, Patagonia! How often had I pictured in imagination, wishing with an intense longing to visit this solitary wilderness, resting far off in its primitive and desolate peace, untouched by man, remote from civilization!' The air was filled with the scent of evening primroses—in that region an early morning scent, and one he would always find evocative. In the sandy dunes by the seashore he waded through a jungle of wild liquorice, a feathery plant with spikes of pale blue flowers. The feeling of 'relief, of escape, and absolute freedom' in this vast solitude filled him with exhilaration. Further inland he found a grey thorny wilderness alive with small birds, some new to him; and with the songs of mocking-birds, shrill-voiced woodhewers and the piercing cries of cachalotes 'like bursts of hysterical laughter'. At once he began to note intriguing habits, like the behaviour of a small whistling bird, 'wren, or tree-creeper, or reed-finch, or pipit', which dropped into hiding at his approach 'with a shyness very unusual in a desert place where small birds have never been persecuted by man'. The egg season was over, but there were nests to be found in the bushes. After a long trudge through the wilderness he came on his second day to the Rio Negro, where he planned to spend a year in watching and collecting the birds of the district. 'Never river seemed fairer to look upon. . . . Far out in the middle of the swift blue current floated flocks of black-necked swans, their white plumage shining like foam in the sunlight'; and on the bank he found his first lodging, a thatched farmhouse in a cherry orchard, with ripe fruit glowing among the leaves, a welcome sight after hours of torturing thirst.

This promising beginning was halted when, two or three weeks later, he handled a revolver which went off unexpectedly, lodging a bullet in his left knee. For the next two months he had to lie helpless, though he still found things to watch and think about: the mysterious intricate dance of house-flies above his bed in a mission house; then, as he lay outside on the grass, the autumn muster of large purple swallows getting ready to fly north. By mid-February he was on the move again, to spend the autumn and winter months exploring the valley, studying its wildlife, its inhabitants, and the buried settlements of the remote past, laid bare by drought and violent winds. In spring he visited 'Parrots' Cliff', where a flock of Patagonian parrots nested in holes in the soft rock—those screaming parrots with 'sombre green plumage touched with yellow, blue and crimson', so well remembered from their winter visits to the plantation. This alone must have made the journey worth while.

His attempts to find the lesser rhea were unsuccessful. These birds, he wrote afterwards to Dr Sclater,

> were formerly exceedingly numerous along the Rio Negro, but a few years ago their feathers rose to an exorbitant price. Gauchos and Indians found that hunting the ostrich was their most lucrative employment, and consequently these noble birds were pursued unceasingly, and slaughtered in such numbers that they have been nearly exterminated. . . . I was so anxious to obtain this bird that I engaged 10 or 12 Indians, by offering a liberal reward, to hunt for me; they went out several times, but failed to capture a single adult bird.

His own hunting had more success. In a journey of 100 miles, he met with 126 species, 33 found only in Patagonia; among them the new species which was to add his name to the lists of science as 'Hudson's tyrant-bird'.

Once, coming on a flock of flamingoes, he crept up to the rushes bordering the water 'in a fever of delighted excitement—not that flamingoes are not common in that district, but because I had noticed that one of the birds before me was the largest and loveliest flamingo I had ever set eyes on, and I had long been anxious to secure one very perfect specimen'. He fired, the bird was retrieved at length by a temperamental old sporting dog, and the rapturous account continued: 'Never had I seen such a splendid specimen! It was an old cock bird, excessively fat, weighing sixteen pounds, yet Major had brought it out through this slough of despond without breaking its skin, or soiling its exquisitely beautiful crimson, rose-coloured, and faintly blushing white plumage!' Another prize was a magnificent horned owl with 'immense tiger-coloured wings' and fiery eyes, 'at which I gazed with a kind of fascination, not unmixed with fear when I remembered the agony of pain suffered on former occasions from sharp, crooked talons driven into me to the bone'. When he aimed his gun the bird sat eyeing him so calmly, 'I scarcely had the heart to pull the trigger. . . . But I wanted that bird badly, and hardened my heart.'

Nor was Dr Sclater to be disappointed in the promised report on the bird-life of the region. In March 1872 there arrived in London an essay 'On the Birds of the Rio Negro of Patagonia', especially memorable for its descriptions of bird-songs and notes. One would like to know whether the scientific gathering to whom it was read appreciated such fresh and vivid passages as:

> When the profound stillness of midnight yet reigns and the thick
> darkness that precedes the dawn envelopes earth, suddenly the
> noise of this little bird is heard wonderfully sweet and clear. . . . I
> have often observed that when a bird, while singing, emits a few of
> these *new* notes, he seems surprised and delighted with them; for
> after a slight pause he repeats them again and again a vast number
> of times, as if to impress them on his memory. . . . When I dis-
> covered that all the strains I had heard had issued from a single
> throat, how much was my wonder and admiration for the delight-
> ful performer increased!

To this essay Dr Sclater's note in the *Proceedings* recorded: 'It
would appear that one or other of his predecessors was fortunate
enough to obtain specimens of nearly all the birds peculiar to this
district, leaving to Mr Hudson only the little *Cnipolegus*.' This
species, of which Hudson had sent four male specimens, was
accordingly named Hudson's tyrant-bird after 'its energetic dis-
coverer'. He had already been honoured by being made a Corres-
ponding Member of the Zoological Society, which gave him the
right to add the letters CMZS to his name. Besides *Cnipolegus
hudsoni* (now *Phaeotriccus hudsoni*), Dr Sclater also named after
him Hudson's spinetail, *Synallaxis hudsoni* (now Hudson's canas-
tero, *Asthenes hudsoni*).

His next contribution to the *Proceedings* was a long essay on the
swallows of Buenos Aires. He had begun to write on this subject
in the twelfth letter, before starting out for Patagonia; and while
there he had made a special study of different song-notes in
species common to both regions. This paper also contained a
striking account of marauding swallows invading the nests of
oven-birds, 'warbling out their gay notes in answer to the out-
rageous indignant screams of the *Furnarii*', and finally taking
possession:

> Thus are the brave and industrious Oven-birds often expelled
> from the house that cost them so much labour to build . . . when
> unable to drive the Oven-birds by force from their citadel, [the
> swallows] fall back on their dribbling system of warfare, and keep
> it up till the young birds leave it, when they take possession before
> the nest has grown cold.

In the next three years, several further papers were to appear in
the Zoological Society's publications. It must now have seemed
to Hudson that his footing in England was secure and friendly;
while changes had begun in Argentina—draining, fencing and
cultivation—to turn the wild pampas into economic cattle

ranches for new markets abroad. This he did not want to see. It was time to go. He had money enough at least for the single fare (£47), and to look about him on arrival. Payment of his share in his father's estate was delayed until June 1874, nearly three months after he left; but this sum he probably anticipated. No doubt he was confident of soon finding work. He was an exile by two generations, but by no means unknown in 'the land of his desire': an Englishman returning home.

In 1868, the year his father died, Hudson had taken down in his notebook some reminiscences of an old gaucho, used eventually in his story *El Ombu*. There the old man, Nicandro, sits day after day under an ombu tree by the ruins of a vanished house. The notes, when Hudson returned to them long afterwards, must have brought memories of the home he had left.

> Do you hear the manganga, the carpenter bee, in the foliage over our heads? Look at him, like a ball of shining gold among the green leaves, suspended in one place, humming loudly! Ah, señor, the years that are gone, the people that have lived and died, speak to me thus audibly when I am sitting here by myself. These are memories; but there are other things that come back to us from the past; I mean ghosts ... sometimes, when a traveller lies down here to sleep the siesta, he hears sounds of footsteps coming and going, and noises of dogs and fowls, and of children shouting and laughing, and voices of people talking; but when he starts up and listens, the sounds grow faint, and seem at last to pass away into the tree with a low murmur as of wind among the leaves ...

Within a few years the distinctive Hudson voice, inherited from their father, would no longer be heard at The Twenty-five Ombus. Brothers and sisters were scattered: Daniel to his ranch on the southern frontier; Edwin to settle as a land surveyor in Cordova, in the western province; Caroline Louisa and Albert to teaching posts, the latter in the National College in Buenos Aires. All except Caroline Louisa married; of these, all except William had children. Though widely different in mind and temperament, the six were united by 'a hidden quality, a something of the spirit' from their mother's side; and they remained an affectionate circle. William's letters, and later his first novel, were passed from one to another. Two nieces were to visit him in London. But after 1874 they were never again together under one roof. The farmhouse by the ombu grove became for them, like Nicandro's haunted ruin, 'a house that died'.

On 1 April 1874 Hudson sailed for Southampton in the *Ebro*, seen off by his brother Albert. The two hopeful young men in their early thirties can hardly have guessed that this was the last time they would see each other; but at the moment of parting Albert broke through their reserve with a strange and valedictory remark, which many were to echo in later years: 'Of all the people I have ever known, you are the only one I don't know.'

Part II
1874–1901

8

Coming Home

*I was following not the Exe only, but a dream as well, and a memory.
Before I knew it the Exe was a beloved stream. Many rivers had I seen in
my wanderings, but never one to compare with this visionary river,
which yet existed, and would be found and followed at last. My
forefathers had dwelt for generations beside it, listening all their lives
long to its music, and when they left it they still loved it in exile, and
died at last with its music in their ears . . .*

The Exe valley and his 'natal city' of Exeter, the river Clyst and the
village of Clyst Hydon, where Daniel Hudson's father had lived
before emigrating—these names, familiar from childhood, must
have been in William's thoughts all through the voyage. The *Ebro*,
a small mail steamship with sails, carrying 127 passengers, took
thirty-three days from the river Plate to Southampton: days of
alternating excitement and boredom, described in five long
letters to Albert. In these pages—the first headed 'Atlantic Ocean
April 14–1874'—one can hear, for the only time, the young
Hudson talking in free, light-hearted vein to his family: about
shipboard scandals and flirtations ('tell it not in Gath, publish it
not in the streets of Nuestra Señora de los Buenos Ayres'); a
blunder by the Captain when 'we came up slap bang against the
rocky island of San Antonio'; a whale hunt in St Vincent harbour
(Cape Verde Islands), where 'a pair of whales were so accom-
modating as to come into the harbour and tumble and blow all
round us.' Early in the voyage a passenger died of yellow fever
and was committed to his 'vast and wandering grave' amid fears
of a general outbreak. On 19 April Hudson wrote: 'Ten days have

flown—dragged—by since we left Rio, and here on the wide desolate sea, no land, but clouds on the round horizon: no birds, but flying fish as they rise up before us glittering like silver in the sun...' Later there were swarms of blue and silver fish seen fathoms down in clear water, and a fleet of Portuguese Man-of-Wars, 'beautiful things—real flowers of the ocean—[that] fly before the wind, all sails set, sails tinted with pearl, rose-purple ...' Near the coast of Africa 'we encountered à Kaka-lani-pandorga-quelanota. You would know just as well what I meant as when I say we had a storm.' There was a glimpse of wild mountain coast with 'white snow patches on its summits'. Then: 'Lisbon, April 29, 1874. At last, we are in Europe, but how long we have been in coming!' They had met head winds after St Vincent, 'a weary tedious time'. Now the sun was 'on the wrong side'. Ahead lay bitter easterly storms in the Bay of Biscay; and the first sight of 'home'.

> Southampton, 5 May 1874.
> ... How can I describe England? Compared even with this town of 55,000 souls, Buenos Ayres now seems to be a poor, filthy, rough, ugly, disagreeable city. Southampton is a beautiful place: wide clean macadam streets, grand old elm and horse-chestnut trees—parks covered with velvety turf—gothic churches and ancient stone buildings, covered to their summits with ivy. Even a Rookery in the middle of the town and Rooks cawing and quarrelling in their nests. The town is full of sparrows and their incessant chirping sounds precisely like the swallows at daybreak in Buenos Ayres. Altogether day in England is like the humid, misty, dreamy fresh morning twilight of Buenos Ayres.

The green countryside, the soft light, even the smell of malt and hops from a brewery, all seemed to him magical; it was 'a land of morning'.

He had made friends on board; one, a student named Abel Pardo, a future Senator of Buenos Aires, was to seek out Hudson whenever he returned to England in after years. These travelling companions expected him to go on with them to London, and were surprised to find him ready to say goodbye at the dockside. In England at last, and in Gilbert White's county, he wanted only to be alone and to look for birds. They arrived on Sunday, 3 May; on the 4th he walked out on the Winchester road—Winchester was to be his first English cathedral—finding trees, birds, grass full of wild flowers. He could identify the daisy—from Burns—wild violet and 'one I took for the buttercup. I heard thrushes, wrens and many others I have heard so much about. I also, to my delight, heard the Cuckoo, and listened to him for half an hour, warbling his mysterious lay from grove to grove—one bird I thought might be the nightingale, but I couldn't be sure.'

The only companion he would have welcomed would have been someone who could answer his questions. Instead, next day, he found himself driving into the country with a persistent shipboard acquaintance who refused to be shaken off, professing an interest in English farming. 'I didn't want him. I wished to goodness he'd leave me alone, but I couldn't say so.' They passed romantic streams, parkland and woods, 'the pretty orchard and green fields of the modest thatched cottage of Rosas', and the ruins of Netley Abbey, where thrushes were singing from the ivy-covered walls, blackcaps warbling and jackdaws cawing like Urracas. There were birds everywhere, but the stolid youth who drove them could only put a name to the robin: 'Please sir, that's Dobbin Dishwater.' By Hudson's eager 'What bird is that? What bird sang that note?' he was as bewildered as by the other man's 'I say, what crop is that?—Yes, but what grass?'

Another Englishman, met on a trip to the Isle of Wight, was equally puzzled by an allusion to Tennyson. 'Who's he? A retired admiral?' Hudson was finding himself the classic immigrant, knowing and caring more about England than the natives. Not that he counted himself an immigrant. Genealogical research in London no doubt soon told him, if he did not already know, how ancient the name of Hudson was, going back to the very roots of English history: to Anglo-Saxon Huddas, a name so old that its meaning was forgotten long ago; to Norman Hughs and Rogers and their sons, known to familiars as Hud, Rodge or Hodge—now the accepted nickname for the farmer's boy; to Gower's army of rebel peasants, including Hobbe and Hudde; even perhaps to 'Robertus Hood [or Hod] fugitivus' and the old forest ballads.

The last letter, dated 'Southampton, 8 May', ended: 'After reading (try) forward this letter to Conchitas—Mrs Denholme [Mary Ellen] will take 15 days to read it, and well she might. If I write on this scale, my London letter will fill 3 vols. . . . Write to the same direction as before till further advice. With love to all, believe me ever yours, William H. Hudson.'

Of his first day in London he wrote some twenty years later:

> I put up at a City hotel, and on the following day went out to explore, and walked at random, never inquiring my way of any

person, and not knowing whether I was going east or west. After rambling about for some three or four hours, I came to a vast wooded place where few persons were about. It was a cold wet morning in early May, after a night of incessant rain; but when I reached this unknown place the sun shone out and made the air warm and fragrant and the grass and trees sparkle with innumerable raindrops. Never grass and trees in their early spring foliage looked so vividly green, while above the sky was clear and blue as if I had left London leagues behind. As I advanced farther into this wooded space the dull sounds of traffic became fainter, while ahead the continuous noise of many cawing rooks grew louder and louder. I was soon under the rookery listening and watching the birds as they wrangled with one another, and passed in and out among the trees or soared above their tops. How intensely black they looked amidst the fresh brilliant green of the sunlit foliage! What wonderfully tall trees were these where the rookery was placed! It was like a wood where the trees were self-planted, and grew close together in charming disorder, reaching a height of about one hundred feet or more. Of the fine sights of London so far known to me, including the turbid, rushing Thames, spanned by its vast stone bridges, the cathedral with its sombre cloud-like dome, and the endless hurrying procession of Cheapside, this impressed me the most. The existence of so noble a transcript of wild nature as this tall wood with its noisy black people, so near the heart of the metropolis, surrounded on all sides by miles of brick and mortar and innumerable smoking chimneys, filled me with astonishment; and I may say that I have seldom looked on a scene that stamped itself on my memory in more vivid and lasting colours.

It was a happy introduction to the city that would seem before long an immense unfriendly wilderness. His enthusiasm recalls Charlotte Brontë's first London exploration and her praise of Kensington Gardens. Both writers enjoyed this experience at the age of thirty-two; both had read *The Seasons* with its optimistic view of city life and labour, 'the sons of Art' and Trade and Joy commingled, successfully getting their living, while 'even Drudgery himself . . . looks gay.' Hudson was to know more of drudgery than of gaiety. The unfriendly note may have been struck at once. Soon he would need work; and his first object in coming to town was probably to make himself known without delay to Dr Sclater, who had given him so much encouragement when he lived on the other side of the world. The acquaintance cannot be said to have progressed on their meeting, or in the future. One of Hudson's essays appeared that month in the Zoological Society's *Proceedings*, and three more in 1876. The two men were later to collaborate in producing *Argentine Ornithology*. Sclater, also, was one of those who signed Hudson's naturalization papers in 1900. But in temperament they remained worlds apart; and from Hudson's point of view 'this eminent professor lacked charm, to say the least of it.'

Soon Hudson was travelling west to visit South American friends at Malmesbury in Wiltshire, that county of low rolling downs where he was always to feel most at home in England. Malmesbury was no more than a hundred miles from Exeter and Clyst Hydon; two days' ride in the old life: in the new, a few hours' journey by train. The main line from Taunton crosses the river Clyst near Exeter. The traveller's feelings on his first journey there may be easily imagined.

As usual, where his personal life and deeper feelings were involved, he left no account of it. But he described with close insight the homecoming of another chance-met immigrant who had traced his family home from a father's description:

> the stream, the village, the old stone church, the meadows and fields and hedges, the deep shady lanes . . . What he was going to do in England he did not consider. He only knew that until he had satisfied the chief desire of his heart and had looked upon the original of the picture he had borne so long in his mind he could not rest nor make plans for his future. . . . how many there must be who come with some such memory or dream or aspiration in their hearts!

At the end of his life, however, Hudson came nearer to self-revelation. In a strange little essay, 'Apple Blossoms and a Lost Village', he recalled how in the previous May he had gone to look again for Clyst Hydon, probably walking from Bradninch station three miles away—

> and how I wouldn't ask the way of anyone, just because it was Clyst Hydon, because the name of that little rustic village had been written in the hearts of some who had passed away long ago far from home:— how then could I fail to find it? It would draw my feet like a magnet!
>
> I remembered how I searched among deep lanes, beyond rows and rows of ancient hedgerow elms, and how I found its little church and thatched cottages at last, covered with ivy and roses and creepers, all in a white and pink cloud of apple-blossoms . . .

Only two old orchards now remain on the outskirts; but living memory bears out this vision of springtime white and pink in the heart of the village. Clyst Hydon was once, and remained until early in this century, an 'orchard village': the church ringed with blossom in May, and more apple orchards spreading over the neighbouring countryside as far as the eye could see.

In other respects, though of course more prosperous, the village must be outwardly much the same as when Hudson first saw it: the deep lanes no longer shaded by elms, but with their banks covered in May by primroses, periwinkles and stitchwort; the church surrounded by yew trees, grass and tombstones, with daffodils fading above sheets of daisies and blue speedwell; swifts shrieking overhead, swallows building, a tawny owl calling at night, and chiffchaffs by day in the willows along the river.

The River Exe too may still be followed just as he described, from its source among bogs and cotton grass under the Exmoor skylarks; first a brown peaty trickle, then a moorland stream bordered with rushes, flowing through sheep pastures, under the mossy bridge above Simonsbath; running wider and deeper through Exford and Winsford, attracting birds and children to dabble on a hot day; down through Somerset, 'singing aloud, foam-flecked, between high hills clothed to their summits in oak woods: after its union with the Barle it enters Devonshire as a majestic stream, and flows calmly through rich green country', circling the city of Exeter, on past the great bird flocks of the estuary to the sea. Many of the riverside paths he walked are there, still lonely and quiet in winter, or by starlight and at dawn in summer.

Stonehenge at first sight was a shock,

> one of the greatest disillusionments I ever experienced. Stonehenge looked small—pitiably small! ... As a child I had stood in imagination before it, gazing up awestruck on those stupendous stones or climbing and crawling like a small beetle on them. And what at last did I see with my physical eyes? Walking over the downs, miscalled a plain, anticipating something tremendous, I finally got away from the woods at Amesbury and spied the thing I sought before me far away on the slope of a green down, and stood still and then sat down in pure astonishment. Was *this* Stonehenge—this cluster of poor little grey stones ... !

Coming nearer, seeing the great circle silhouetted against the sky, he began to experience some of the awe and wonder the place has evoked for centuries; though, characteristically, he was soon interested in a colony of sparrows nesting in the stones—a practice later discouraged by wire-netting. No doubt he remembered Gilbert White's note on the daws that built there. Later, seen in a midsummer dawn, Stonehenge appealed to him 'more than any place builded by man'.

Selborne brought no disillusionment. He saw it at the end of a fifteen-mile walk, on a wet summer day with yellowhammers calling, and felt that he knew it already—

> the little old-world village at the foot of the long, steep, bank-like hill, or Hanger, clothed to its summit with beech-wood as with a green cloud; the straggling street, the Plestor, or village green . . . and, close by, the grey church, with its churchyard, its grand old yew-tree, and overhead the bunch of swifts rushing with jubilant screams round the square tower.
>
> I had not got the book in my knapsack, nor did I need it. Seeing the Selborne swifts, I thought how a century and a quarter ago Gilbert White wrote that the number of birds inhabiting and nesting in the village, summer after summer, was nearly always the same, consisting of about eight pairs. The birds now rushing about over the church were twelve, and I saw no others.

Wandering about the village and the Hanger, watching a flock of greenfinches in the evening light, he thought of White continually and felt that he was in some mysterious way still living, 'an unseen presence near me'. In the churchyard, after long search, he found the little headstone and knelt to put aside the long rank grass half-covering it, 'as when we look into a child's face we push back the unkempt hair from its forehead', and read the brief inscription; G.W. 26 June 1793.

After his travel diary ended on 8 May 1874, there is a gap of nineteen months until the next recorded date in Hudson's life. In this time he may have travelled to Scotland, and also to Ireland to look for relations of his grandmother (Daniel's mother), the Malonys. In London he stayed at some time with a family named Poland: one of the daughters, Hannah Poland, was to be a founder member of the (Royal) Society for the Protection of Birds, and its first honorary secretary. On 22 December 1875, he received a ticket for the reading room at the British Museum, giving his address as 40 St Luke's Road, Bayswater: evidently a lodging-house, kept by a Miss Wingrave.

Tower House, so called from the campanile design of its central block, stands at the corner of two roads close to Westbourne Park railway station in West London. In May of the following year he married Emily Wingrave. From 1878, No. 40 St Luke's Road is listed under his name in Kelly's street directory, together with a house in Leinster Square, a few streets away, in which the couple made their home. In the mid-1880s they returned to live at Tower House, which remained his London home until he died there in 1922.

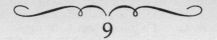

9

Staying On

There was something of the hand of destiny, Morley Roberts said, in the way Tower House remained the background of Hudson's life. The same hand seems to have shown itself fifty years later when the site was chosen in Hyde Park for his memorial. It stands, according to another close friend, 'almost on the exact spot where Hudson often slept when he first came to England, lonely and penniless'. What then had become of his hopes and plans?

Hardy's biographer Dr Robert Gittings suggests that, early in his career as an architect, Hardy, an 'unconnected young man from the country', met with a setback because he did not belong to 'the right public school and university background'. Hudson's failure to find the professional niche he deserved may have been due to a similar élitism. In the world of natural history, as David Elliston Allen points out, 'The first half of the century had been devoted to revealing the variety in nature; the second half was to be devoted to explaining how and why this variety had come about.' This period saw the rise of a generation of new scientists, much more intensely and self-consciously professional than their predecessors; many of them 'militant anti-amateurs' dedicated to the laboratory and the microscope, recording their researches in an exclusive specialist language and ignoring all 'aesthetic implications' in their work. Up to now Hudson had been eager to ally himself with the professional scientist, often suppressing his own feelings about the aesthetic implications. His contempt and hostility towards the indoor naturalist may have dated from his first days in London, and in particular from a visit to the distinguished ornithologist and artist John Gould, a member of the Zoological Society's Council and an authority on humming-birds. Gould showed him with pride a collection of mounted specimens. Hudson had 'just left tropical nature behind across the Atlantic'. Every summer of his life he had watched the humming-bird, 'an exquisitely beautiful little creature in its glittering green mantle, and in its aerial life and swift motions a miracle of energy'—darting and hovering over the acacia blossom, flashing in and out of the house, always too alert to be trapped; the tiny male birds carrying on ferocious challenges and chases in mid-air. What he saw in the dusty room in Bedford Square was a travesty. 'Those pellets of dead feathers, which had long ceased to sparkle and shine, stuck with wires—not invisible—over blossoming cloth and tinsel bushes, how melancholy they made me feel!' No doubt his feelings were evident, and did not flatter Humming-bird Gould, or help his chances of finding a patron. Gould, despite 'a certain jollity and bonhomie ... was a harsh and violent man,' Edward Lear found many years earlier. Now, a sick man in his seventies, he was said to 'hate the sight of a stranger' and saw few visitors; and he behaved badly to the proud, shy young newcomer, treating him as 'some astounding intruder who dared to believe he knew anything of birds'. Hudson later expressed what he thought of Gould in a savage little sketch lampooning their interview. This, for him, was an unusual reaction; as a rule he preferred to bury the past and avoid all mention of anything painful or humiliating. In later life he could rarely bring himself to speak of Gould or Sclater. 'Turn failure into experience, and experience into success', might have been his silent precept. But the sense of disillusionment must have been deep.

Eighteen years had passed since he first faced the problem of living. In that time he had travelled a long way, physically and mentally. His mind was stocked with ideas and experiences, and he had already distinguished himself as a naturalist and writer. But the years of bird-collecting, and even his published essays, had after all given him little standing in England. Perhaps he had hoped to be sent abroad again as a collector. The Zoological Society Reports show, however, that fieldwork was often a part-time interest for men in the services and other occupations overseas. Professional collectors probably had to finance themselves, as Hudson himself had done in the past, hoping for profits from the sale of specimens. Now his money came to an end with no offer of work; though it is hard to believe that no post could have been found for him in the world of natural history, had goodwill prevailed. His audacity in setting Darwin right about the woodpecker may have been remembered against him (though not, of course, by the great man himself); and, like the young Hardy, he was not one to 'push his way into influential sets'. Without professional backing, he was up against the academic barrier. To study at Cambridge was obviously out of the question, not only financially but from his lack of formal education. In London the School of Mines at South Kensington, which did not demand Latin or Greek, offered courses in natural history for a fee of only £3 or £4; also immensely popular free evening lectures for working men, to which Hudson might have gained admission, as Karl Marx had done in 1862. The prospectus laid down, however, that the object of the course in natural history was 'to convey to the Students of the School of Mines such a knowledge of the principles and of the details of Biological Science as is necessary to the right understanding of the nature and import of Fossil organic remains'. To Hudson this concept would have seemed as dead and unreal as Gould's stuffed humming-birds. So far as earning a living went, his prospects were bleak. He loved and understood children, especially little girls, and would have made an excellent tutor: no doubt there were many in London far less qualified. No such post seems to have come his way. He had shown that he could write, but lacked the newspaper experience and connections through which, in the mid-1870s, Richard Jefferies was working his way into the literary world. Hudson could only turn to freelance writing, self-education and whatever odd jobs he could pick up.

At one point a bankrupt archaeologist named Chester Waters engaged him as a secretary, probably less for his secretarial aptitude than for his formidable looks. Waters was trying to live by tracing, or perhaps concocting, genealogies for Americans interested—like Hudson himself—in their family origins. As his house was in a constant state of siege from creditors and bailiffs, he could not leave it to carry on his affairs. Hudson, employed to 'look up pedigrees and the like', found himself involved in the problems of Waters's life, tying food to cords let down from upper windows, when he could not get back into the house without being followed; and sometimes unable to go out at all. With his taste for odd situations, he may have found this amusing for a time; but he needed money, and his salary was rarely paid.

The pair had fierce quarrels, Waters asserting flatly, 'It's no good asking me for money, I haven't any.' Finally, still unpaid, Hudson threw a batch of papers in his employer's face and left, to return to an even more precarious way of life; wandering about London, watching the crowded streets, the rooks of Kensington Gardens and Gray's Inn, the tame ravens and visiting robins at the Tower, and two or three pairs of wood pigeons—then almost unknown in London—nesting in the parks; reading at Free Libraries; listening to music whenever he had a shilling to spare; and writing all the time, in lodgings or on park benches, filling countless small pocket notebooks. The long novel was still in its heyday, and family magazines were on the increase: fiction must have seemed the most promising market, and in the first flow of creative energy he wrote copiously. One script, or pile of notebook pages, stood two feet high; another, a long *History of the House of Lamb*, was pruned down to the two-volume novel that became his first published book, *The Purple Land that England Lost*. Ten years were to pass before he saw it in print. In that period, apart from his bird essays in the Zoological Society's *Proceedings*, some fifteen stories, articles and poems appeared in magazines. A mere handful; yet they represented years of effort, perseverance and patient self-discovery.

His poems meant a great deal to him; above everything he wanted to express himself in verse. First of these to be printed was a ballad in a short essay, 'Wanted—A Lullaby', which appeared in March 1875 in *Cassell's Family Magazine*. Either he or the editor obviously felt that this subject called for a feminine pseudonym; the one Hudson chose, 'Maud Merryweather', is interesting. The name Merryweather, as he may have discovered from his researches, comes from Mereworth in Kent (spelt Merryworth by Cobbett) close to the village from which the Merriams, his ancestors on his mother's side, emigrated to Massachusetts in the seventeenth century. 'Maud' might have been suggested by Tennyson's 'Birds in the high hall garden':

> Maud, Maud, Maud, Maud,
> They were crying and calling.

As for the essay itself, this curious production might almost be classed as fiction. Hudson threw himself into the part of a rather self-righteous Victorian matron who has lived in South America and regrets that there should be no English lullaby to compare with the Spanish mother's crooning she has heard there. A widely travelled man has told her, she says, that American Indian mothers also put their children to sleep by singing; the cradle song of the Tehuelches, the wandering tribe of Southern Patagonia, being the most pleasing. Still in character, she quotes her husband's views, takes a side-swipe at the higher education of women, and enquires, 'Is it not that the artificial life of our time has the effect of weakening the genuine mother-nature?'

Whether or not there was laughter behind this impersonation, there was certainly real concern. Somewhere, in an English home or lodging-house, Hudson had come across a bored, impatient woman dosing a wakeful child with spoonful after spoonful of some opiate, so that she could go out, leaving it in a drugged sleep. (Anna Sewell in *Black Beauty* (1877) also gave a warning about dangerous infant 'soothing syrups'.) It appeared, however, that even his own mother had failed to find the perfect lullaby: she would sing her children to sleep with the hymn, 'There is a happy land', which was not altogether a restful tune. With the right air, he maintained, a child might be sung to sleep with any words, 'even if profound and obscure as any Mr Browning writes'; yet the right words would be an asset, and he hoped some poet might perform this service for English children. The accompanying ballad had been composed to suit the 'simple pretty air' to which Spanish mothers would croon the line *A-ro-ro mi niño*, over and over without variation. However, he explained, his own words would be of no interest to an English mother, since they belonged to a distant land:

> Once an Indian mother
> Left alone her child
> In the rushes lying
> Sleeping in the wild.
>
> When she came to seek him
> Loud and clear she sung
> As a bird comes flying
> Singing to her young.
>
> Once an Indian warrior
> In the desert found
> All alone, a baby
> Sleeping on the ground.
>
> In his breast he hid it
> And he fled away
> Fled o'er hill and valley
> Fled by night and day.

113

And the mother mourned it
As the ewe doth mourn
For the lamb the eagle
To the hill hath borne...

In such tentative flights the future writer of the South American romances was trying his wings. Meanwhile the future English naturalist was shaping his course. Poverty was to keep him for years from seeing much of the English countryside, but in London he became an expert on the bird-life of the parks, squares and the green spaces beyond Bayswater, many of which were to vanish in the building boom of the next twenty years. As in South America, he found his interest unshared, though later he would come to know other London bird-watchers. The first time he heard a willow wren's song in the suburbs he described it eagerly to acquaintances, thinking they would tell him the name of the singer. No one could do so. In his lonely wandering he would hearten himself at times with the fancy 'that I was on a commission appointed to inquire into the state of the wild bird-life of London'.

The autumn of 1875 saw a great influx of visiting birds. On 26 November, after heavy rain and floods, the weather correspondent of *The Times* recorded: 'During the last two nights the mercury has fallen to freezing point and the indications of an early winter are plentiful, more especially on the Thames, where the presence of the porpoise and sea gull and flocks of wild fowl point to the probability of severe weather.' This forecast proved accurate. A heavy snowfall in early December was followed by months of fog, frost, snow and hail. Hudson, coming from the milder winters, pure air and sun of the pampas, suffered severely from the dark foggy days and the midwinter nights 'seventeen hours long', as he noted with feeling. But though sick and poor, he was no longer friendless. He had met Emily Wingrave, and was soon to marry her—'because', he once said, 'her voice moved me as no voice had ever done before, though I had heard all the great operative warblers of the time, Patti included.'

This was a cool and simple explanation of a step which later seemed to others lamentable. They were married on 18 May 1876, at St Matthew's, Bayswater, then an elegant Regency chapel. J. H. Wingrave and Louise Hanmer Bassett were witnesses. Daniel Hudson's profession was given as Farmer; that of Emily's

father, John Hanmer Wingrave, as Accountant General, HM
Civil Service (formerly the highest post in the Accountants'
division at the Excise Office, where he held senior posts from 1834
to 1850, and where others of the family also worked). Hudson
himself gave only the formal Gentleman. The bride, of course,
claimed no profession, but supported them both by running their
married home as a boarding-house: first at No. 16 Leinster
Square, Bayswater, then, by 1878, at No. 11. The former was
Emily's address in the marriage register. In the early 1870s it had
been a school for young ladies, and she may have come there
originally to teach singing. She had a pleasing soprano voice, and
had appeared on concert platforms with Sims Reeves and other
stars in her younger days, sometimes in Paris. Later she took
pupils, and Roberts's account suggests that she was an excellent
teacher, exacting, patient and good-humoured.

On the marriage certificate Hudson's age was given correctly
as thirty-four; Emily's as thirty-six. In fact she was eleven years
older than her husband; but he did not know this until late in life.
In appearance she was 'curiously ageless', with a type of looks,
fair-haired and fresh-skinned, which often shows little change
between the thirties and late fifties. Talented, hard-working,
unassuming, courageous, she was also in her own sphere shrewd
and capable; and devoted to Hudson. Roberts, when they met,
was struck by her 'beautiful look of kindness'.

The narrator of *The Purple Land* remarks that in all countries,
even England, 'it is permissible for women in some circumstances
to propose marriage.' Those circumstances may well have arisen
through his illness and destitution the winter before: '. . . great
many people died this winter,' a friend of George Gissing's wrote
in April 1876. Without Emily, Hudson might have been among
them, passing unnoticed from a workhouse infirmary to a
pauper's grave. She gave him a home, companionship which in
those years was protective and unexacting, and a chance to devote himself to the slow unfolding of his gifts; something of the
security of the mother and child relationship which, as his
writings show, was often in his thoughts. Hudson never forgot
this debt, and he was very fond of her. For all its pathos, it was a
kind and timely marriage, and when it had lasted forty-five years
he wrote:

> It is kindness that counts in the end—the feeling for another that
> outlives short-lived passion. Now I was never in love with my

115

wife, nor she with me. But we became friends. . . . And after these
eight years of her illness, and after we have been so much apart, I
feel that the one being who knew me and whom I knew as I can
know no other, has left me very much alone.

In one sense he was alone from the first. Emily was deeply
attached to him and believed in him as a writer; but, unlike his
mother, she 'understood little or nothing of him or his work and
the wider reach of his big spirit'. Later he would find women
friends who could do so. Solitude was his natural element; he
needed freedom to pursue his thoughts and give life to the
themes taking shape in his imagination. But he also needed
contact with a lively and sympathetic mind, and at length he was
fortunate in meeting Morley Roberts, who became a lifelong
friend.

It was on an evening of late summer in 1880 that Roberts,
calling on another man, rang the bell of the Leinster Square
boarding-house and gazed with interest at the stranger who
answered his enquiry. Unconscious power seemed the keynote
of this man's personality, together with an impressive and warm-
ing friendliness.

> His height was about six feet three inches when he stood upright,
> which he rarely did [Roberts recalled]. He wore a short cropped
> beard and an untrimmed moustache: his hair in his youth was dark
> brown. . . . His eyes were more or less hazel and deeply set, with
> heavy brow ridges and well-marked eyebrows: his nose, large and
> prominent and by no means symmetrical. [It had been broken at
> some time.] His complexion was sallow, and his ears, though
> well-formed, as large in proportion as his hands and feet. . . . But it
> was Hudson's whole aspect that showed the man. It marked him
> with a rare stamp. It was at once kindly and formidable. He looked
> like a half-tamed hawk which at any moment might take to the
> skies and return no more to those earth-bound creatures with
> whom he had made his temporary home. His sight was keen: his
> curiosity insatiable. As he walked the streets he observed every-
> thing and everybody. He was as much the field-naturalist in
> London as in the country. In town, for beasts and birds he substi-
> tuted the whole race of man. This gave him his air of interested
> armed detachment. . . .
>
> Though many photographs of him are good and often better
> than good, none will ever see again Hudson's brooding smile,
> suffused with humour, nor catch the light in him which warmed
> and illustrated his talk. His power and size, the roundness of his
> skull, its shape and index, showed there was much in him of
> Beaker ancestry, those powerful men with round skulls and big
> noses, whose round (or long) barrows with drinking beakers in

them are found from Torquay to Caithness, men whose descendants are still strong, men who 'get there', who do things and are
not born to be hewers of wood and drawers of water. . . . With
good health he would have been a marvel of strength.

Rheumatic fever, however, had left him with a permanently
damaged heart and an alarmingly irregular heartbeat.

Roberts, aged twenty-three, had just returned from four years
in Australia. Though not a naturalist, he had 'watched the
platypus swimming in the flood of the Lachlan, nursed the
"dinged joey" of a kangaroo rat into tameness, and had visions of
the thousand coloured, screaming, whistling birds' of the bush.
Later, he was to work as 'civil servant, Indian office clerk,
shepherd in Texas, railroad navvy in Minnesota, lumberman in
Oregon and vineyard worker in California', besides writing many
books. He was a good listener, and the age gap made no
difference to their friendship. In time he won Hudson's
confidence, hearing of his work and his hopes, of *The Purple
Land*—some of which Hudson altered at Roberts's suggestion—and of his essays and poems. It was when Roberts read an
essay, 'The Settler's Recompense' that he became convinced of
Hudson's latent greatness. Wilfrid Meynell, editor of a literary
journal, *Merry England*, also recognized his quality, printing this
and other work. Later rewritten as a chapter for *Idle Days in
Patagonia*, the essay described the 'war with nature' awaiting
hopeful immigrants, and it ended in typical Hudson vein:

> The man who finishes his course by a fall from his horse, or is
> swept away while fording a swollen stream, has spent as bright,
> useful and happy, if not happier, life than he who dies of apoplexy
> in his counting-house or dining-room. . . . Certainly, the dreary
> refrain concerning the vanity of all earthly things has been less
> frequent on his lips.

It was this sweeping contempt for all that was petty in civilization that captivated Morley Roberts, as it was later to captivate the
high-spirited Cunninghame Graham. Until he went abroad
again, Roberts was a regular visitor at the boarding-house. He
was welcomed gratefully by Emily Hudson, because, with one or
two other young men—engineers and planters from abroad—he
helped to enliven the sombre evening dinner hour. It seemed
dreadful to Roberts to find Hudson at that table, among colourless or shiftless people, 'ancient widows and dodderers'. There
he would sit, brooding and silent, sometimes irritable, but

sometimes 'suddenly glowing, bitter or humorous' in response to his friend. Then he would get up to squeeze and drink fresh lemon juice at the sideboard; and he and Roberts would go out to sit for hours under the plane trees in the dusk, while Hudson talked of the pampas, the gauchos, horses and long horseback journeys. Roberts 'tried to repay him with tales of the wide salt-bush plains of the Lachlan Back-Blocks, of the myriad sheep and cattle, of the emus and the snakes, of kangaroos, trap-door spiders and iguanas and horned lizards'. Hudson as yet had seen little of England, and Roberts, who as a child had lived in several counties, also told him about the Sussex downs, Wiltshire and Salisbury Plain and the coast of Cornwall.

Wandering far afield in London, Hudson had discovered the grassy flats of Hackney Marshes that, with the illusion of distance, with lark and kestrel overhead and swans on the River Lea, could sometimes bring him a moment of exhilaration. In Richmond Park and Highgate woods he heard nightingales, watched the green woodpecker and jay, and found thickets where he could spend whole days alone, out of sight and hearing of London. But often he walked for miles on pavements and saw no birds but sparrows. These he had loved from the first day at Southampton, when their notes reminded him of the swallows of Buenos Aires; and in London he found their chirruping refreshing to his tired brain. On dreary walks they formed the background of his musing: 'I had them for butterflies, seen sometimes in crowds and clouds, as in the tropics, with no rich nor splendid colouring on their wings, and I had them for cicadas, and noisy locusts of arboreal habits'—or as brown hawk moths, suspended in air with vibrating wings. He had begun a long poem, *The London Sparrow*, which he read aloud to Roberts. Nothing else written at this time gives such a frank picture of his feelings:

> A hundred years it seemeth since I lost thee,
> O beautiful world of birds, O blessed birds,
> That come and go!—the thrush, the golden-bill
> That sweetly fluteth after April rain,
> In forest depths the cuckoo's mystic voice,
> And in the breezy fields the yellowhammer . . .
> Nor in this island only: far beyond
> The seas encircling it swift memory flies
> To other brighter lands, and leaves behind
> The swallow and the dove: in hot sweet woods
> The gaudy parrot screams; reedy and vast
> Stretch ibis- and flamingo-haunted marshes . . .

London is seen as a prison:

> I from such worlds removed to this sad world
> Of London we inhabit now together ... a desert desolate
> Of fabrics gaunt and grim and smoke-begrimed
> By goblin misery haunted; scowling towers
> And castles of despair ...

He describes the companionable ways of the sparrow:

> At dawn thy voice is loud—a merry voice
> When other sounds are few and faint. Before
> The muffled thunders of the Underground
> Begin to shake the houses...

and goes on to recall the past:

>   ... for thee
> 'Tis ever Merry England! Never yet
> In thy companionship of centuries
> With man in lurid London didst regret
> Thy valiant choice—yea, even from the time
> When all its low-roofed rooms were sweet with scents
> From summer fields, where shouting children plucked
> The floating lily from the reedy Fleet,
> Scaring away the timid water-hen...

In the end he sees the city falling into ruins—a theme Richard Jefferies too was exploring in *After London*—and the sparrow remaining as 'Nature's one witness', when

>   ... the murmuring sound
> Of human feet unnumbered, like the rain
> Of summer pattering on the forest leaves
> In everlasting silence dies away.

The London Sparrow was accepted by Wilfrid Meynell and printed in *Merry England* in 1883. Two others followed. 'In the Wilderness', also in nostalgic mood, described his longing for wings to fly away:

> Many a heron-haunted stream
> And many a plain I'd pass,
> A thousand, thousand flowers behold
> Strew all the wayside grass ...

'Gwendoline' shows even more clearly how much he lost in using the form of verse:

119

Like a streamlet dark and cold
Kindled into fiery gold
By a sunbeam swift that cleaves
Downward through the curtained leaves—

So this darkened life of mine
Lit with sudden joy would shine;
And to greet thee I would start
With a great cry in my heart.

Emotion and images, fresh and truthful in his mind, seem trite on the page. Hudson saw this, and made himself give up his dream of excelling as a poet: 'I could never satisfy myself that I would ever be able to master that delicate and difficult instrument.'

In prose, however, he was already finding his own voice, as well as trying to turn out some conventional work that would sell. *The Purple Land that England Lost*, published in the same year as 'Gwendoline' (1885), reached a standard incomparably higher. Before this book appeared he had also placed two stories in widely different styles.

All his life Hudson was haunted by the idea of a mysterious bird-woman, benign or malevolent. A gaucho legend on this theme was the first of his short stories to be printed, and remained a favourite of his. 'Pelino Viera's Confession' appeared in the *Cornhill Magazine* in 1883, and in the following year in the *Naçion* of Buenos Aires. Pelino Viera, the narrator, discovers that his wife is a sorceress. One night he secretly watches her transform herself into a great bird, then follows her to a coven and accidentally stabs her. She regains human form, but dies, and he is convicted of her murder, writing his account in prison while awaiting execution. One sentence at the end is in Hudson's own idiom, where the prisoner lies awake in his cell, 'thinking of the great breezy plains, till I almost fancy I hear the cattle lowing far off, and the evening cry of the partridge'. The rest seems no more than skilful retelling of a folk tale, familiar at one point to readers of *The Golden Ass* and Andersen's *Travelling Companion*. But the fantasy took a deep hold on his imagination. Traces of it reappear in the reason he gave for his marriage—the charm of Emily's singing—and in his attacks on 'feathered women' who followed the fashion of wearing birds' wings or plumes. Rima in *Green Mansions* is first heard as a strange bird-voice; in *Marta Riquelme* the transformation produces a climax of horror.

'Tom Rainger', published by *Home Chimes* in 1884, is a boyish story amusingly written. It was supposed to be set in Trinidad, which suggests that readers in Buenos Aires might have been reminded of a true incident. Young Tom, three years out from England, and 'engaged' to half a dozen local girls, hears that his English fiancée is arriving on the next boat. In panic he consults a friend, Philip, who meets the boat in his place. The fiancée proves to be extremely pretty and cheerfully releases Tom. The story then follows a predictable course until Tom, by now in love with her again, receives a letter from Philip beginning, *I am the happiest man in the world*. 'Slowly, like a withered autumn leaf, the letter fell fluttering to the floor . . .'

Ralph Herne, a much longer story, centred on the yellow fever epidemic of 1871. At the outset Hudson reversed his own experience; an Englishman arrives in Buenos Aires to start a new career, but finds himself unable to do so. He is a doctor, but must qualify all over again; however, the epidemic quickly removes this veto. Having been away in Patagonia during that 'plague year', Hudson had to blend fiction and family reports to describe the fever-ridden city. The result is a striking account of terror and delirium, agony and sudden death, grass-grown streets, a grinning pedlar with a load of coffins, the rumble of death carts and 'that desolate cry, "Bring out your dead!" so long unheard in Europe'. This tale was not printed until 1888.

Harsh experience as well as imagination went into his picture of London poverty, *Fan: the Story of a Young Girl's Life*, published later under a pseudonym. The interest lies in the early chapters, set in his own part of London and describing familiar things: the ragged girl 'selling matches'—the cover for begging—and cleaning doorsteps for a penny, walking through half-built streets into 'real country', watching the 'minstrels, quacks and jugglers' of the Saturday night street market—where Hudson went to study, among other things, 'the colour of the British eye'. Fan's situation at her mother's death recalls that of Ida Starr in Gissing's early novel *The Unclassed* (1884); and Hudson might not have tried this experiment with the realistic novel had he not come to know this author and his work.

Roberts, who had been with Gissing at Owens College, Manchester, introduced him to Hudson before leaving for America in 1884. Though widely different in many ways, Hudson and Gissing had in common their experience of poverty and of writing, as well as the love of books and the habit of solitary wandering. As a boy Gissing had delighted in long country rambles—sometimes shared with his father, a keen amateur botanist—and he still

121

loved the countryside. Later, like Hudson, he was especially happy in Exeter and the Exe valley. At this period, however, he was writing chiefly from inside knowledge of seedy urban scenes. Probably no men in London knew the street life of the eighties better than these two, the naturalist and the social observer. Hudson introduced Gissing to Spanish literature, and encouraged him to learn the language so as to read *Don Quixote* in the original. They also exchanged their own books as these appeared, and in Hudson's work Gissing found 'something alien, strange and yet soothing'. But for Hudson it was not a happy association. He admired the truthfulness and social awareness of Gissing's books, particularly *Born in Exile* (1892); but he also found them painful, since they often stressed poverty and misery, recalling the dark years of the mid-eighties—a reaction later shared by Gissing himself. At the time, conscious of his powers, Hudson could not resign himself to failure, or tolerate Gissing's bitter jokes about their lack of prospects. Gissing would pretend to accept defeat as inevitable, and to look forward with amusement to a future in Marylebone workhouse. For Hudson and Emily, between 1884 and 1886, the joke would have become reality had they not preferred to endure hunger—'so very different', as Gissing wrote, 'from appetite'—in silence.

It was a period of such wretchedness that, as with the shadowed time of his late teens, Hudson could afterwards hardly bear to speak of it. The Leinster Square boarding-house failed, perhaps because Emily was too kind to get rid of non-paying guests. This seems to have happened some time in 1884, the year when Hudson's name was listed for the last time as householder there. Tower House at that time was also in other hands. Somehow they managed to open another boarding-house near by in Southwick Crescent (now Hyde Park Crescent); but this too was a failure, and they found themselves in lodgings further west, in the suburb of Ravenscourt Park, trying to exist on the proceeds of his articles and Emily's music lessons: 'Emily trudged about teaching girls without voices and temperaments to howl opera, and those without music to beat a wretched piano, while Hudson sat at home and wrote what was mostly rejected.' As he later grimly admitted, they once lived for a week on a tin of cocoa and milk: at a time when a day's food could be bought for a few pence, a large loaf, for instance, costing 5½d and sprats sometimes as little as a farthing a pound. In *Fan* he showed how well he knew that knife-edge existence of 'the unclassed', in a limbo outside society, staving off—with penny loaves, twopenny screws of tea, half-penny bundles of firewood—the last resort of the workhouse, 'where those who were unfit to live, and could not live, yet would not die, were put away out of sight'.

The workhouse guardians were alert to distinguish between 'God's poor' and the reverse, and to keep wastrels and cadgers off the rates. Out-relief was officially frowned on, even for the sick—a policy that inspired an angry ballad whose first line, 'It was Christmas Day in the workhouse', is still remembered, though the context has been forgotten. Task-work could be exacted in return for lodging, or as a test before a rare grant of out-relief. For men this was still usually stone-breaking or oakum-picking (pulling old tarred rope to pieces for use in caulking ships). No doubt Gissing was witty about these tasks. The hard times early in 1886, with many skilled men out of work and mass demonstrations in London, did elicit an official circular pointing out the need for new forms of task-work without 'the stigma of pauperism', and which could be done by all, 'whatever their previous avocations'. Meanwhile the system was fatal to those who clung too long to their self-respect. The Charity Organization Society also existed to help deserving cases: in some districts the Poor Law relieving officer and the Society's local committee worked together in helping 'fit objects of private charity'. This would of course entail close questioning and form-filling by a COS district visitor. Hudson had also probably heard of the Royal Literary Fund. In later years he was to apply to the Fund on behalf of others; he did not do so himself. Only a hungry child, perhaps, could have driven the Hudsons to any of these shifts. They had no child.

When there was bread, he shared it with the sparrows that came to their window—forty or fifty of them daily—and in the breeding season he noted the different alarm reactions in the parents and young birds. His only other pleasure was in looking down into Ravenscourt Park, then a wilderness of grass and ancient trees, 'beautiful even in the cold dark winter months, when it was a waste of snow, and when, despite the bitter weather, the missel-thrush poured out its loud triumphant notes from the top of a tall elm'. The place was still private property—later, like other such homes near London, to become a public park—and Hudson could not walk there; but he remembered the view with gratitude, and the coming of spring and summer with glimpses of wild flowers, green shade and the sound of the birds.

If the 'darkling thrush' brought a message of hope, it was to be justified; but not yet. Throughout the winter of 1885/6 he had to endure not only semi-starvation and exile from the country, but what must have been from its timing the worst blow of his career: the failure of his first book. It was the climax of many lesser disappointments.

> When I had not a penny [he wrote later] and almost went down on my knees to editors, publishers and literary agents, I couldn't even get a civil word, and of ten—or perhaps twenty—MSS sent nine (or nineteen) would be sent back. And now that I don't want the beastly money and care nothing for fame and am sick and tired of the whole thing they actually come to beg a book or article from me.

'The notice which you have been pleased to take of my labours, had it been early, had been kind . . .' Dr Johnson's words, once quoted to Roberts in one of these brief moods of bitterness, apply with particular force to the fate of *The Purple Land that England Lost*. This is a picaresque tale, like the Spanish romances Hudson had read as a boy; the hero, Richard Lamb, leaving his young wife in Montevideo while he rides off through Uruguay in search of a job, meeting every kind of character and becoming involved in civil war, political conspiracy and enjoyable philandering. His journey is the thread connecting a sequence of tales about crafty plainsmen, bloodthirsty ruffians, patriots and beautiful women, usually in some measure of distress. The chapter headings—'Manuel, Also Called the Fox', 'A Ghastly Gift', 'Mystery of the Green Butterfly', 'Lock and Key and Sinners Three'—underline the mood of each anecdote. The light touch of 'Tom Rainger' had developed into a satiric gift that enlivens many incidents, as when he mockingly describes an opportunity missed:

> Love cometh up as a flower, and men and charming women naturally flirt when brought together. Yet it was hard to imagine how I could have started a flirtation and carried it on to its culminatory point in that great public room, with all those eyes on me: dogs, babes and cats tumbling about my feet; ostriches staring covetously at my buttons with great vacant eyes; and that intolerable paroquet perpetually reciting 'How the waters came down at Lodore' in its own shrieky, beaky, birdy, hurdy-gurdy parrot language.

Not that Lamb is given to missing opportunities. To the women he meets—mysterious Margarita, passionate Dolores, tragic Demetria, enticing little Cleta—he usually responds with frank admiration and manners 'so very disengaged' that he can hardly escape some awkward scenes:

> 'Speak, Richard!' she exclaimed. 'Your silence at this moment is an insult to me!'
> 'For God's sake have mercy on me, Dolores. I am not free—I have a wife.'

But there is a great deal in the book besides sentimental adventures. Both human and wild life—sparkling fireflies, gold and scarlet wasps, flame-coloured orioles, lizards and spiders—are observed and drawn with beautiful directness; and there are passages which foreshadow the ease and authority of Hudson's mature style. Describing the pastoral bliss, the 'liberty and dirt' of a Scottish exile and his family, he passed judgement on late Victorian England:

> O civilization, with your million conventions, soul-and body-withering prudishnesses, vain education for the little ones, going to church in best black clothes, unnatural craving for cleanliness, feverish striving after comforts that bring no comfort to the heart, are you a mistake altogether? . . . We had only to conquer Nature, find out her secrets, make her our obedient slave, then the earth would be Eden, and every man Adam and every woman Eve. We are still bravely marching on, conquering Nature, but how weary and sad we are getting! . . .

This was his brief: the theme of all his serious work from 'Wanted—A Lullaby' to *A Hind in Richmond Park*, his last book. Similar ideas had already launched him into a second novel, *A Crystal Age*, picturing a better kind of life for the human race. But in the autumn of 1885 his hopes must have centred on *The Purple Land that England Lost*. That much-travelled manuscript had been on his hands for ten years. Even at that time, with a large fiction-reading public, it was hard to get a first novel accepted unless the author paid towards the cost of publication; it was also hard to sell a book by an unknown author unless the reviews were favourable enough to impress the library subscribers. Gissing, as Hudson no doubt knew, had gambled and lost a small fortune—£125—on his first book. Hardy and Barrie also paid their publishers. Hudson's first publishers, Sampson Low, seem to have been discerning enough to take a risk with *The Purple Land*; but it did not pay off.

Hudson had first approached the firm in April 1885, and within six months the book was ready: two slim volumes, priced at a guinea, bound in blue with red decorations and green-and-white floral endpapers. All now depended on reviews; but it had a bad start, being advertised in *The Times* on 26 October with two travel books. This, and the unhelpful sub-title, 'Travels and Adventures in the Banda Oriental, South America', placed it firmly in the wrong category, bringing a peevish outburst from the influential *Saturday Review*:

> Never was so absolute a misnomer given to a book. *The Purple Land* is no record of genuine travel performed by a real traveller, but a very silly story of the imaginary adventures of an imaginary Mr Lamb. . . . We feel bound to say that we have seldom been called upon to express an opinion on a more vulgar farrago of repulsive nonsense than is contained in the volumes to which the author has given so misleading a title.

This blow fell on 14 November. On the 26th the *Whitehall Review* described it as 'a capital representation of men and manners', but also made dispiriting judgement on the 'jerky' style and 'disjointed' anecdotes. A month later the *Athenaeum* reviewer, like nearly everyone else, objected to the title, but added:

> His various adventures are described with great spirit and gusto, giving what we can well believe to be a faithful, as it certainly is a vivid, portrayal of the spirit and character of the society into which he was thrown. The reader who has followed the author's fortunes so far will heartily wish him a prosperous ending to his troubles.

This was better, but not persuasive enough; the book was not selling. Then in the new year the *Graphic* gibed, 'his main object in penning the record seems to have been to prove that he was a donkey, and he has here succeeded admirably. . . . As Mr Hudson is not the real author of these experiences, these strictures do not touch him.' They touched him enough to make him give up writing stories for many years.

Figaro considered that, even if the title had been happier, *The Purple Land* would not have made a noise in the world. The romance that did so this season was *King Solomon's Mines*, singled out by *The Times* on 2 November for a special article. It was a pity that Hudson, who must have seen this, could not know that

Rider Haggard's manuscript had been turned down by one publisher's reader as 'a farrago of obscene witlessness'; still more that he could not foresee the reception of *The Purple Land* in 1904, when the *Spectator*—describing it as an 'enchanting romance', and Lamb as 'a most attractive and versatile personage; chivalroue, sympathetic, susceptible and impulsive'—would condemn the first reviewers for discouraging his unique talent in this genre.

At least one of them, however, must have been exempt. Before the first edition vanished, leaving the author still penniless and the publishers £30 out of pocket, it received one long and wholly enthusiastic notice by A. H. Keane in the *Academy*. This appeared on 26 January, too late to make any impression, except on Hudson's feelings. It was his first taste of praise; and there was a flattering sequel. Keane was so taken with the book that he invited Hudson to dinner and offered to make him a present of his own life story. He too, it appeared, had had an adventurous youth which would make a wonderfully romantic tale; and on reading *The Purple Land* he had exclaimed, 'That's the book I have been trying so long to write and can't do it!' Now he urged Hudson to take his notes and journals and set to work.

The proposal had of course to be declined, Hudson tactfully explaining that any such attempt 'would read to him much as *The Purple Land* would to me if he had written that book after getting his facts from me'. But the encounter must have been cheering.

The Purple Land later brought him a proposal of another sort, and one that could not be turned down without heartache. He had sent a copy to Albert in Buenos Aires. It was passed on to Edwin, who responded with kindness and devastating candour:

> Why are you staying on in England, and what can you do there? I have looked at your romance and find it not unreadable, but this you must know is not your line—the one thing you are best fitted to do. Come back to your own country and come to me here in Cordova. These woods and sierras and rivers have a more plentiful and interesting bird life than that of the pampas and Patagonia. Here I could help you and make it possible for you to dedicate your whole time to observation of the native birds and fauna generally . . .

This was the old Edwin, shrewd, dictatorial, sure of what was best for his young brother. The plan must indeed have seemed at first glance to offer 'a prosperous ending to his troubles', at least as he rated prosperity. And near the end of his life Hudson recalled, 'I read the message with a pang, knowing that his judgement was right. But the message came too late; I had already made my choice, which was to remain for the rest of my life in this country of my ancestors, which had become mine.'

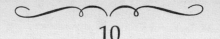

10

Looking Back

So England held him. The place where he first touched English earth remained his 'beloved Southampton'; and in the future he would bring to the countryside a unique blend of fresh, almost childlike vision with experience and mature writing talent. He had still seen little beyond the city that continued to treat him so coldly. But, apart from stubborn ancestral feeling, there were strong reasons for the decision not to return. Pride was certainly one. Having set out as a young man to 'seek his fortune', he could hardly have brought himself to turn back in middle age with a sense of failure. Another bar was the change overtaking the pampas. There was also the major problem of Emily, who would surely have been out of place in South America, if he could have persuaded her to go there. By the time Edwin's message arrived, however, she had been for some years the owner of Tower House in St Luke's Road, which came to her on the death of a sister, and where Hudson was first listed as householder in 1878. She clung to her property and would never sell it or agree to live elsewhere so long as her health lasted.

In 1873 the Victorian diarist and barrister A. J. Munby noted dining with a friend in 'St Luke's Road, Westbourne Park, in the wild Bayswater desert'. Though remote from the fashionable world, and so 'a desert', Westbourne Park was until the mid-seventies a highly respectable neighbourhood inhabited by professional middle-class people. Tower House in 1871 was still a family home, occupied by a retired 'merchant', his son (a law student) and nephew (a bank clerk), together with a servant and a twelve-year-old house boy. By 1875, as the district began to go down in the world, it had begun the long career as a lodging-house which first brought Hudson there.

Reviled for many years by Hudson's admirers, the house has nevertheless in the 1980s regained something of its former status. Height, ornate design, heavy-looking structure and elaborate 'belfry' windows combine to give it the dignity of a survival. It is now a period piece as typical as St Luke's Mews at the end of the road, where the old pattern of stables, coachmen's quarters and paved yard remains today, seventy years or more after the horses left. A plaque to Hudson's memory was placed on the front of the house in 1938. In the narrow front garden, one acacia tree also survives, planted perhaps by Hudson in memory of the past. 'Stale and gloomy outside and dim with ancient paper and paint within', Roberts found the place when he returned from America at the end of 1886 to find them settled there. When success came at last, friends were to deplore this 'cracked belfry' imprisoning their eagle. They deplored too the boarding-house relics that furnished the sitting-room, where the only gleam of colour came from a glass case holding his books; the monstrous horsehair circular settee, ugly 'lace' curtains and antimacassars, chairs and sofas 'with the leather peeling off, hanging in flaps like the wattles round the neck of a vulture', as Violet Hunt wrote in exasperation. Such indignation was wasted. None of this meant anything to Hudson. The house and its trappings were Emily's affair, and he scarcely saw them. His thoughts were elsewhere; and, by the time these critics appeared, the periods of imprisonment were often short and voluntary, except in illness.

In 1886, when they had existed for two years on the edge of pauperism, the house was a refuge to which he returned thankfully. It was mortgaged for £1,100, evidently since 1882, two years before the Leinster Square failure. By letting off the rooms on the lower floors—which brought higher rents—they were able to pay the interest, though with little or nothing to spare for improvements. This time, it seems, they discarded the boarding-house pattern, that polite semblance of family occupation, with 'guests' and communal dining-room. A housekeeper was installed in the basement, presumably to wait on the tenants. The Husons took the garret flat for themselves; though the long climb can scarcely have been helpful to the attacks of 'palpitations, dizziness, nervelessness and general imbecility' from which he suffered. Nor could he hope for peace and pure air

at that height. Smoke and smuts, together with 'rumbling, puf-
fing and shrieking noises', poured from trains passing less than
fifty yards away; the 'ever-lasting brain-worrying noises of
traffic' came up from the crossroads below. But he had what he
needed: a roof over his head, bread to eat, time to watch the
seasons and to get on with his work.

Not surprisingly, after their privations, Emily had begun to
show her age. Young Roberts noticed that her bright hair and
complexion were fading, though this may only have meant that
she could no longer afford cosmetics. But she was still active and
busy, running the house, guarding her husband's privacy—often it was she who came down the four flights to answer
their bell—and drilling her music pupils. She and Roberts were
always good friends, and when her own voice failed she taught
him to sing some of Hudson's favourite arias and lieder: 'La
donna è mobile', 'Che farò', 'The Erl King', songs by Schumann,
Beethoven and Handel.

> Sometimes [Roberts wrote] he laughed when his wife pulled me
> up and ragged me, and then sang to show me how to do it, and
> often he said, 'Sing that again', and lay back in a higher state of
> contentment than my own, as Emily Hudson often gave me very
> plain opinions as to my want of progress. ... These hours are
> happy hours to remember. They seemed to help him. And after
> singing came tea, when we discussed and fought over a hundred
> questions about Darwin and Wallace, questions of habit and cus-
> tom, of mimicry and protective resemblance, of migration, per-
> petually a mystery and a big interest for him, of variation and
> structure and ornament, of dancing and singing in birds and their
> relation to music and dancing in man.

At such times the garret with its low sloping ceiling became
'a little home of strange knowledge, of speculation and
enthusiasm'.

Hudson had gone back to pure natural history and was steadily
producing the essays which were to make up *The Naturalist in La
Plata* and *Idle Days in Patagonia*. Writing itself was a grinding task,
'long to learn, hard to learn, and no gift of the angels'. Ideas were
first jotted in pencil on scraps of paper or the backs of envelopes,
then worked out at length and ceaselessly rewritten. As in earlier
years, discussion with Roberts helped him to develop his
thoughts and arguments, but in this field at least he was becoming sure of himself despite continual rejections. The work
had that real excellence and originality which, in John Clare's
words, must be its own creation, 'the overflowings of its own

mind, and must make its admirers willing converts from its own powerful conceptions and not yield to win them by giving way to their opinions'. Admirers by now included the editors of *Longman's* and the *Gentleman's Magazine*, who published some of these essays between 1884 and 1891.

Meanwhile, in the spring of 1887, *A Crystal Age* appeared anonymously; no doubt to avoid comparison with the earlier failure. This slim volume, bound in black, with a device on the cover like red frost crystals, must have given him some pleasure; and the publisher's printed motto—*Vita Sine Literis Mors Est* ('Life without literature is death')—a moment's wry amusement. He would not see another of his stories in book form for fifteen years. Here too he had taken great pains with the writing; and again there was an appreciative review in the *Academy*, observing that such a graceful style 'ought not to be wasted on transcendental fiction'. Like *The Purple Land*, it was later to have distinguished admirers, among them Hilaire Belloc, who once declared that it was the book he had read most often and liked best.

A Crystal Age was Hudson's contribution to the utopian romance of the period. He much admired Samuel Butler, and the tale has more than one echo of *Erewhon*. The hero, Smith, travelling in a remote country, finds himself among people leading an idyllic pastoral life; living in fine houses, eating fruit and herbs and honey, wearing easy and graceful garments. The men spend their working hours in farming, forestry or handicrafts, and their leisure riding spirited horses and enjoying the beauty of nature. Illness is looked on as a misdemeanour, and they survive far beyond the usual human life span. Hudson said this was written as escapism rather than prophecy. In fact he was looking back, not forward: the *Crystal Age* is his childhood world without the dreadful deeds, the slaughter of men and animals; and with some of the 'aesthetic' ideas current when it was written. But this is not the airy fantasy that it at first appears. Hudson had grasped the great problem of the future, the threat from human over-population; just as, a few years on, he would be among the first to realize the long-term menace of the motor car. Butler, and Morris in *News from Nowhere* (1891), skimmed over the whole question of living space: Hudson tackled it as frankly as the time—and his own reticence—allowed. In the 1880s he could not be explicit; but he later explained that the central theme of *A Crystal Age* is sex, or rather family limitation, which he saw chiefly in terms of shedding the male sexual drive.

Tickner Edwardes in *The Lore of the Honey-bee* (1908) asked, 'Will a time come when we must learn from the honey-bee or perish? . . . unless the world comes to an end, our earth will eventually become too small to hold us.' Twenty years earlier, Hudson based his 'ideal' community on the beehive, headed by a single fertile couple, the Father—promoted from drone to king—and the revered Mother. The rest are workers; not sexless, but with all sexual instinct in abeyance. When the parents die, another pair will be chosen to produce the next generation. This change—the 'great renunciation', Edwardes called it—was to come about, not by medical science, but in the long course of evolution, as a quotation from Darwin on the title-page indicates. Smith, falling in love with a girl who cannot understand his courtship, finds himself in a strange predicament. The writer's predicament was that he could explore the situation only in veiled terms; but so far as it goes this is skilfully done.

Despite the serious underlying theme, the story has its lighter moments, as when the brash young hero shatters musical sensibilities by roaring out 'The Vicar of Bray': a little episode that sounds authentic, remembered perhaps from some concert or even from the Leinster Square drawing-room. In another passage Hudson lists his antipathies with obvious enjoyment—'politics, religions, systems of philosophy, isms and ologies of all descriptions; schools, churches, prisons, poor houses'—and hopes they will be consumed to ashes.

The despised isms and ologies were at present personified in Dr Sclater, with whom in 1887 he was compiling *Argentine Ornithology*. The first important book on the subject since that of Don Felix de Azara over eighty years before, its appearance was an event in the world of ornithology; but the book was always a sore subject with Hudson, who felt he had done most of the work while Sclater took the credit. Without Hudson's contribution, Roberts agreed, it would have been merely 'an arranged bone-heap'. Dr Sclater in his Preface courteously implies equal collaboration—'All the personal observations recorded in these pages are due to Mr Hudson, while I am responsible for the arrangement, nomenclature and scientific portions . . .' But on the title-page the work is styled: 'A descriptive Catalogue Of The Birds Of The Argentine Republic. By P. L. Sclater MA, PhD, FRS, etc. With Notes On Their Habits by W. H. Hudson, CMZS, Late Of Buenos Ayres.' The book itself makes this seem disproportionate. In the entry for each species, the scientific data—some lines of

names, dates, references to written reports and localities—are
followed by pages describing the birds in their natural surroundings, based on Hudson's early field notebooks and his contributions to the Zoological *Proceedings*. For example, the entry for
Molothrus rufoaxillaris, named by Hudson the screaming cow-
bird, is headed: Scl, et Salv. Nomencl. p. 37; Hudson, P.Z.S. 1874
(Buenos Ayres); White, P.Z.S. 1882, p. 601 (Catamarca); Barrows,
Bull. Nutt. Orn. Cl. viii. p. 134 (Enterios); Scl. Cat. B. xi. p. 338.
Then come nine pages by Hudson, including the splendid
account of cow-birds' parasitical habits and how he found them
out, which had earned high praise from Darwin (see p. 91). From
his diary he quotes an excited entry made when he first saw one
laying an egg in the nest of a fostering species. It begins, 'Today I
have made a new discovery, and am as pleased with it as though I
had found a new planet in the sky . . .'

To underestimate Dr Sclater's part would obviously be absurd.
The earlier work of classifying and naming specimens, together
with his bibliography and list of localities, all entailed a vast
amount of patient and detailed labour, after many years of study
and preparation. But this applied also to Hudson: and with an
added grace. It is one thing, as C. E. Montague said, to note down
facts—'Both of us once lived on the Doon. He is now in the
States'—and another to write:

> We twa hae paidlet i' the burn
> Fra' morning sun till dine;
> But seas between us braid hae roar'd
> Sin' auld lang syne.

Hudson's creative gifts transformed the project from a slim
catalogue of purely academic interest to a two-volume work
which many bird-lovers would delight in, and for which some
would pay 3 guineas. According to Roberts again, Dr Sclater had
'a keen regard for royalties somewhat repugnant to a much
poorer collaborator'. However, he must certainly have helped to
obtain from the Royal Society the donation of £40 'which has
enabled Mr Hudson to devote a portion of his time to the compilation of his interesting notes'. One can only regret that he had not
apparently been able to do something of the kind a dozen years
before.

The first volume of *Argentine Ornithology*, with coloured plates
and line drawings, was published in a limited edition of 200
signed and numbered copies early in 1888. The printer's device of

a Roman lamp appears after the title-page, with the words *Alere Flammam*, 'to feed the flame'. Two years earlier the dying Richard Jefferies had used this motto for the name of an artist in his last completed book, *Amaryllis at the Fair*. Jefferies was dead now, burnt out before he was thirty-nine, but he had left his mark on the great tradition of country and nature writing. No one prose writer before him had had such wide knowledge of English labourers, farmers, gamekeepers, poachers, of the downs and woods and wild creatures. In the last decade, as London sprawled out over fields where Hudson and Jefferies both wandered and never met, country writing had found a new public. The spread of bicycling would greatly increase this interest, heralding a rediscovery of nature and the countryside by townspeople of a second and third generation. Hudson was to carry on Jefferies's work: even to write the book about the Sussex downs for which Jefferies had no time, some of it in the very room at Goring on the Sussex coast where *Amaryllis* was painfully scribbled or dictated. Now he began to prepare for that new phase of life in brief escapes to the home counties. This was the period of which he wrote:

> The walks, at a time when life had little or no other pleasures for us on account of poverty and ill-health, were taken at pretty regular intervals two or three times a year. It all depended on our means; in very lean years there was but one outing. It was impossible to escape altogether from the immense unfriendly wilderness of London simply because, albeit 'unfriendly', it yet appeared to be the only place in the wide world where our poor little talents could earn us a few shillings a week to live on. Music and literature! but I fancy the nearest crossing-sweeper did better, and could afford to give himself a more generous dinner every day. It occasionally happened that an article sent to some magazine was not returned, and always after so many rejections to have one accepted and paid for with a cheque worth several pounds was a cause of astonishment, and was as truly a miracle as if the angel of the sun had compassionately thrown us down a handful of gold. And out of these little handfuls enough was sometimes saved for the country rambles at Easter and Whitsuntide and in the autumn.

Ironically, to reviewers of *Argentine Ornithology*, this half-starved aspirant was already the acknowledged expert in his own field. 'Mr Hudson has been known for many years as one of the best living observers of the habits of birds . . .' (*Nature*). His notes and observations, said the *Saturday Review*, were not merely interesting in themselves but 'suggestive of curious questions of

135

evolution and heredity and origin of species'. Such questions were also the basis of the travel essays on South American natural history that would, over the next few years, pay for his first sight of rural Surrey, the Thames valley, the Sussex coast and the south downs.

In this daily toil he continued to look back. He would later declare that his life ended when he left the pampas; yet in one sense he never did so. And it was not only the brilliant birds of his native land that haunted him, but all the fauna he had known there. Spiders in a Hampshire meadow brought an aching sense of loss:

> It made me miserable to think that I had left, thousands of miles away, a world of spiders exceeding in size, variety of shape and beauty and richness of colouring those I found here—surpassing them, too, in the marvellousness of their habits and that ferocity of disposition which is without a parallel in nature. I wished I could drop this burden of years so as to go back to them, to spend half a lifetime in finding out some of their fascinating secrets. Finally, I envied those who in future years would grow up in that green continent, with this passion in their hearts, and have the happiness I had missed.

Far from having missed it, he had had over thirty years of learning and passionate involvement, now distilled through relentless desk work into his best book so far, and the one that was to make his name, *The Naturalist in La Plata*. The chapter on spiders is a masterpiece. He remembers them in loving detail, from the 'fairy gossamer, scarce seen, a creature of wind and sunshine', to hairy monsters of ferocious habits. Early in life his compassion had been roused by small spiders as helpless victims of the blue wasp, 'lithe and sinister, of a slender graceful figure—the type of an assassin'. The spider's pain, the boy's protest, can still be felt, together with his heartfelt interest in their lives. Timid bush-dwelling spiders, with 'soft, plump, succulent bodies like pats of butter', are preyed on by mason wasps, and combine protective colouring with a most subtle aerial deception. Vivid green spiders live in green bushes, yellowish ones in faded leaves. When disturbed, each spider drops to earth on a thread: the green one 'just as a green leaf would drop', the other more slowly, like a withered leaf. 'How many tentative variations in the stiffness of the web material must there have been before the precise degree was attained enabling the two to complete their resemblance to falling leaves!' And how many hours the watcher must have spent in noting this minute triumph of evolution; the threat gestures of larger species, 'balancing themselves on their head and hands, and kicking their legs about in the air' while 'they hum a shrill warning or challenge, and stab at the air with their naked stings'; or the autumnal migration in gossamer spiders, and the 'modified structure' of the waterside spider that, when hard pressed in a quarrel, escapes by dropping into the stream and rowing rapidly to land with its long, paddle-shaped legs.

Some species were venomous. Hudson had known a woman who still suffered acute pain from a bite received fourteen years earlier. He recounts his own narrow escape from a man-hunting spider of a species so 'active, swift and irritable' that he thinks nature for once may have overshot her mark:

> Riding at an easy trot over the dry grass, I suddenly observed a spider pursuing me, leaping swiftly along and keeping up with my beast. I aimed a blow with my whip and the point of the lash struck the ground close to it, when it instantly leaped upon and ran up the lash, and was actually within three or four inches of my hand when I flung the whip from me.

The whole book is on this level. He describes the puma, so curiously friendly to man, yet in tropical places 'a great hunter and eater of monkeys, which of all animals most resemble man'; the burrowing *vizcacha* that will travel long distances to dig out its friends from 'villages' buried by men; the armadillo, the versatile 'Brer Rabbit' of gaucho fables; the iguana that can break a dog's leg with a blow of its tail; a strange ride across country where large green snakes rushed at him hissing fiercely; an even stranger encounter with a man whose teeth, sharp and pointed like a shark's, made him seem like 'a savage animal of horrible aspect'. Writing of animal 'weapons', he tells how a frog had given him a surprising nip, and he thought it might be a new species, a 'wrestler frog' (in fact this was normal mating behaviour). In a chapter on the desert pampas—'my "parish of Selborne"'—he remembers a March evening in 1874 when he rode for the last time through miles of stately pampas grasses, and saw a band of Indians leap on to their horses' backs to scan the plain for stray animals, looking in the sunset light 'like bronze men on strange horse-shaped pedestals of dark stone'.

This blend of travel, adventure and evolutionary debate had a strong appeal for the late Victorians. *Idle Days in Patagonia* has an opening scene like that of *The Tempest*, with a storm at sea, a ship running aground, a voice crying 'We are lost.' It also has an absconding crew and a young Englishman with a revolver and a 'quiet but determined voice' who saves the situation. The next chapters deal with life among settlers and Indians. For the intending immigrant, 'the young enthusiast rushing about London to speak his farewells and look after his outfit', there is a lively description of the war with Nature he will find, with pumas raiding his sheep and cattle, and upland geese descending 'in millions' on the harvest fields. But, rich in experience of many kinds as that year had been, these Patagonia essays are often in deeper and quieter vein, dealing with adventures of mind and spirit. Recollecting in tranquillity, Hudson develops patterns of thought on a wide range of themes, many of which would recur in his later work; on bird-music in South America, which he can now compare with that of nightingale, thrush and lark; on eyesight in civilized man and savage; eyes and their colouring in birds, animals and man; on scents and their power to call up the past. Patagonia had given him his first experience of a snowfall, his only taste of the true Southern winter. Discussing whiteness in nature and its effect on the mind, he speaks for the first time of the 'animism' that had haunted him since childhood, the poetic sense that 'all nature is alive and intelligent, and feels as we feel.' Also he analyses Herman Melville's ideas on this subject in *Moby Dick* (1851), a book then little appreciated, which he helped to make famous. Though quotation is never intrusive, his wide reading is now shown in allusion to scientific authorities, to modern poets and to prose writers from Bacon and Johnson to Kingsley and Lewis Carroll.

More striking than anything else is an account of an experience during the 'idle days' of his ambiguous title. Like Darwin, he realized that the grey monotonous wastes of Patagonia had left a deeper and more lasting impression on his spirit than any other region. That winter on the Rio Negro, he had found himself riding out alone day after day into the wilderness, returning there each morning 'as if to attend a festival' and remaining until sunset, in a kind of trance far beyond thought, yet with a sense of suspense, watchfulness and strong elation; listening to the silence, and aware of 'something there which bade me be still . . .' What he had experienced, he now felt sure, was a return to the mental state of the pure savage. Others, as a modern writer on Patagonia remarks, have called it the peace of God.

The same fascination with desert places was felt by Charles

Doughty, whose *Travels in Arabia Deserta* appeared in 1888, and who became one of Hudson's favourite writers. The feeling was shared by a number of later friends—Cunninghame Graham, Wilfrid Scawen Blunt, T. E. Lawrence—and by D. H. Lawrence, an 'avid reader' of Hudson's South American writings.

Today, despite modern transport, Patagonia remains remote and mysterious, much of it still the vast grey desert of rocks and thorns that Hudson found; and still a sanctuary for the large purple swallows he watched, for swifts and sparrows, falcons, hawks and owls, the condor, the great eagle of the Andes and the albatross of the far south.

And La Plata? Hudson said a hundred years ago that many large species—rhea, flamingo, crested screamer—would soon be lost to the pampas, together with their ancient habitats. One of his readers, the naturalist Richard Lydekker, had been so impressed with his account of the huge flocks of crested screamers that, visiting Buenos Aires on business, he rode out over the plain, eager to see them for himself. He came too late. To his bitter disappointment he glimpsed only two specimens a long way off, and was told that Hudson's account was 'pure romance', that the screamer was a rare bird and had always been so. He determined to return to England and discredit *The Naturalist in La Plata*; but before leaving Argentina he met an old countryman from whom he learned that Hudson had told the truth. In a quarter of a century the screamer had been almost wiped out.

Grief at what was happening so permeates Hudson's work that one tends to assume—as he did not—that this was true of all bird-life there. Many years later another reader, Louis Halle, had a happier experience than Lydekker. Visiting Hudson's birthplace in 1947, he found the plain still alive with birds, including many of the marsh-dwellers Hudson loved. A hundred miles south, he was told, he could see black-necked swans and flamingoes; and in the 'Purple Land' he found other large birds, even groups of rheas. Today, driving out from Buenos Aires, the traveller can see oven-birds nesting on telegraph poles, and bands of snowy egrets, herons, storks, ibises, jacanas. Just as the rock-pools and something of their marvellous life remain on our shores, more than a century after the crowds began to arrive, so on the pampas many birds have adapted and survived in what has become an endless vista of wire fencing.

Hudson no doubt hoped this would be so. But in writing of his homeland he thought not only of enclosure, dwindling numbers and the loss of noble species, but also of the spirit that dies when man overruns a wild and lonely countryside. A place open to all is in that sense lost to all.

Travelling alone one summer day on the pampas, he came to a lake ringed with immense flocks of crested screamers, many thousands of birds resting there in undisturbed possession. Each separate flock would sing melodiously in turn, one taking up the powerful chant as another let it die away, so that the sound travelled in great waves around and across the water. It was scenes like this that were in his mind when he wrote: 'I am glad to think I shall never revisit them, that I shall finish my life thousands of miles removed from them, cherishing to the end in my heart the image of a beauty that has vanished from earth.'

11

Protecting Birds

One day at the beginning of the eighties the artist Sir John Millais called on Hudson's old acquaintance, 'Humming-bird Gould', now an invalid confined to a couch. After being kept waiting for half an hour in the hall Millais was admitted to his room, and found him 'evidently got up for the occasion, apparently working on a water-colour drawing of a humming-bird recently discovered'. Amused as he was at this pose, Millais thought it 'a fine subject', and afterwards painted a picture of an old man on a couch, surrounded by a collection of stuffed specimens. Millais called his painting *The Ruling Passion*, and Ruskin was said to have admired its 'sentiment'. Later it came to be known more prosaically as *The Ornithologist*: a title that now seems more suited to a portrait painted forty years later, showing Hudson bird-watching in the New Forest. Hudson—who never called himself an ornithologist, preferring the modest term field naturalist—had spent those years, the second half of his life, in helping to bring about this change of attitude. There was no such thing, he would quote, as a dead bird: 'the life is the bird.'

The bird-collector's 'ruling passion' is seen today as a curious thirst for loot, often obtained by atrocious means, and regardless of the danger to rare and beautiful species. Gould's collections included many birds of paradise from New Guinea. In the breeding season the cock birds in their brilliant plumage would gather each morning at sunrise on particular trees, to display by a complicated dance. Native hunters would wait under these trees and bring down the birds one after another with blunt arrows; as early as the 1840s, large numbers were being taken in this way for sale.

Gould, like other collectors, must have been aware of this, but chose to disregard it; just as he bought specimens of the Dartford warbler, knowing that—as he himself wrote in 1873—collecting had already made it rare on the heaths near London, from one of which its name was taken. His pleasure in his specimens was real enough, as Hudson noticed. Another collector saw his fingers 'trembling with emotion' as he handled the birds of paradise.

Bird-skins were needed for the study of ornithology, and in their place—the museum cabinet—they had value and interest. This was the trade by which Hudson had tried so hard to make a living. Now he realized that English birds were even more at risk than those of the pampas: not from scientists, but from the looting spirit of the times. Private collectors were a serious menace. Birds all over the country, from the goldcrest to the golden eagle, were being persecuted—first for their beauty, then for their increasing rarity—by gamekeepers, wildfowlers, shepherds and others in the collectors' pay. Any countryman with an eye for a rare bird could find customers; the rarer the prize, of course, the bigger the reward, until the trade destroyed itself. In the mid-eighties, Hudson wrote, 'the honey buzzard was a breeding species in England, and had doubtless been so for thousands of years. When the price of a "British-killed" specimen rose to £25 [a year's wages for a farm labourer] and of a "British-taken" egg to two or three or four pounds, the bird quickly ceased to exist.' The Dartford warbler or furze wren was still numerous on Milford common in Surrey, until a local bird-stuffer offered a shilling a clutch for the eggs, and set every village boy hunting for them. It was the same man who supplied Gould with his specimens. Rare visitors were shot on sight. In May 1870 a flock of forty golden orioles, arriving in woods near Penzance, was quickly wiped out: 'everyone in the place was up and after them.' Thirty years later, Hudson thought it would be safer for a hobby, oriole, hoopoe or harrier to nest in a London park than in the wildest part of the New Forest.

This spirit of destruction prevailed everywhere, taking many forms and running through all classes. Ironically, a new fashion for the study of natural history caused some of the worst havoc. An army of 'well-meaning, idle-minded' collectors ravaged the seashores. Amateur botanists, on summer outings, vied with each other to make the 'best' collections, meaning those with the most rare plants. Sportsmen of all types were equally remorseless. After 1835, as the breech-loading gun came into general use, there was ever-increasing slaughter. One Highland sportsman, who boasted of shooting 'everything that moved', accounted in 1868 for 1,900 head of game, including grouse, golden plover and hares, besides 'vermin' like owls. Gamekeepers were bribed to kill ravens, crows, buzzards and other predators. Townsmen took excursion trains to the coast to amuse themselves by shooting kittiwakes and other sea-birds; nesting colonies on the cliffs afforded easy sport. Later, when dealers were offering a shilling each for white gulls to decorate women's hats, there was profit as well as mass slaughter. Fowlers would tear the wings from their screaming victims and fling them into the sea 'to struggle with feet and head until death slowly came to their relief'. The fledgelings were left to starve in thousands. In London, in the hard winter of 1892/3, gulls flocking on the Thames were shot from the bridges. In many country places, men and boys joined in bush-beating and bird-netting on winter nights. On the Cornish coast, starving birds were trapped with teagles, long strings set with baited fish-hooks. Villagers, Hudson said, 'thought birds were only made to be destroyed'; and he had read of one gentleman at Ringmer in Sussex who, in about 1850, had all the nightingales in his grounds put down: 'their late singing disturbed his rest.'

Nor could the birds of the London parks live and nest in safety. In Kensington Gardens, in 1880, the authorities cut down the grove of 700 fine elms where Hudson had watched the rooks on his first morning in London. The reason, he was told, was that grass would not grow well in the shade, and people walking there got their boots muddy. Cats and bird's-nesters roamed many parks; boys went hunting with stones in the Bayswater squares. One East End park was the haunt of chaffinch fanciers, each carrying a caged bird blinded with red-hot needles: ostensibly looking for a wild chaffinch to give their pets 'a little practice in the art of singing', but adept at using limed twigs and decoys. The unthinking pet owner, who killed nothing himself but liked to have a tame bullfinch or goldfinch, kept the trade in wild birds flourishing, and made these species rarer for a time. Bird-catchers from Whitechapel or Bethnal Green spent their spare time trapping in the lanes or on the commons near London; on Sunday mornings in the 1880s, Jefferies wrote, one could meet four or five of them in the space of a mile in the country around Surbiton. *Enquire Within*, a popular home manual first published in 1856, gave hints on looking after caged blackbirds and thrushes, linnets and skylarks. (It also had a recipe beginning, 'Take a dozen

larks'.) Hawks with clipped wings were bought from gamekeepers and kept tethered in country gardens for their 'amusing
tricks'. Hudson once failed to rescue a white owl from captivity in
the hot, bright kitchen of an inn at Chichester. It remained one of
his bitterest memories.

For many of these people, no doubt, the idea of cruelty never
arose. If it did, there were time-honoured excuses. Boys robbing
nests knew from their elders that 'where there's no sense there's
no feeling'; or, when chasing and stoning a blackbird, that the
quarry 'enjoyed the fun'. One lad, seen to shoot at a singing
thrush, argued that 'If I don't do it, someone else will.' Sporting
and farming interests took a heavy toll. Gilbert White had
recorded how a poultry-keeper trapped a raiding sparrow-hawk,
cut off its wings and talons, put a cork on its beak and threw it
down for his hens to tear to pieces. A hundred years later this 'law
of retaliation' was as powerful as ever. Highland eagles, then as
now, were said to take new-born lambs. Hawks, jays, magpies
and squirrels, unwelcome in game coverts, made showy ornaments in glass cases, replacing the earlier displays of wax fruit
and flowers. Owls, both white and brown, were shot by the
'country loafer' and the gamekeeper, and fell victim in hundreds
to the pole-trap, which exploited the predator's liking for a high
isolated perch.

Yet all through the nineteenth century the climate was slowly
changing. There had always been a few, more thoughtful and
sensitive than the rest, who condemned sports like badger-
baiting and cock-fighting, and protested at cruel treatment of
horses and cattle. Maria Edgeworth in her children's classic
Rosamond (1821) even touched on the rights of wild animals.
Humane feeling, like callousness, could be found in all walks of
life. There were villagers who fed small birds in winter from
kindness, and welcomed swallows nesting in their eaves; as well
as the others John Clare knew about, who were as ready to kill a
wren or robin as a sparrow. Bloomfield in his *Farmer's Boy* anticipated *Black Beauty* by nearly eighty years with an angry account of
the way post-horses were overworked, 'the dreadful anguish he
endures for gold'. Charles Waterton (1782–1865) banned the gun
on his estate, which he enclosed with a high wall, creating the
first wildlife sanctuary. Waterton, like Hudson, had hunted
animals as a boy, travelled and collected as a young man in South
America, and in his thirties turned to protection. Other
ornithologists were exchanging the gun for spyglass and hide.

The Society for the Prevention of Cruelty to Animals, founded in 1824, became Royal in 1840. In the 1850s Anna Sewell's aunt was teaching boys in Norfolk about bird-life, to discourage them from bird's-nesting. In 1863 Queen Victoria wrote to her daughter in Germany: 'I wonder you could go to see the poor seals shot at! Papa could not bear their being shot, he was so fond of them!' The first British law protecting seals was not passed for another half-century. Bird protection meanwhile had a long start: the impetus coming from reaction to mounting slaughter in a purely frivolous cause, the use of wings, feathers or stuffed birds in women's fashions.

Most game, even when shot for amusement, ended as food. Furs and seal-skins, however cruelly obtained, were put to practical use as human clothing. Collectors could claim a scientific interest. No such excuse could be made for a hat trimmed with gulls' wings or the plumes of great crested grebes, or a ball dress set off by a spray of goldfinches or robins. Bird-lovers, revolted at this heartless waste, were already making themselves heard in the 1860s. From the first, the campaign attracted distinguished leaders and supporters, among them Professor Alfred Newton, the leading Cambridge ornithologist. In 1868 Professor Newton made a historic speech to the British Association, describing the raids on sea-birds by plumage-hunters, and warning that many species would soon be in danger of extinction. He put the blame where it belonged, on the heads of women customers: 'fair and innocent as the snowy plumes may appear on a lady's hat, I must tell the wearer the truth—she bears the murderer's brand on her forehead.' His speech had a curious and enlightening sequel. A woman in the audience sprang to her feet and 'passionately protested against the injustice done to her sex in holding ladies responsible for the murder of the white gulls. "Much mischief", she concluded, "was done in the world through ignorance. No lady would willingly wear the feathers of a bird that was destroyed in the act of feeding its young."' As she was speaking, some of the learned audience—no doubt hardly able to believe their eyes—noted that she was wearing a kittiwake in her hat. A friend of Hudson's had a similar experience, meeting in a train another woman who spoke 'with very great warmth' about endangered bird species. She was wearing an aigrette; and was shocked when told that it was made of the plumes of white egrets killed while nesting.

These innocents, however blind where their own headgear

was concerned, were at least aware that the problem existed, and anxious to save the birds. Unfortunately, they were not typical. Despite ever-widening publicity, women continued to wear feathered hats, and year after year millions of birds were shot 'in the act of feeding their young'.

The first campaigners put their faith in legislation. The Sea Birds Preservation Act was passed in 1869, the year after Newton's speech, and other Acts followed. In 1872, protected species for the first time included the cuckoo, robin, wren and goldcrest. This meant only that it was illegal to kill them in the breeding season; but it was a landmark. In 1876, Professor Newton returned to the attack with a letter to *The Times* revealing that protection in Britain had been followed by carnage abroad. Vast bundles of herons' and white egrets' feathers, with tropical birds by the thousand, were being imported. If these species were to survive, the Governments concerned must follow Britain's example and impose a close season; but the most effectual remedy would be for all right-thinking people to discountenance the fashion. He went further, suggesting that those who wore feathers deserved to be tarred as well.

In 1880 the Wild Birds Protection Act gave all British species a close season; but killing for the feather trade went on. In December 1885, when Hudson was watching for reviews of *The Purple Land*, he no doubt read a broadside in *The Times* from another old campaigner, the Rev. F. O. Morris. Even by the Thames, Morris wrote, 'idle and ruthless gunners' were taking kingfishers, sandpipers and snipe for women's headgear; and he urged support for a new Plumage League to fight the fashion.

'Alas!' a woman writer commented, 'he little knows the hardness of some of us when fashion is in question.' Women, however, were now starting a crusade of their own, hoping that, in matters of dress, female persuasion might have greater success than the more familiar male disapproval. When the Plumage League merged with another Society, Mrs Robert Williamson of Manchester formed her own Society for the Protection of Birds. About the same time, in February 1889, a close friend of Hudson's, Mrs Eliza Phillips, began to hold meetings in her Surrey home for women interested in protecting wildlife: fifteen voices against millions, as Hudson said. Calling themselves the Fur, Fin and Feather Folk, they took a pledge to refrain from wearing the feathers of any bird not killed for food; the ostrich excepted, since

146

ostrich plumes could be taken without killing. A note of moderation, good sense and accurate information, typical of their later history, was thus struck at once.

One of the supporters of the Manchester group was a young woman, Hannah Poland, daughter of the family Hudson had known ever since his arrival in London. The Manchester and Croydon groups were on friendly terms, and in 1891 they joined forces in London, keeping the name Society for the Protection of Birds. Hannah Poland—that 'brave young girl', Hudson called her—became honorary secretary, at the request of the Manchester founder, because of the active interest she had shown in the work. It seems likely that it was Hudson who had inspired and encouraged this interest; and it was perhaps through the Polands that he met Mrs Phillips and her friend Miss Catherine Hall, who lived not far from the Hudsons in Bayswater. Mrs Phillips and Miss Hall became the Society's first vice-president and treasurer; the president being Winifred, Duchess of Portland, another keen campaigner. Though Professor Newton 'gave them their first guinea', and male co-workers were not lacking, membership to begin with was still confined to women; but an exception had always been made in Hudson's case. From the first he was their supporter, adviser and guest of honour at the meetings in Mrs Phillips's house at Croydon, then a country town with woods nearby, where in spring he could hear the nightingale and cuckoo. And on those days at least he fared better than the crossing-sweeper. Another founder, Mrs Frank Lemon, recalled that at luncheon before their meetings 'dishes and wines that we knew were his favourites' accompanied the planning of the agenda.

The bird protectors, like the legislators, began with high hopes; thinking that, if only enough women could be persuaded to join, 'the demand for ornamental plumage would cease and the supply would automatically come to an end.' With strong press support, the Society's numbers grew to over 5,000 in the first year, and continued to increase; and there was rejoicing when, in September 1891, a professional gull-hunter was reported as saying that 'this ladies' association' had stopped the demand for sea-birds. But the fashion trade had its own powerful line of propaganda, giving out that aigrettes and other ornaments were now being made up from domestic hens' feathers. To counter this, Hudson wrote a pamphlet setting out the facts about the massacre of the white egrets abroad:

The feather-hunters consider it a rare piece of good fortune when they discover one of these breeding-places, when the birds . . . are fully fledged, but not yet able to fly; for at that time the solicitude of the parent birds is greatest, and, forgetful of their own danger, they are most readily made victims. I have seen how they act when the heronry is approached by man; their boldness, broad wings, and slow flight making it as easy as possible to shoot them down; and when the killing is finished, and the few handfuls of coveted feathers have been plucked out, the slaughtered birds are left in a white heap to fester in the sun and wind in sight of their orphaned young, that cry for food and are not fed.

There is nothing in the whole earth as pitiable as this—so pitiable and so shameful—that for such a purpose human cunning should take advantage of that feeling and instinct, which we regard as so noble in our own species . . .

Five thousand copies of the first printing were distributed by the Society, and the pamphlet was quoted in many papers. In May 1892, *Punch*, which had been denouncing the fashion for years, published a cartoon showing a monstrous female decked with wings and a vast feather boa. Again it seemed that success was near. But in October 1893 Hudson wrote to *The Times*:

Since last autumn many of us have been rejoicing in the belief that bird-wearing was at last going out. So marked was the decline that many of the best millinery establishments at the West End and in country towns ceased to supply birds. . . . The change was attributed to that better feeling so long desired; to the literature which the Selborne, the Bird Protection and other societies had been industriously disseminating; and to the increased regard for bird life which comes with increased knowledge. Is it possible any longer to cherish such a belief when we see the feathers displayed in the windows of milliners and drapers in London and every country and seaside town at the present moment; when we read in all the ladies' journals that wings are to be 'all the rage' during the coming winter; and when almost every second woman one sees in the streets flaunts an aigrette of heron's plumes on her bonnet? . . .

This letter, headed 'Feathered Women', was reprinted as a pamphlet, and seemed to make its mark: feathers were out of fashion for the next two seasons. At the Society's annual meeting in February 1894 Hudson was thanked for his valuable work; and the report for 1894 stated confidently that, while women of 'the 'Arriet class' still wore sparrows painted blue or scarlet, the fashion had declined among gentlewomen. But, far from being over, the struggle had hardly begun. The autumn of 1895 saw the shops refilled with plumage; the trade announced that robins would again be fashionable on ball dresses; and churches everywhere during Sunday services became 'forests of waving feathers'. Hudson's next move was to write an open letter which was sent to more than 10,000 clergymen and ministers, enlisting their support. He felt that these men were committed to teach mercy, and that some might be led to preach and practise it: as Morley Roberts drily commented, he had a great imagination. But this 'Macedonian cry' was not listened to. Hudson's own comment appeared in another letter to *The Times*: 'Clergymen, like men in other professions, "must live", and find it easier to do so by keeping on pleasant terms with their lady parishioners...'

The bitter struggle was to continue for thirty years; slowly, one after another, the objectives were gained. In 1899 Queen Victoria confirmed an army order that officers should no longer wear egret plumes; in 1902 the export of bird-skins and feathers from British India was prohibited; six years later the New Guinea trade in birds of paradise at last ended. The Society (Royal since 1904), had to work for another thirteen years before an Act in 1921 banned the importing of foreign plumage. Hudson, Miss Hall, Mrs Lemon and Hannah Poland (Mrs Lemel) all lived to see this achievement.

By the 1920s the feather boa had become a symbol of absurdity, worn by stage charwomen and by eccentrics like Auntie in the Pip, Squeak and Wilfred cartoons. But the feathered hat continued to reappear; the 'Edwardian' fashion of 1938/9, and the 'new look' ten years later, brought popular revivals. In 1951, Phyllis Barclay-Smith, Secretary of the International Committee for Bird Preservation, warned that fresh propaganda might be needed 'to bring to the observer the picture of a nestful of young birds slowly dying of starvation, or the extinction of a lovely species'. Television now made this literally possible; it also gave large numbers of people their first experience of watching wildlife, later sending many of them into the country to wildlife parks and other observation centres.

This was what Hudson, with his great imagination, had wanted to do for the urban Victorians: the millions for whom 'the divorce from nature was absolute, and ... the divorce from all dignity and beauty and significance in the wilderness of mean streets in which they were bred, whether in the well-to-do suburb or the slum'. Hudson knew these streets. Now he was coming to know the countryside beyond, with some woods,

downs and commons almost unchanged since White's day, and
still filled with birds, if only they could be saved:

> The jay, the 'British Bird of Paradise', displaying his vari-coloured
> feathers at a spring-time gathering; the yellow-green, long-
> winged wood wren, most aerial and delicate of the woodland
> warblers; the kingfisher, flashing turquoise blue as he speeds by;
> the elegant fawn-coloured, black-bearded tit, clinging to the
> grey-green, swaying reeds, and springing from them with a bell-
> like note; and the rose-tinted narrow-shaped bottletit as he drifts
> overhead in a flock; the bright, lively goldfinch scattering the
> silvery thistle-down on the air; the crossbill, that quaint little
> many-coloured parrot of the north, feeding on a pine-cone; the
> grey wagtail exhibiting his graceful motions; and the golden-
> crested wren, seen suspended motionless with swiftly vibrating
> wings above his mate concealed among the clustering leaves, in
> appearance a great green hawk-moth, his opened and flattened
> crest a shining flame-coloured disc or shield on his head . . .

He believed that, if others could share his pleasure, the Society
would gain the strongest possible asset in public enlightenment
and concern. A Londoner who watched the skylarks soaring over
Hackney marshes would know better than to keep one in a cage
only 15 inches high, the roof arched and padded, as one manual
advised, 'so that the bird may not injure itself by jumping about'.
When people realized that stuffed birds were, compared to the
living creature, 'a libel on nature and an insult to man's intelligence', dead kingfishers would no longer be displayed in cottages, or peregrines and buzzards in large houses. Women would
give up 'murderous millinery', and bird collections would
become a source of embarrassment to the collectors' heirs.

Time was to prove Hudson right to a great extent. But, as the
plumage campaign made clear, there could be no short cut to this
change in public feeling. If, in the 1890s, films of the worst
cruelties practised by the plumage-hunters could have been
shown to a mass audience, it is doubtful if they would have made
much impression. For the great majority, life was too hard to
allow leisure and energy for any such imaginative effort. The new
ideas had to struggle against vested interests on one hand and
deep-rooted indifference on the other.

Because of this, legislation, however powerful in theory, often
proved ineffectual in practice. In the 1890s, hotel-keepers were
still advertising 'Sea-bird Shooting' to attract visitors. Few cul-
prits could be caught in the act. The haunts of birds and policemen were usually far apart, and many rural policemen in the

early years would 'wink at illegal bird-catching'. When law-breakers were brought to court it was hard to prove that birds had been 'recently killed or taken' in Britain. Poultry-dealers found it worth their while in the close season to send large consignments of newly killed wildfowl to the Continent and bring them back for sale in Leadenhall Market. A Welsh country postman, stopped while carrying fifteen live goldfinches, was predictably successful in giving the court 'various explanations how he came by them'. A Bethnal Green dealer, summoned for possessing a clutch of young larks, also had his case dismissed: though the birds were 'beating themselves against the bars of the cages', the magistrate found no evidence that they were not cage-bred but trapped in the wild. Such cases were typical. Many magistrates, Justices of the Peace and other men of standing were amongst the keenest collectors, and contended that the new Acts 'interfered with the liberty of the subject'. The bird-dealers too had learned to argue that their trade was a boon to farmers, and that to stop it would mean 'the ruin of England', as a linnet-catcher told Hudson: 'for what would there be then to stop the birds increasing? It stands to reason that the whole country would be eaten up.'

When Hudson met this man on a Berkshire common, he sat down and smoked with him, talking about stoats and other predators, and lending him his field-glasses to watch a red-backed shrike: 'How near it brings him!' the man exclaimed, delighted. In the same way Hudson spent many hours inducing London dealers and knowledgeable countrymen—land-owners, clergymen, gamekeepers—to talk to him. These researches confirmed his belief that private collectors, gamekeepers and bird-catchers were the chief danger to British species; and he went on writing pamphlets setting out the hard facts needed to press for effectual measures. Even in the early years there were some successes. In 1894, in a note added to his pamphlet *Lost British Birds*, he wrote that collectors had wiped out the St Kilda wren. However, there were survivors, and Sir Herbert Maxwell—a notable scientist and writer, now vice-president of the Society—secured an Act to protect them. In 1895, when the SPB republished Charles Waterton's essay defending the barn owl, Hudson in a preface quoted some grim evidence from a gamekeeper. Twenty-five years earlier, this man told Hudson, both white and brown owls had been common on the estate where he worked; now all were gone, accidentally caught by pole-traps set for other predators. ('The buzzards, once common, he had exterminated, and was proud to tell it.') Hudson urged that pole-traps should be banned, and in 1904 this was done; a measure sponsored by Sir Sydney Buxton (another name well known in the world of natural history) who had become treasurer of the Society.

The first women-only phase had been short-lived. It soon gave way to reorganization on a more secure basis and with wider scope, bringing in distinguished men in public life to increase the Society's powers and prestige. Their readiness to lend support was heightened by a remarkable change in Hudson's own professional standing. In the spring of 1892, just three years after the modest beginning in Mrs Phillips's drawing-room, *The Naturalist in La Plata* was published, and hailed as a masterpiece. The Society's official writer had emerged from obscurity to wide acclaim by the scientific and literary world.

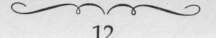

12

Coming Through

The Naturalist in La Plata had a splendid press. Alfred Russel
Wallace, in a three-page review in *Nature*, called it a remarkable
book, unique in that it was written, not by a traveller or visitor,
but by one born in that country, who had been familiar from
childhood with its fauna, and had spent twenty years in careful
observation. Never, he said, had he derived so much pleasure
and instruction from a book on the habits and instincts of
animals. He praised its originality, earnest spirit and clear,
delightful style, and wished it a success in proportion to its
merits. Richard Lydekker, later to confirm Hudson's accuracy for
himself, wrote with equal enthusiasm in *Natural Science*; and
reviewers in a dozen literary papers spoke at length of their
pleasure, interest and gratitude, calling it 'a capital book', 'a rich
treat', 'a beautiful work', and classing it with the works of Darwin, Bates and Wallace. *The Quarterly Review*, more unexpectedly, mentioned Balzac, describing it as 'a comedy of animated
tropical nature'. In the *Morning Post* Hudson was compared,
perhaps for the first time, to Jefferies. The critic of the *Saturday
Review*—to which he would soon become a regular con-
tributor—was also generous with praise, while seizing the
chance for a pleasant dig at the naturalists; remarking—on the
question of reason versus instinct—'the difficulty appears to
arise from denying to the brute creation the privilege of being
idiotic, or of doing very foolish things, like the great mass
of human beings': and adding, rather in the vein of Mr Listless,
'He would appear to have spent years as a settler on the Pampas.
Dreary and monotonous his surroundings must have been,

although, as a naturalist, he found inexhaustible sources of interest.'

Others, however, were captivated by the sheer contrast with their own lives. A reviewer of *Idle Days in Patagonia*, which followed in 1893, was clearly impressed by Hudson's adventures: the escape from near-shipwreck, the risk so casually taken in that first blind cross-country trek, his endurance of heat and thirst, his tolerant attitude to a deadly snake that had shared his cloak all night. Dr Johnson said that every man thought meanly of himself for not having been a soldier or sailor: to this a Victorian might have added an explorer or frontiersman. Many of Hudson's readers must have longed to change their way of life. Two who actually came near doing so were Sir Edward and Lady Grey, who discovered the books in 1893 during Grey's first summer as Parliamentary Under-Secretary for Foreign Affairs. Grey, then thirty-one, had from a sense of duty followed a famous grandfather into political life, to which he felt wholly unsuited. A born field naturalist, he had by the usual route—boyhood love of shooting and fishing—developed a passionate interest in all country things, a 'genius for bird observation' and a special love of water-birds. These feelings, shared by Dorothy Grey, were making them both 'increasingly miserable at the tie to London' during his first months in office. Hudson brought them to crisis point. Lady Grey sent a message to her husband one night at the House of Commons:

> first about the Hudson book, I have read a good deal: it touches very fine notes of feeling for nature. I felt first sad because it was such a long way off from what we are doing. . . . I read on and on and old Haldane came in in the middle. After the usual common-places I sort of let out, and we talked from 5 to 8 and the result is that he has gone away saying 'I understand at last. You must not stay in politics. It is hurting your lives.'

Haldane later went back on this, recalling them to duty: 'We are all soldiers in a great struggle, and cost what it may to our feelings let us storm the breaches. . . . It is a religious question with us.' But the Greys sought out and befriended Hudson. Whenever they first met, it must have been something of a shock to realize that their oracle was a man over fifty, living only a mile or two away, and more firmly tied to London than themselves. Grey did not escape until he too was in his fifties, ill and almost blind, so that Hudson's latest book had to be read to him; but he found ways of helping Hudson to greater freedom, through a Civil List pension and the loan of a country cottage. So far as their disparate ties allowed the three became close friends, and Lady Grey's death in 1906 was a great grief to Hudson.

One of the *La Plata* essays had already brought him another distinguished friend. Robert Bontine Cunninghame Graham, a Scottish aristocrat, was also in Parliament in the early nineties, though even less suited than Grey to the restricted life of a politician. Sympathy with the underdog brought him there. Descended from Scottish kings and Spanish hidalgos, and known to his friends as Don Roberto, he seemed destined to live—in the words of a biographer—'in the romanticism of a Byron and the idealism of a Don Quixote'. In 1890, when he and Hudson met, Graham was well known for his gallant support of John Burns in the Bloody Sunday meeting in Trafalgar Square three years earlier, and his subsequent imprisonment. In later life he came to look strikingly like Van Dyck's equestrian portrait of Charles I, from whom he could claim direct descent. At this time, however, his photographs, showing keen eyes, fine features, an air of vigour and sensitive pride, are remarkably like the early pictures of Hudson. The two had a great deal in common. Graham had spent years as a young man in South America. A natural horseman, speaking fluent Spanish, he was in his element on the pampas, where he had worked and mixed with the gauchos, picking up their dialect, learning their sayings, songs and dances. In February 1890 he read Hudson's essay 'A Naturalist on the Pampas' in the *Nineteenth Century* and wrote to suggest a meeting. They were friends at once, and this had far-reaching influence on both men as writers. Ten years younger than Hudson, with health and energy unimpaired, Graham evoked in him a more vital self. In a sense other than the literal one, they spoke the same language; while their use of Spanish, and of gaucho and Indian terms, was an obvious bond. Together they relived past adventures and campaigned against current atrocities—the massacre of Indians in South Dakota, and of albatrosses by English sportsmen at sea. Graham signed an early letter to Hudson with his own horse-brand. In his reply, Hudson did the same, writing, 'Should you ever revisit those distant lands and come across some mancaron about a thousand years old . . . with the above marca, please accept him as a gift from me . . .'

Mutual enthusiasm and understanding gave Hudson confidence to go back to his South American stories. Soon after their first meeting, Graham, who had so far written little, sent Hudson an article of his own about the pampas. Hudson in return sent *The Purple Land*, and wrote: 'I shall by and by attempt to spin another little yarn entitled *El Ombu*, for which I have some tempting materials.' Already, evidently, he had been looking up the notebook in which, more than twenty years before, he had written down the old gaucho's story. *El Ombu*, published in 1902, was dedicated to Graham, and *The Purple Land* was republished at his insistence. Meanwhile, all through the nineties, a tale of a different kind—'the Venezuelan romance'—was taking shape in Hudson's imagination, to emerge as *Green Mansions*.

When in London, Graham rode every day in Hyde Park on Pampa, a temperamental Argentine mustang which he rescued from a Glasgow tramcar—to the evident relief of the tramway staff—and which carried him for twenty-five years. This fiery beast, with flowing mane and tail, reminded Hudson of his own boyhood favourite, and it was one of his pleasures to watch them in the park. Speaking of this to a friend, he called up with an airy gesture of the hand 'the handsome cavalier on his prancing horse'. But once, overcome by memories, he exclaimed 'Oh Pampa!', put his arms round the horse's neck and wept.

Did he ever ride again after his journey through the desert pampas in March 1874? Once, in his sixties, walking in Wiltshire with the Ranee of Sarawak, he suddenly leapt on a hunter in a field, sat 'like a centaur' while it reared and bucked, then rode it about, his hand on its mane. The Ranee, astonished, asked him, 'Do you often do that?' If he did, it was in secret. But he was sometimes at home again in the horseman's world. Through Cunninghame Graham he met Wilfrid Scawen Blunt, who with his wife Lady Anne Blunt (Byron's grand-daughter) had founded a famous Arabian stud at Crabbet Park in Sussex. Blunt, another keen politician (or political rebel), poet and traveller, had lived in Buenos Aires in the 1860s, crossed the pampas with rifle held so that 'even distant enemies might see and mark its silhouette', watched birds at the foot of the Andes and narrowly escaped death in a pampero blizzard. These three were linked by the past as closely as the 'three very poor Bohemians', Hudson, Gissing and Roberts, by literary poverty.

After 1888, when Roberts went to live in Chelsea, he and Hudson came to know many painters, including Alfred Hartley, 'the best fellow in the world', A. D. McCormick and Bryan Hook, who were soon among Hudson's favourite illustrators. Hartley drew him in his poncho on the coast of Patagonia, and Hook on the bridge in St James's Park, feeding the gulls, for *Birds in London*; pictures that must have pleased him, as they underline his youthful appearance even in his fifties. He seems to have been less gratified—after reading the book—by McCormick's using him as a model for six wash and charcoal illustrations to Roberts's novel *The Earth Mother*; a sombre, Poe-like tale of a Chelsea sculptor who kills an enemy in a duel and hides the body in a cast from a statue. The rugged bearded 'Garth' is certainly recognizable; so too is Roberts's admiring description: 'he dwarfed and rendered insignificant all the men with whom he sometimes walked; and though no one said that he was handsome, women were always impressed by him.' Hudson told Cunninghame Graham, 'The artist got me to pose for him, and the consequence of my good nature is that I appear as the hero, who is a murderer and everything that is bad, in the confounded book.'

McCormick did please him, however, by walking fully dressed into the sea at Shoreham 'from sheer joy of the sea and longing for it', as Hudson himself would greet the sea on arrival by scooping up a handful of salt water to drink. In the early nineties he and Roberts, with their friends, stayed several times at this little town on the Sussex coast, then a favourite haunt of painters. Even today, Shoreham has some of the features that appealed to him; boathouses at the water's edge, little shipyards and yachts building or repairing or lying at anchor; the 'queerly named street Raptigal'—Rope Tackle—leading down to wide mud flats with sea-birds at low tide; the shelving beach, fringed with sea bindweed and wild borage, where Hudson and Roberts had a memorable adventure. Three young girls were swept into deep water while bathing, and Roberts swam out to the rescue. Hudson could not swim, and the state of his heart was always precarious, but he waded down to his neck and somehow kept his footing in a rough sea on the steep treacherous shingles, helping Roberts to bring them in one after another. The third girl, and Roberts himself, were both unconscious when he and another man got them ashore. But for Hudson's height and strength they would have drowned.

Up to now holidays had been brief; but the spring of 1892 at last brought a long stretch of freedom. In February 1,000 copies of *The Naturalist in La Plata* were published in London and New York; by June the English edition was reprinting. It meant that he could afford to spend seven or eight weeks in the country, from May to early July, the time of nesting and full song. *Birds in a Village*, the title essay of his first book on the English countryside, caught his sense of novelty and excitement.

He came to the haunts of birds, wrote a sympathetic reviewer, as a leading theatre critic would come to the play. In the Thames valley he found Cookham Dean, a bird-watcher's paradise: a leafy, straggling village surrounded by gardens, elm groves, cherry orchards, deep lanes and hedges, a beechwood and a rough, thorny common. Kingfishers flashed over buttercup fields, bluetits darted in the apple blossom, birds of all kinds perched on a rustic bridge over a stream, close to a pool covered with water-lilies and overhung by wild roses. From his window at dawn he heard cuckoos babbling in chorus and watched them chasing each other; later he watched a hedge-sparrow feeding a young cuckoo. A dozen nightingales sang about the village; reed warblers by the river kept up a low 'gurgling and prattling like musical running water'; grasshopper warblers on the common produced 'a mysterious trilling buzz or whirr' affecting the nerves of hearing like 'the vibrations of the brake of a train'. Hearing the cry of a wryneck—already a rare bird—he searched for it in quiet, grassy orchards with hollow trees where it might be nesting, and by the woods at twilight; and eventually saw one. The jay, another favourite of his, was also rare in that heyday of the keeper's gibbet. He heard one in the early mornings, foraging around the village; stalked it to the wood, and lay on the dry moss watching it in the tree-tops through his field-glasses—evidently a new possession:

> I had the wild thing at my thumb, so to speak, exhibiting himself to me, inquisitive, perplexed, suspicious, enraged by turns, as he flirted wings and tail, lifted and lowered his crest, glancing down with wild bright eyes. What a beautiful hypocrisy and delightful power this is . . . thus to fool this wild elusive creature, and bring all its cunning to naught!

'Nightingale days, cuckoo and blackbird and tree-pipit days' gave way after midsummer to greenfinch days 'filled with the perpetual airy prattle of these delightful birds'. Altogether he sighted fifty-nine species; and, according to the *National Observer*, probably got two out of every three wrong. 'He has written so well of what he knows,' wrote this anonymous critic of *Birds in a Village* (under the heading 'Strange Birds'), 'that it is regrettable indeed to find him babbling thus of English birds.' He doubted whether Hudson could tell a rook from a crow, and thought he had even 'mistaken his Philomel': not surprisingly, since Hudson said that 'at my own cottage, when the woman who waited on me shook the breakfast cloth at the front door, the bird that came to pick up the crumbs was the nightingale, not the robin.' But the writer's 'true objection' to the book, it appeared, was not 'mere error' but Hudson's wrath against ornithologists and collectors. The reviewer's own bias seems equally obvious, and Hudson could afford to smile at the charge of 'simple ignorance', or advice against allowing 'ecstasy' to take the place of sober observation. He had been careful to make clear his status as 'one from foreign parts'—warned perhaps by experience with Professor Newton, with whose help he was compiling his pamphlet *Lost British Birds*: 'old Conservative academic Newton', he recalled long afterwards, 'who glared at me, an Argentine, who dared to come to England and write about [English] birds...'

Other reviewers of *Birds in a Village*, which came out in August 1893, showed more percipience. The *Graphic* welcomed him as a writer who might do for England what Thoreau and Burroughs had done in America; and *Nature* commended him as a close and loving observer, while looking back with regret to the grand scope of his South American work, and the accounts of 'riding at a swinging gallop through rustling seas of giant thistles ... or gazing up at the starry skies of Patagonia.' When *Idle Days* appeared earlier in the same year, Wallace had again written a sympathetic review, though he felt that even this book was something of an anti-climax after *La Plata*; and other critics concurred. *La Plata*, he was still assured by *Nature* in 1900, would always be reckoned as his best work, because 'it treated of animal life among which *he* was entirely at home, and of which *we* knew little or nothing.' The *Saturday Review*, however, maintained that in *Idle Days*, and now in the slender *Birds in a Village*, there was excellent work, together with developing powers in new fields. In a full-page review, a knowledgeable critic praised both books in enthusiastic terms, and especially noted his mastery on the subject of bird-song: 'We know of no writer on it who approaches him in descriptive power, in the choice and accuracy of phrase, in subtlety of perceptive faculty, and sensibility to all sounds in nature.'

It was Emily's hand, perhaps, which stuck these columns in his early press-cutting book; but Hudson was not yet indifferent to critical approval. He must have been glad of such discriminating praise, and of continued support from the *Academy*: 'his readers must often have wished he would bring his poetic insight to bear upon British bird-life.... He has done so; and the result is that everyone will greedily wish for more.' The publisher Charles James Longman, who as editor of *Longman's Magazine* had been using Hudson's essays since 1886, now commissioned a textbook, *British Birds*, which the firm brought out in 1895; followed in 1898 by *Birds in London*.

British Birds is an efficient compilation, listing 375 species (including rare visitors), quoting widely from leading authorities, and coming to life when Hudson writes from his own experience; for instance, of the foraging tree-creeper:

> His procedure is always the same: no sooner has he got to the higher and smoother part of the bole up which he has travelled than he detaches himself from it, and drops slantingly through the air to the roots of another tree, to begin as before. The action is always accompanied by a little querulous note, which falls like an exclamation, and seems to express disgust at the miserable harvest he has gathered . . .

—the red-backed shrike:

> its movements on its stand, as it turns its head from side to side and jerks and fans its tail, frequently uttering its low, percussive, chat-like chirp or call-note, give the impression of a creature keenly alive to everything passing around it . . .

—or the spotted flycatcher:

> silent and motionless, listless and depressed in appearance . . . like a silent grey ghost of a little dead bird returned to haunt the sunlight.

His descriptions of bird-song and call notes are equally meticulous; from the wren's 'loud bright lyric, the fine, clear, high-pitched notes and trills issuing in a continuous rapid stream'—to the 'storm of extraordinary sounds' with which young herons in the nest greet the arrival of food, 'grunts and squeals and prolonged screams, mingled with chatterings and strange quacking or barking notes'.

'Wren' was also, and long remained, the common or country name for several other small birds, of which he lists five: the goldcrest ('golden Christian wrennie', he later heard it called in Cornwall), wood and willow wren (warbler), furze wren (Dartford warbler) and red craking night wren (Savi's warbler). At Cookham Dean he had heard the old name prettichaps used for both garden warbler and blackcap, and cuckoo's mate for wryneck. He also records develing and screecher for the swift; fallowchat, whitetail, stonecracker, chack-bird and clodhopper for the wheatear; chit or chit-perle, Norfolk names for the little tern; and others still locally familiar, yaffle, goatsucker, whaup.

Savi's warbler he gives as a lost species, together with avocet, bittern, honey buzzard, black-tailed godwit and marsh harrier; hen harrier and kite are described as 'on the verge of extinction'. The bird protectors, happily, were to change this; he himself, within a few years, could have heard the bittern in Norfolk. The osprey, too, he lists as near extinction; it was soon to disappear as a nesting species for half a century, before its return in the 1950s. The corncrake, on the other hand, he describes as 'one of the commonest British birds'; the evening cry of the partridge was as familiar as that of the blackbird; white owls were a common sight in barn or belfry; and puffin and peregrine flourished in their ancient coastal retreats.

Besides black and white drawings, by G. E. Lodge, *British Birds* has eight fine colour paintings by Thorburn—who was paid £40 for them—and a rather dim photograph of rooks at their nest, by the pioneer bird photographer R. B. Lodge, who in 1895 achieved the first close-up of a bird on its nest. *Birds in London*, coming three years later, has several more of Lodge's early photographs: cormorants in St James's Park, a dabchick on the nest, a starling at a nest-hole. The rapid progress of nature photography in the next decade may be seen from the much better illustrations in *The Open Air* (1907), a countryside collection edited by Edward Thomas, to which Hudson contributed several essays.

Hudson himself was soon trying his hand with a camera: his own copy of *Birds and Man* was to be 'extra-illustrated' with many photographs of Wells in Somerset, and he spoke of 'taking snapshots' of picturesque country people. But it seems likely that he soon found wildlife photography, with its technical demands, too distracting to a dedicated watcher, and did not persevere with this.

His note on the early spring assemblies of the jay brought a rebuke from one reviewer of *British Birds*, stating that it was a solitary bird except in late summer and early autumn. 'If I had not made it a rule never to reply to a critic,' Hudson commented, 'I could have informed this one that I knew exactly where his knowledge of the habits of the jay was derived—that it dated back to a book published ninety-nine years ago.' In his introduction he pointed out the value of first-hand observation: 'so long as they are watched for, fresh things will continue to appear.'

The book was meant especially for the young, and as such

warmly recommended by *Nature*, while *Popular Science* wrote: 'One who would know the birds of Britain can hardly do better than allow himself to be introduced to them by Mr Hudson.' Reprinted in 1897 and 1902, it was used by several generations of schoolboys, and one early reader remembers:

> For a lot of us it was our first bird book. Hudson was to us what the Rev. J. G. Wood was to my father's generation. Hudson you have to be patient with; he's no use for the instant bird spotters of today, out for a big score each sortie, but he imparts delight in birds. He did truly love the bird in the landscape. He sat still and watched and listened and enjoyed. I learned a lot from him and so did many others.

Birds in London took him back to his old haunts. In the spring of 1897 he was getting up early on fine mornings to spend a whole day in revisiting parks, heaths and open spaces. It was not meant as a guide-book, which would quickly have been out of date; but was chiefly an account of bird-life as he saw it in 1896 and 1897, both in the central parts and on the outskirts, updating his observations over more than twenty years. The book remains of great interest to Londoners today, when many species have returned or moved in, some even nesting in densely populated areas. The tendency then seemed to Hudson towards steady loss and decline, not only from new housing, with increasing population and smoke, but from relentless clearance of cover in the parks. Since 1874 he had seen not only the rooks but the missel-thrush, nuthatch and spotted woodpecker leave Kensington Gardens, his nearest resort; while blackbirds, tits, wrens and robins were becoming rarer. Yet in the dense shrubberies of Battersea Park, where birds were encouraged and protected, these last four species were on the increase, and the lesser whitethroat, reed warbler and cuckoo bred in 1897. In those twenty-odd years he had seen wood pigeons establish themselves all over London, moorhens and dabchicks colonize the lakes, and seagulls become annual winter visitors. The history of the gulls gave him special pleasure; showing that public habits could change. Until the nineties the gulls would come up the Thames only during hard weather, to be greeted with shotguns by sportsmen on the bridges. In the long frost of 1892/3 this dangerous sport was stopped, and workmen began to feed the gulls with scraps on the Embankment. Soon this became a popular amusement. Hudson thought he was the first to feed them on sprats: 'The very sight of the little silvery fish thrown up would bring the birds screaming with excitement about me, and I would soon have a pushing crowd of people round me to see the fun. By and by others—ladies and gentlemen—began to come with their baskets and parcels of sprats.' It was a good omen for the future of bird protection.

But losses in recent years had far exceeded gains. Peregrine falcon and kestrel were gone from London, and it seemed to him unlikely that they would ever return. A local bird-stuffer had killed the 'last' magpies on Hampstead Heath. Kensington Gardens alone of the central parks still had the owl and jackdaw. Even old residents like the great tit (or oxeye, as Hudson calls it) had vanished, and fewer summer migrants were nesting.

Ravenscourt was no longer a secluded wilderness but a public park; though still to him, through his grateful memories, one of the most beautiful in London. In 1888, when it was opened, the birds at first fled in terror, but many had since returned, among them the missel-thrush. The wild flowers did not survive; but today in spring the grass is full of crocuses, thrush and blackbird sing, and great trees give shade in summer. Cedars and ancient thorns that he knew are still there; as are many London trees, including half a dozen immense black poplars in Finsbury Park, the last of an avenue then 'all uniform in size and trimmed to the same height', a practice to which he strongly objected. He detested artificiality, and urged that weeds and wilderness were needed not only for birds but for man: 'To exhibit flower-beds to those who crave for nature is like placing a dish of Turkish delight before a hungry man: a bramble-bush, a bunch of nettles, would suit him better'—a concept probably better understood today than at any time since this was written. In 1898 such ideas seemed fanciful, and he was lightly chaffed in *Nature* for saying, 'in his enthusiasm for his subject', that the sight of wild birds not only brightened the city dweller's existence but added to his well-being.

He received an outright payment of £150 for *British Birds*, and £100 on publication for the first 2,500 copies of *Birds in London*, with a 15 per cent royalty thereafter. If he could have produced a book a year he would now have had a sufficient income; but his researches were too thorough and his writing methods too painstaking for this. With books, articles and lodgers' rents he still had less than £100 a year. But country lodgings were cheap—one cottager gave him 'big fires, three or four meals a day and every luxury she could get' for £1 a week—and he could now afford to travel further and stay away for longer than in the lean years of the eighties; going west to Savernake Forest and north to Northumberland and Yorkshire, searching for Dartford warblers on Dorset heaths, and returning to Cookham Dean in three successive summers. In 1892 a reader of *The Naturalist in La Plata* had invited him to Dublin, offering 'a hearty welcome to our Saturday morning breakfasts at the Zoological Gardens'. His fifty-third birthday, in August 1894, was spent at a country house in the Wicklow hills, where there were stables with nesting swallows and a wild garden full of bird-life, and where he saw misselthrushes travelling in flocks of some hundred birds. Earlier that summer he was at Abbotsbury in Dorset. In 1895 he was away for long intervals from March to November. Spring was spent in the west, watching ravens on the Somerset coast, sheldrakes on the river Axe, and the jackdaw colonies of the Cheddar valley and Wells Cathedral: the latter so numerous at nesting time that a man with a barrow had to clear up the dropped sticks before morning service. He was at Wells in April, listening to the returning migrants—willow wren, chiffchaff, blackcap—and to green woodpeckers near the cathedral: 'you will not hear that woodland sound in any other city in the kingdom.' In May, 'brown as an Indian', he was on Exmoor, drawing out his gamekeeper friend about pole-traps. That summer he and Emily rambled along the Thames from Maidenhead to Wargrave and Sonning. Later he went to Stratford-on-Avon, and on into Gloucestershire, where he roamed about in the dark autumn evenings listening to wood owls and correcting Shakespeare's *tu-whit to-who*: 'there is no *w* in it, and no *h* and no *t*.'

In the early spring of 1896 he was back at Savernake, staying in a cottage deep in the forest, wandering alone with red deer and fallow deer, or coiling himself down out of the wind to bask like an adder in the sun's first warmth. That summer he visited Selborne, and the forests of Alice Holt and Wolmer; and Morley Roberts went with him to Cookham Dean, where they crawled about the common on hands and knees until he sighted a grasshopper warbler. In June 1897, at Beaulieu in Hampshire, he corrected proofs of *Birds in London*; later he took a sea trip to Norfolk and watched herons, curlews and whimbrels on Breydon Water with another friend, 'a poor naturalist who has a wife and seven children and £80 a year . . . and manages to keep a boat and houseboat, mostly his own work, and all his time is spent on the water.'

Always he was looking for 'home', and finding a sense of home-coming: on the green levels of Somerset and East Anglia, in Berkshire forests, and in small villages as far apart as Glouces- tershire and Norfolk, where, as at Clyst Hydon, there were cot- tages 'ivy and rose and creeper covered, with a background of old oaks and elms'. He loved the cathedral cities of the west, especi- ally Wells, 'the rustic, village-like city' surrounded by wooded hills and streams, and alive with bird-song and bell music. On his first visit, on a Sunday evening in spring, when the bells of St Cuthbert's church were 'filling and flooding that hollow in the hills', he followed a 'streamlet' that still runs westward out of the city, and came through a cleft into a narrow valley. The following sound of the bells, a 'musical roar', now suddenly changed, and echoed back from the high woods in front 'as if every one of those thousands of oak trees had a peal of bells in it'. The effect was so magical that at first he thought he would never return to blur the impression; and he did stay away ten years. Another time he insisted on going into the belfry of the same church while a peal was being rung: an experience remarkably like that of Lord Peter Wimsey in *The Nine Tailors*. The ringers, he found, had been right in trying to deter him.

> the sound was truly awful and horrible. I do not mean the musical waves of sound, but one awful steely note that pierced my brain like a hot arrow. I stayed in the belfry perhaps twenty seconds, and got out upon the leads. Again and again I went in, and this most awful sound absolutely hurt me and drove me out . . .

At times he was as 'scared of a wetting as a cat', knowing that a bout of bronchitis could kill him; yet often he disregarded bad weather, illness and fatigue. In his sixties he still took morning bathes in a cold sea, and in late November 'quite enjoyed going for long walks and getting thoroughly wet'. During the London autumn, he wrote, 'a person who elects to spend his nights on the roof, with rugs and umbrella to keep out cold and wet, may be rewarded by hearing far-off shrill delicate noises of straggling sandpipers or other shore-birds on passage, or the mysterious cry of the lapwing, "wailing his way from cloud to cloud".'

Emily, equally stoical, was still for a time 'the companion of his walks'; though Roberts once heard her object to this description, asking why he did not refer to her as his wife? Because, Hudson retorted, a wife was often no companion. They left town in April 1900 with bad colds, feeling too ill to walk; and after curing themselves by rambling about the Petersfield district in 'furious

165

cold winds', spent the Easter Saturday in a long walk down the Portsmouth Road, turning off to lodge at Havant.

Easter 1901 was equally strenuous. He and Emily trudged in a bitter east wind through daunting red-brick suburbs from Reading station to Three Mile Cross, Mary Russell Mitford's much-changed village, and on to see her grave at Swallowfield; where Hudson was rewarded by meeting a sexton who as a boy had known Miss Mitford, and 'remembered her well, and she was a very pleasant little woman'. He often had luck of this kind; and sometimes the sun shone. One spring day in 1894 they walked in a Surrey wood 'with clear sunbeams shining through old leafless oaks on the floor of fallen yellow leaves, listening to cuckoo and willow wren'. In the depths of the wood they came on a procession of rustics to a small ancient church (at Oakwood, near Ockley), and afterwards heard a strange story about this church from their village landlady. This was what he loved—the unexpected discovery, the charm of surprise—and he liked to find it out for himself, or to hear of it from genuine country people. This was one reason for preferring cottage quarters. The people who took them in 'were mostly poor people, and we too were poor, often footsore, and in need of their ministrations, and nearer to them on that account than if we had travelled in a more comfortable way'. Emily, despite her age and increasing weight, would march steadily along the road while he was scrambling through hedges, climbing hills and exploring woods. By the end of the day he would often be exhausted, so that she had to slacken her pace. Then she would sit patiently on village greens while he searched for a frugal lodging.

His lodgings in more prosperous days remained simple; even a village inn was a last resort for Hudson, and hotels he mostly avoided. There, as Roberts put it, 'the birds wore the same plumage and sang the same social songs, especially in the evening, when Hudson preferred to seek in some country bar or kitchen for new plumage and new wild music.' As for the amenities, there had been no baths on the pampas. Roberts himself in later life came to appreciate comfort, and found Hudson's ways trying; but at Cookham Dean in the 1890s, still under forty, he stayed without complaint in a brick-maker's cottage and went with their host to the clay-pit to learn brick-making, 'much to Hudson's delight, for though he was strangely lacking in every kind of manual dexterity he loved all the primitive arts and handicrafts'.

Edward Thomas, soon to be one of his greatest friends, wrote amusingly of the intellectual in the country, trying 'to chat with the poor and see them *au naturel*'. Hudson's rapport was genuine and unthinking; though sometimes, naturally, he could make a mistake. Talking to some men near Cookham Dean, he asked, 'Are there no badgers about here?' and was puzzled when this innocent question seemed to cause embarrassment, even hostility. Later he found that 'badgers' was the local idiom for 'a rough lot', including poachers. In Wiltshire, some years later, he had a long talk in a graveyard with an old church cleaner, afterwards giving her some money: 'and to my surprise after taking it she made me an elaborate curtsey. It rather upset me, for I had thought we got on very well together and were quite free and easy in our talk, very much on a level.' Most of the time that was true: he could break through reserve or class feeling to immediate trust and liking. Late one summer evening he and Emily arrived in a remote hamlet, to find that the only spare room had just been stripped by the bailiffs. Never mind that, he told the tearful housewife: it was a very good room, 'and we are going to stay.' And at once she fell in with his plans. The room was refurnished with loans from neighbours, potatoes were dug and supper cooked for them; afterwards he and Emily sat resting in the dusk, watching the moon rise and listening to the reeling of nightjars. Such elemental pleasures were sharpened by uncertainty. One evening when he was alone, weary and famished, it seemed he must spend the night under a hedge; but a village baker invited him in for a cup of tea:

> I could have told him that I should like a dozen cups and a great
> many slices of bread-and-butter, if there was nothing more sub-
> stantial to be had. However, I only said 'Thank you', and followed
> him in to where his wife, a nice-looking woman, with black hair
> and olive face, was seated behind a teapot. Imagine my surprise
> when I found that besides tea there was a big hot repast on the
> table—a ham, a roast fowl, potatoes and cabbage, a rice pudding, a
> dish of stewed fruit . . . 'You call this a cup of tea!' I exclaimed
> delightedly.

He stayed a week with the baker and his wife, and soon knew their life history. It was a familiar experience; and in return he would be patient, as he might not have been elsewhere, when interest flagged. One ancient cottager wanted him 'to go on listening for ever' to her village reminiscences, holding him with a gaze 'like the luminous eyes of an animal', while he longed to be out of doors; and from kindness he did stay on with her for several days.

Patience was once most severely tested, when memory failed to recapture something beyond price. At Wolmer he lodged in the forest with an old woman, 'a great talker', and a native of Selborne: her mother as a child had known the Reverend Gilbert White and had told her 'many interesting things about him'—but, try as she would, she could recall none of them. Again and again he questioned her, always in vain, until in desperation he would jump up and rush away to get over his chagrin in the open air.

Ford Madox Hueffer (later Ford Madox Ford), meeting Hudson at the turn of the century, said he was equally at home in Soho, or Carlton House Terrace, or in a shepherd's kitchen, drinking strong tea and eating poached rabbits. But in London, with writing to be done, he was more sparing of his time and energy; perhaps reluctant, also, to accept invitations he could not return. 'I could no more dine with you and your friends,' he wrote to Cunninghame Graham, 'than with the Fairies and Angels. . . . The fact is, being poor I long ago gave up going to houses and dining. One of the apostles, a certain Paul, warned us against "unequal" alliances, and Aesop touches instructively on the same subject in one of his parables . . .' But, despite St Paul and Aesop, he did attend gatherings of writers and painters at the house of Graham's mother, Mrs Anne Elizabeth Bontine: like her son an exceptional person, beautiful, intelligent and amusing, and quick to appreciate Hudson's qualities. Informal gatherings probably best suited his aloof bird-watching temperament. At a similar affair he met a writer and minor poet, Coulson Kernahan, who confirms his likeness to Graham: '. . . the words *Grand Seigneur* were the first to come to mind. Not because he was tall, gaunt and bearded, with a touch of the Spanish hidalgo about him . . . but because of the almost chivalrous courtesy of his bearing, did I recall Cervantes' great romance, and murmur to myself "Don Quixote, surely!"'

A lonely man, even in congenial company, Kernahan thought him; though keenly observant of his fellow guests.

His observation came as naturally to him as did his courtesy. In conversation his eyes met yours frankly, and with a kindly, keen, human interest in which was nothing of impertinent curiosity. Shy men—and as shy he struck me always—are sometimes self-conscious, but self-conscious Hudson was not; he was too natural in all he said or did . . .

He said he was a recluse, and was out of his setting at such a social function as that at which we had met. . . . Once when he asked me 'Who is that?' and I mentioned a well-known name, and offered to introduce him, he replied (almost hastily for a man who, I imagine, was never in haste): 'No! please don't. I am interested to know it is he, and to see him, but let us leave it at that.'

They met during an At Home given by Louise Chandler Moulton, an American poet from Boston, who spent part of each year in London between 1876 and 1898, and knew many of the literary figures of the day. These included a popular novelist, Margaret Raine, whose daughter Violet Hunt was to become a friend and admirer of Hudson in his later years. She described her first sight of him—grizzled, dark-skinned, foreign-looking—at a tea-party when 'I was a lively child too much brought forward for her age, allowed to pour tea for her mother's old friend Mrs Louise Chandler Moulton.' Mrs Moulton probably also knew, or knew of, Hudson's New England relatives, the Merriam family. He must have been glad to meet her, too, for another reason: her book of verse, *Swallow Flights*, includes a poem on releasing a caged bird. He himself would do this whenever possible, buying a finch or a linnet for a few pence in a market, or persuading someone to give a pining bird its freedom. Many people were afraid that, if released, a bird would be set on and killed by others; but he saw no such attacks, and later published a pamphlet to say so.

Hudson's blend of striking looks, reticence and melancholy was often attractive to women; Mrs Moulton was no exception.

'He struck me [she told Coulson Kernahan] as such a lonely—almost tragically lonely—man! I suspect that for some reason his life is unhappy. If it were only that he is poor, which I also suspect to be the case, one might be privileged to help, but he is, I imagine, intensely proud, and in the case of so sensitive a man, one can't go too carefully where money is concerned. Besides, there is strength, character, determination, written on that gaunt and somewhat grim face of his, and I can't think that mere money cares account for the loneliness—the soul-loneliness—which is also written there . . .'

Mrs Moulton was not alone in her concern, nor was hers the only impulse of practical sympathy to be daunted for fear of touching his pride. Cunninghame Graham must have felt this problem acutely when Hudson wrote to him in 1897 or 1898:

> Besides being poor in this world's goods, although of course rich in accumulated treasure where neither moth nor rust corrupt, I have for the last two or three months been afflicted with neuralgia of the eyes, which makes work 'with book and pen' wellnigh impossible; yet to live I must work. Do you remember Yeobright in Hardy's best work, 'The Return of The Native'—how when his eyes failed he took to cutting heath for an occupation, and was very happy in his rough toil? That would suit me better than writing.

By the end of the nineties, influential friends were insisting that he should have official recognition and help; among them Sir Edward Grey, Edward Clodd, a banker, writer and friend of writers, and the artist William Rothenstein, also noted for generous help to those in need. The idea of a Civil List pension seems to have originated with Clodd. Grey arranged an approach to the First Lord of the Treasury, Arthur Balfour, suggesting Hudson's name for a 'literary pension' to enable him to spend more time in the country. Before this could be awarded he had to be naturalized as a British subject. He was persuaded to take the necessary steps, and by 30 April 1900 the papers were ready.

Appropriately, the signatories met in the library at 3 Hanover Square, Dr Sclater's home, which was the headquarters of the Zoological Society and also—in rooms on the top floor—of the Society for the Protection of Birds, to which Sclater was a good friend. The papers were signed by Dr Sclater himself, by Morley Roberts, and by a Mr Waterhouse (probably the Zoological Society's Librarian, Frederick H. Waterhouse). On 5 June 1900 Hudson became officially an Englishman. Five days after his sixtieth birthday, on 9 August 1901, he was awarded a Civil List pension of £150 a year, 'in recognition of the originality of his writings on Natural History'.

After visiting Warwickshire and Gloucestershire Hudson had written, 'I should like a good ten years of such rambles in each county in England. One remembers Ruskin's expressions of defeat at the thought of death coming just when you are beginning to live . . .' Death was still a long way off; and the next ten years were to bring him not only wider fame but the greatest freedom and happiness he ever knew in England.

Part III

1899–1922

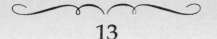

13

High Summer

In the brilliant summer of 1899, and the autumn and winter following, Hudson explored the Sussex downs and completed his first full-length book on the English countryside. The downs gave him a sense of strong elation. On a hot June morning near Lewes he met a 'genial ruffian' just out of gaol, swinging along with a bunch of yellow flag irises in his coat: 'he must indeed have been happy and seen all familiar things with a strange magical beauty in them.' It was his own mood. To escape from London always made him feel 'as if I had sloughed off a frayed and rusted envelope and come out like a ring-snake in new green and gold'.

In those miles of hills and valleys, from the bare chalk of the east to the wooded slopes and hollows of the west, he rarely met anyone but shepherds and an occasional tramp. The silence was broken only by bee and dung-fly, whinchat and stonechat, and sometimes by more distant sounds: larks by the hundred, singing out of sight, their high notes carrying perhaps three miles on every hand, 'filling the whole air like misty rain'; the scattered cries of sheep and sheep-dogs, and the far-sounding calls of a young shepherdess left in charge of a flock 900 strong at harvest time. After days of solitude, a small village at evening would seem as noisy and bustling as a town.

In *Nature in Downland* he draws a wide landscape filled with heat and light; describing the 'living garment' of the ancient turf, bright herbs, teeming insects, the hair grass ('ur-grass') of the high downs, spring bugloss and forget-me-not, the flowers of high summer and the wildlife of furze and blackthorn patches. Sitting on the grass, he could count thirty or forty blue butterflies

173

at once. Roaming through the scrub, he found badger earths, turtle-doves nesting in the blackthorns, hunting stoats and swarming rabbits, and saw four foxes in one morning—

> and where I saw four there must have been forty: I doubt that foxes are anywhere in England more numerous than in some of the furze-grown places on the South Downs. It is true they are hunted in their season, else they would not be in existence at all, but I do not think that more than one fox in every six or eight born each year is killed by the hounds. How they are kept in reasonable limits I cannot say. .... I have found foxes at midsummer, in fine condition and with a splendid coat of hair, lying dead among the furze, and could only say, 'Careless fellow! you have gone and got yourself bitten by an adder, and there's an end of you.'

One reviewer, taking this mild joke literally, objected: 'We should have imagined "Charlie's" field craft would have protected him from that kind of calamity, even if his thick fur failed to keep out the venom.' The sheep evidently had no field craft; a good many, he found, did really die of adder bites, sometimes from lying on a sluggish adder, more often from nosing up to one out of curiosity. He also studied the reaction of downland lizards to snakes—far from being 'hypnotized', they escaped by running up bushes—of moles to drought, and of a 23-three-year-old shepherd to subversive remarks on his poor pay and prospects, which the young man seemed to accept with dignified philosophy.

Hudson was interested in cases of 'pre-natal suggestion' and an older shepherd told him of a ewe in his flock, some time in the 1880s, which had dropped a lamb with 'a round flat face with two round staring eyes' and a beak-like nose. The man thought the pregnant ewe had been startled by one of the long-eared owls then common in the furze; and that another lamb was born with hare-like fur because the mother had been frightened by a hare. Hudson was impressed that the shepherd, 'with only the light of nature to go by, had found the right interpretation'. He evidently knew Frederick W. H. Myers, who coined the term 'pre-natal suggestion', and in his notebook he was collecting reports of similar cases in human beings. One, heard at Savernake, described an infant born with an adder-like face, and making hissing sounds, after an adder had struck at the mother. Others were about children born respectively one-handed, albino, or with the face resembling a dog, a calf or a monkey; all following alleged incidents of the same kind. A similar case, dated 1726, of

174

a one-handed child, appears in the Clyst Hydon parish records, which Hudson would certainly have examined: this entry may have aroused his interest in the subject.

On these parched hills he carried no water-bottle, preferring to call at some cottage for a drink and talk, or to dip his tweed hat into a farmyard well. One week he lodged in a fine old farmhouse, let out to cottagers when the land changed hands. He would come down at night to this cool, tree-shaded place, to eat and rest in the brick-floored kitchen among the labourers, all drowsy from their long day in the sun. In September he was at Goring, staying in Jefferies's last home, listening to the last sounds he heard, the garden-birds and trees, the sea beyond the stubble fields; watching ringed dotterels on the lonely shore, and a kingfisher fishing from a groin. He saw the autumn gatherings of pewits above the Cuckmere valley, as many as 2,000 together; the bright leaves and crimson berries of a hawthorn wood on the high downs of Findon; missel-thrushes feasting on yew berries in Kingley Vale; and the beeches of West Sussex standing in winter sunsets like high pale columns on floors of red and gold. In January, walking over the snowy downs from Harting to Cocking, and on to Selsey, he found mild weather and early bird-song by the sea, and flocks of wintering birds around Chichester harbour. But except for the shepherds, and a few others, he was not really at home with Sussex people, or they with him. He preferred the dark Iberians of the west, or a finer-featured type which he met with in Somerset, to these sturdy Anglo-Saxon 'peasants'. His account of Willum, Tummas, Gaarge and their fellows, singing in their village inn on a Saturday night, though kindly meant, for once strikes a patronizing note. And in West Sussex he attributes rustic lack of response to 'stupidity', where a more sympathetic ear might have found something different: youthful diffidence, instilled perhaps at the village school, or an older man's dislike of being questioned by a stranger.

Wandering south of Chichester, he liked to see the distant cathedral spire changing colour in the winter landscape, and to hear the great bell; but a closer look at that city of 12,000 souls (3,000 adult males), 20 churches and 70 public houses produced a chapter recalling Cobbett in caustic mood. He found the muddy streets filled at all hours with 'drink-degraded wretches', while the 'ghostly men', the clergy, seemed to live apart. Even the cathedral depressed him, except for the carving in the choir, the merry fox, screaming goose and gravely listening ape: and a

175

verger with a sense of humour, who, acting as guide, gave a slant of his own to the usual recital. Hudson put down his depression to a local malady, 'the chichesters', as well as to his surroundings; but there was a deeper cause. It was here, in the kitchen of the inn or hotel where he stayed, that he found a white owl caged in atrocious conditions. After persuading the landlady to let him set it free, he spent several days finding a good home for it in an ivy-covered barn; only to be told that she had changed her mind. Pleading was in vain. It was not surprising that, on leaving the city, he wiped its mud off his boots, wishing the owl a merciful death and its gaolers a suitable reward.

Many years after publishing this malediction, he went back, and heard from the same verger that, not surprisingly, his chapter had given great offence. Thereupon he called at the inn. The owl was gone, but the two sisters who ran the place were still there, and at first he was unrecognized and affably received. But before he left suspicion began to dawn: 'I noted a sudden strange chill towards me. . .'

Bird protection was never far from his thoughts. In *Nature in Downland*, as in all his work, the theme often appears; notably in the chapter 'Shepherds and Wheatears'. These beautiful little migrants, with their 'wild delightful warble', bred here and there on the downs; once he found a colony nesting in rabbit holes in a valley near the sea,

> a rough flinty place, honeycombed with rabbit holes, and thickly grown over with big sea-poppy plants in full blossom. Lying coiled up in a hollow of the ground I had this garden of poppies, which covered about half an acre of ground, all round and above me, and looking up, the higher graceful grey plants, blossom-crowned, were seen against the sky. The great flower, as I then saw it for the first time, its purest yellow made luminous and brilliant with the sunlight streaming through it, seen against the ethereal blue beyond, had a new unimaginable loveliness. The wheatears were all around me, some with grubs in their beaks, but not venturing to enter their nesting-holes, flitting from place to place; some remaining in one place to keep watch, others coming and going. But as time went on, and I still refused to stir, they grew tired of waiting, and of uttering their chacking alarm-note and flirting their pretty tails, and began carrying food into the burrows. . .

At the late summer migration, when wheatears rested in thousands in the downs, shepherds in the past had made more than their year's wages—sometimes as much as £50—by trapping them for the 'ortolan' markets of Brighton and Eastbourne. After about 1880, farmers began to frown on this practice, saying that the men neglected their proper work; and bird-catchers from the towns had taken over:

> The bird-catcher spreads his nets as far from the road as he can, and gives out that he is catching starlings with the farmer's permission . . . Catching wheatears for starlings has gone on unpunished until now, or rather to the end of the last close time in East Sussex, September 1, 1899, and ought not to be any longer tolerated. . . . Lark-eating, which revolts us even more than wheatear-eating, is, alas! too common and widespread in the country to be suppressed in the same easy way. But . . . we may look forward to the time when the feeders on skylarks of today will all be dead and themselves eaten by worms, and will have no successors in all these islands.

Reports like this, and others in *Birds and Man*, published in 1901, reached a much wider audience than his SPB pamphlets, valuable as they were. Scientific reviewers might complain that he left out the names of species—the *St James's Gazette*, for instance, pointing out that there were five blue butterflies common on the south downs; Hudson was not writing only for specialists, but also for the kind of reader who declared, 'Unless there be a stout plate of glass between us, I do not share Mr Hudson's hilarious joy in adders, and I cannot say that I keep a warm corner in my heart for the mole, but I don't mind reading about him.'

Others felt the same. It was part of the fashion for the country, for rambling and cycling, and the literary cult of 'the open road' and 'the open air', wander-thirst and romantic wayfaring, handed down from the Romantic poets by Borrow, Matthew Arnold, Jefferies and Stevenson. Sir Edward Grey, still longing to escape from 'the rack of public affairs', almost parodied the whole concept when he told a friend in 1908: 'Some day when there is a storm and you are all hugging your houses and reading your Timeses, I shall take the road and be no more seen, and wander till I cease upon the midnight somewhere in the open air.'

Hudson wrote from his own inner compulsion, but his writings were a strong influence. *Nature in Downland* set the pattern for half a dozen other country books in which he blended field notes and social history, poetry and science and imaginative musings, in an easy, anecdotal, highly readable style. For many readers he was discovering or rediscovering not only the beauty of the countryside but a way of life left over from the past. Up to the First World War, many villagers still lived as their ancestors had done for centuries. On downland slopes in Sussex he saw corn reaped with sickles and carried in wagons drawn by long-horned oxen. In a small Cornish farmhouse he spent winter evenings by a turf fire, with a loaf baking on a hot stone, the lamplight enlivened from time to time by a glorious blaze of dried furze. Lamps and candles, the well and the outside privy, were to last in many places long after his time. Men's smock frocks had for the most part given way to corduroys or 'rusty black', but country women still wore white sunbonnets and gathered at the village well 'like Ancient Britons' with brown earthenware pitchers. He heard the old forms of speech, as in 'I did tell she where to bide', 'leetle' for little, 'a Christian' for a reasonable being, the familiar or affectionate 'maidie', 'nestie', 'ghostie'. Also primitive ideas: in remote Gloucestershire, owls and crickets were taken seriously as messengers of death. For the elderly villager, away from the railways, walking or the carrier's cart were still the usual ways of getting about. The young, in spite of their schooling, could be equally unsophisticated. One farm boy hid from him in shyness, while another, a bird-scarer, ran a quarter of a mile just to see him pass, as young Bloomfield might have done over a century before.

Those friends of his first solitary reading were often in his thoughts. He visited Bloomfield's Suffolk birthplace, Honington, and nearby Sapiston where he had worked in the fields. Strolling under the trees in Troston Park, he remembered Capel Lofft, the patron who gave the farm boy his brief fame. At Bishopstone on the south downs he thought of another country poet, Hurdis, and wished he could wake to feel the sun again. At Easter 1900, at Buriton, he remembered Gibbon; crossing the border from Sussex into Hampshire, he spent that spring at Boldre in the New Forest, where Gilpin, whose travels he often quoted, had been vicar at the end of the eighteenth century.

He stayed at Roydon House, an old manor near the river, with grounds given over to nesting birds and other wildlife. Shrew mice, field voles and bank voles ran about, hornets nested in the wood-pile, a harvest mouse fed on dock seed by the back door, a squirrel danced in through his bedroom window at dawn. It was splendid adder country, and he watched them basking in the woods and on Beaulieu Heath. In 'Hints to Adder-Seekers' he described how he would sometimes pick one up by the tail to measure it with a tape—the longest was 28 inches—and to admire the beautiful blue colouring of the underside. However, he did not recommend this practice to timid or awkward persons. Here too, in May and June, he spent many hours watching a young cuckoo hatched in a robin's nest: Alfred Russel Wallace had asked him to find out 'exactly what happened' and how the young cuckoo behaved, as doubts had been cast on previous accounts.

In late June he stayed for the first time with the Greys in their fishing cottage on the Itchen; another green retreat, scented by a sweetbriar hedge and a lime tree grove in flower. He returned there with Emily to spend the late summer in 'coolness, silence, melody and fragrance', far removed from Westbourne Park, writing about the birds and flowers of the river valley.

He now had a bicycle, and in the autumn of 1900 he was spinning through drifts of leaves on wooded roads in north Hampshire and Berkshire, sometimes dreaming that he was on horseback. On 2 November, by a happy chance, he lodged in the house at Hurstbourne Tarrant where Cobbett had begun to write *Rural Rides* on 2 November 1821. Bicycling gave him immense pleasure, taking him quickly over barren ground so that he could see more birds: sometimes thousands in a day where, walking, he would hardly have seen hundreds. The migrant flocks—pewits, finches, buntings, larks—delighted him by their great numbers, and from the thought that they were at last becoming safe from persecution 'so long as they remained in England'.

His bicycle was 'a very solidly constructed machine, with a big frame and double bars', unwieldy to push up hills. This must at times have taxed his shaky heart; but the increased range was exhilarating. 'Flying along at a reckless rate of very nearly nine miles an hour', he sometimes missed the old days afoot, when he was closer to the earth. But as a rule he went at a gentle pace, amusing himself by tailing a stoat or weasel as it ran by the roadside, stopping to let a flock of finches scatter, or to watch a green woodpecker taking a dust bath, and, when he ran over a grass snake, going back to make sure it was unharmed.

In the next two years he rode about the Hampshire lanes and villages, exploring the New Forest, the oaks of Alice Holt Forest, the beech hangers on the hills, the fir plantations of Wolmer. *Hampshire Days* is Hudson's forest book: the forests of the insect world, grass, heather and wild hedgerows, and of spider and glow-worm, as well as the deep woods where he watched red squirrels 'flying and gliding' in the tree-tops and listened for the haunting call of the oriole. In those years he was also completing *Green Mansions*, his romance of the tropical forest. Both works are imbued with his feeling for trees, for shade and undergrowth and their mysterious life.

He was also gaining deeper insight into human affairs. In *Downland* he described a young shepherd cheerfully contemplating marriage on 12s 6d a week. To an old cottager with whom he stayed at Wolmer this seemed a life of ease, compared with her struggle to bring up ten children in the hungry forties and fifties. But he could see for himself how poor and underfed the farm men often were, their children 'stunted and colourless', the housewives thin and pale, keeping themselves going on tea. The backyard pig had gone, and with it a long era of cottage economy. Yet there were still a few living in something like pre-enclosure independence, with more drive and energy and better health than their neighbours. One of these, a vigorous old woman in her seventies, held forthright opinions on past and present:

> 'I've made elderberry wine years and years and years. So did my mother; so did my grandmother; so did everybody in *my* time. And very good it were, too, I tell 'e, in cold weather in winter, made hot. It warmed your inside. But nobody wants it now....Nothing's good enough now unless you buys it in a public-house or a shop. It wasn't so when I were a girl. We did everything for ourselves then, and it were better, I tell 'e. We kep' a pig then—so did everyone; and the pork and bacon it were good, not like what we buy now. We put it mostly in brine, and let it be for months; and when we took it out and boiled it, it were red as a cherry and white as milk, and it melted just like butter in your mouth. That's what we ate in *my* time. But you can't keep a pig now—oh dear, no! You don't have him more'n a day or two before the sanitary man looks in.... In my time we didn't think a pig's smell hurt nobody.... We had beer for breakfast and it did us good. It were better than all these nasty cocoa stuffs we drink now. We didn't buy it at the public-house—we brewed it ourselves. And we had a brick oven then, and could put a pie in, and a loaf, and whatever we wanted, and it were proper vittals. We baked barley bread, and black bread, and all sorts of bread, and it did us good and made us strong ...'

But such views would be out of fashion until revived by the Women's Institutes, the shortages of the Second World War, and later ideas on diet and self-sufficiency.

From the woman at Wolmer and her eighty-year-old sister,

natives of Selborne, he heard also about older and grimmer Hampshire days. Their father, an ex-soldier, had acted as horn-blower or rally-man to the villagers when, in another hungry time, about 1820, the 'Selborne mob' carried out a pathetic demonstration against their wrongs. Many who took part were transported; but the horn-blower escaped for a time, and, when at last brought to trial, he was pardoned. His grave can be seen under the ancient yew in Selborne churchyard, where his children had him buried apart so that his story should not be forgotten. When Hudson first noticed the grave it was, like those of most poor villagers, only an unmarked green mound. But interest was strongly revived by his account in *Hampshire Days*, and the place was then marked by a short wooden post inscribed 'The Trumpeter'.

Downland had appeared in 1900, and by 1906 it was reprinted three times. In 1903, after the publication of *Hampshire Days*, he had four requests for a book within a few weeks from different publishers, and many more for articles. He was being paid at the rate of 2 guineas a 1,000 words by *Longman's Magazine*, and a respectable 15 per cent royalty on the earlier books in print; also for *Birds and Man* (1901), a collection of essays on bird protection and on his travels in the nineties. The very fact that he now had a Civil List pension 'seemed to bring more money in its wake', and with it the possibility of wider travel, even of crossing the Atlantic. Stirred by the energy of Cunninghame Graham, who was never content to let journeys remain mere dreams, he wrote: 'If I can get up energy enough I may go to America for a few weeks. The Leland steamer will take you direct to Boston, so that I could visit some relations in New Hampshire and Maine . . .' And to the Rothensteins, who wanted him to join them in France:

> I tried to drag Mrs Hudson to Calais, but she would not . . . The only place out of England I wish to go to (and hope to go before long) is New England—Maine and New Hampshire and Vermont where my mother's relations are. I've never seen any of them nor her native place and have a sort of desire—a kind of pious or superstitious feeling—to pay it a visit. It is the red man's feeling and I am a red man, or at all events a wild man of the woods.

But the voyage was never taken. He was ill, or Emily could not be left, or there was some other hindrance. Always, too, there was a book—and then another book—for which to save his strength; dreading, as he started each, that he would not live to finish it. Often he was too ill to write; yet at other times his vitality seemed inexhaustible.

In the nineties he had been out of touch with his brothers and sisters; but his family feeling never diminished, and after this gap—due perhaps to the troubles of Mary Ellen, his younger sister—letters were again exchanged. He heard about the break-up of her marriage, and her decision to leave Buenos Aires and take her son and seven daughters to Cordova, where Edwin was settled; and Hudson sent her money. In 1903 a newly married niece visited England, and he planned to meet the couple at Southampton and take them to stay in the New Forest, as they wished to see English country scenery before visiting the husband's people in Scotland. In 1908 Mary Ellen's youngest daughter Laura married Takeo Shinya, a Japanese; they also took a honeymoon trip to England, staying at Tower House, and Hudson enjoyed talking Spanish with them.

To his friends this must have seemed the right time for him to get away from that house, in its 'desert of macadam', and find a more congenial home. He had once dreamed of a 'lodge' among the Quantocks overlooking Exmoor; and in 1908 he was looking at cottages for sale near Wantage in Berkshire, and finding the prices 'impossible'. He was never to have a country home of his own: it seems that Emily Hudson clung to Tower House and would not leave it. In fact this arrangement suited both. Emily, so long as her health lasted, had her home and her familiar occupations, and enjoyed seaside holidays in Kent, Sussex and Norfolk. She also stayed with him in the New Forest, and when she was not well enough to walk he hired a fly to take her for drives. Hudson had his London base, and also regained much of his youthful liberty; wandering where he pleased, finding new subjects and habitats, getting to know a succession of people, yet enjoying a privacy and detachment seldom possible to the fixed country-dweller. Walter de la Mare, who met him only once, remembered him vividly in 1955—'his looks, his talk, everything. He somehow reminded me of a bird pining to be free—yet was there ever any one in many respects freer than he?'

If this strikes a wistful retrospective note, from one who as a young poet had a city job and family responsibilities, so too at times do Hudson's descriptions of children; and especially his remark, at the end of his life, that in Edward Thomas he had seen the son he wanted. Meeting in 1906, they had over ten years' friendship before Thomas was killed at the battle of Arras. Writing to another friend, Thomas said Hudson was 'a personality most dear to me'; and 'I love the man.' His letters to Hudson show the ease and confidence of a natural bond where affection, regard and 'likeness of thought' were taken for granted. When he began work on his biography of Jefferies in 1907 Thomas at once asked Hudson to accept the dedication—'it gave me so much pleasure to think of connecting the book with you that I had to speak of it'—and during the writing he would develop his ideas in letters. At times the letter-writer might have been Hudson himself; as when, later on, he admits ruefully that he has applied for a lecturing post, well knowing that he could not really take it. To Hudson, too, constant requests to 'say a few words' were a burden and 'an everlasting worry', even at the Royal Society for the Protection of Birds (RSPB) meetings: 'I would gladly give all my talent with the pen', he told the secretary, 'to be able to bellow like Colonel Coulson or any of them.' Again, Thomas writes of his dislike for crowded club dinners: 'I was not born to make acquaintances, or friends either, I sometimes fear; at least I am never half as much at home in company as out of doors alone.' Hudson's admirer Arnold Bennett said in 1910 that probably no literary club would ever give 'a banquet' in his honour; adding—'but, after all, it is well that he should be spared such an ordeal.' Hudson would certainly have agreed. There were no banquets.

But both he and Thomas had a host of friendly acquaintances. It was Thomas who took him to the gathering at Naomi Royde-Smith's house where he met Walter de la Mare: their hostess wanted to tell the famous bird man of a hawk that she had seen in Devon. There were other gatherings that both enjoyed. The friendship with Thomas, and much else, Hudson owed to Edward Garnett, an enthusiast for his books, whom he met in September 1901. Garnett wrote:

> Hudson soon formed the habit of lunching with me, nearly every Tuesday, one of my two days in town, and he would tell me innumerable stories and anecdotes and discuss books with me. Literary acquaintances that I made about this time would also come to the Mont Blanc [a Soho restaurant chosen for 'its utter emptiness' and because one could lunch there for tenpence] and in this way a small circle of habitués was formed.

Besides Garnett, Hudson and Edward Thomas, these included W. H. Davies, Hilaire Belloc, Ford Madox Ford, 'occasionally

John Galsworthy and rarely Joseph Conrad'. Hudson 'liked being in touch with this set of writers, whose interchange was free and cordial'; and he made a deep impression on them. Ford said he moved like an Indian and went up and down stairs 'almost as swiftly and silently as a bird'.

There were also country visits; to Conrad and Ford in Kent; to Henry James at Rye; to painter friends in Dorset and at St Ives in Cornwall; to the Tennant family at Wilsford—probably the country house where Hudson tried to persuade the gardener not to kill earth-worms in the lawns; to Woburn Abbey, where the Duchess thought the exotic animals might interest him: 'does any woman or man know what does or would interest me, I wonder?' As always, what chiefly interested him was solitude in some wild place; but he was not kind only to birds. When Ford had a serious breakdown and wanted to get out of London, Hudson not only sent him details of various country lodgings, but also invited him to visit his own 'secret' retreat in Wiltshire, and took him out for walks. Ford recalled watching a rookery with him at Broad Chalke for 'half an hour at least' while Hudson talked in his 'slow, low, keen tones' on the habits of rooks. It was evidently good therapy: Ford said rather pathetically that Hudson was 'a healer who brought you good luck merely by looking at you'. It was also true charity. For Hudson, 'a day in company was usually a wasted day.'

Children, however, were the exception: he often sought them out and talked to them. Country boys who took eggs and fledgelings, and one who tried to cage a kingfisher, came in for a lecture; but he could understand their hunting instincts, while detesting the young collector, armed with butterfly net, poison bottle and vasculum, getting off the train with the London crowd at Lyndhurst to plunder the New Forest. This concept of nature study, linked with the classroom, 'tadpoles and chestnut twigs', was as alien to him as the world of a 'British Museum gentleman' who innocently told him, 'I wish that when you are out in the woods you would put a dozen or two of young blackbirds, fledged and unfledged, in a bottle of spirits and send it up to me.'

Staying with Edward and Constance Garnett at their home in the woods on the Kentish–Surrey border, he found in their nine-year-old son a boy of his own stamp. 'My solitary pursuits must have brought back memories of his own boyhood,' wrote David Garnett. 'He treated me from the first as an equal, invited me to accompany him on his walks and to show him my dis-

High Summer

coveries', which included a rare phosphorescent centipede and an 'unusual frog' that proved to be a natterjack toad. 'What was wonderful was that he had complete faith in my story. Anyone else would have brushed it aside as a child's invention.' Before a later visit Hudson wrote, 'I hope David will come over to Westerham and meet me at Little Squerries in the afternoon. His woodcraft and weapons would be guidance and protection in that wilderness dark.' One summer evening he took the three Garnetts out to hide under some bushes while he imitated the nightjar's rattle. 'One after another the puzzled birds answered him, and soon they were flying to and fro over our heads like great, silent paper darts, dimly seen in the darkness...'

He was very handsome, David Garnett remembered,

> with high prominent cheekbones, a small grizzled beard, grizzled dark brown hair, with a very flat top to his broad head, and deep-set red-brown eyes, which were usually extremely gentle, but blazed up suddenly, very fiercely indeed.... Hudson was invariably neatly and, for that date, correctly dressed, with a white starched stand-up linen collar and cuffs, a pepper and salt or brownish tweed morning coat, with pockets in its tails, and trousers to match. With his pair of excellent field-glasses slung over his shoulders, he would not have appeared out of place at a local steeple-chase or point-to-point.

It depended where he was. Among villagers, his clothes were companionably shabby. Violet Hunt noticed his ancient weather-stained raincoat; but when he 'shrugged it off', he appeared to her shrewd and critical eye as well dressed as John Galsworthy, 'and that is saying a great deal'.

Did these friends sometimes borrow, perhaps unconsciously, from one another's talk and experience? Hudson as a rule was reticent about his private life. The Rothensteins, for instance, had known him a long time before they even knew that he was married: 'his interests all surged outward away from himself.' But some details of his past became known. Galsworthy, describing the early poverty of Bosinney in *The Man of Property* (1906), says that he 'once lived for a week on cocoa'. Henry James used the name Wingrave. 'Our echoes roll from soul to soul.' Hudson himself, in 'Following a River', seems at one point to be remembering de la Mare's *Epitaph*:

> I think she was the most beautiful lady
> That ever was in the West Country...

185

Apparently he never met the greatest West Country writer; and this at first seems a loss. He and Hardy were contemporaries—Hardy a year older—and had much in common: authorship, family roots in the west, their passion for nature and for protecting wildlife. Friendship might have brought other links to light: early love of music and of their native folk lore, strong maternal influence, loss of youthful religious faith, the sense of exile from the past. Hardy, on going to London, had lived in Westbourne Park. Friends in common included Louise Chandler Moulton: Hardy, to whom success came comparatively early, might have been that celebrity whom Hudson fought shy of meeting at one of her parties. Hudson especially admired *The Return of the Native*, always a theme of deep interest to him, and borrowed the title for one of his anecdotes. Hardy in later life knew Hudson by reputation and also knew his work, 'though not', he said, 'as well as I should like'.

On 18 July 1903 Hudson wrote to Roberts from Stour Provost in Dorset saying that he was going on to Dorchester: 'You might run down and join me there for a few days, and we could visit Hardy together. By the bye, Tess of the d' Urbervilles' village is only two miles from here. . .'

Next day he told Garnett of visiting Marnhull,

> called Marnle . . . the village where Tess was born, and the country, and the cows and the people are very much like Hardy's description. The 'Pure Drop', the little public where old Durberville boasted of the greatness that was coming to him, is close to the general shop; the shopkeeper, who is the post master also, told me he had not read 'Tess', as he never reads books, but he had bought a copy for his boys to read!

He added that he would probably see Hardy within a few days. Roberts could not join him; and back at St Luke's Road, on 29 July, he again wrote to Garnett: 'I walked by Hardy's house two or three times and though I'm quite sure he would have received me kindly I went not into his gate.'

Perhaps he was right. A failed meeting could have been painful; and with two such reticent men the risk of failure was great. Edward Garnett was fascinated by Hudson's 'bigness of nature', his warm-heartedness, his intense zest for life and 'the living fact'. But Garnett knew him well, and knew he took some knowing. He would not show these qualities at once; and neither would Hardy, though they shine through his work. There was also a wide gulf of temperament and outlook which might have precluded friendship. Hudson's work for bird-protection was based on anger and optimism; Hardy's similar work sometimes on sad resignation:

He strove that such innocent creatures should come to no harm,
But he could do little for them; and now he is gone.

In another poem Hardy summed up his view of life:

'What do you think of it, Moon,
As you go?
Is Life much, or no?'
'O, I think of it, often think of it
As a show
God ought surely to shut up soon,
As I go.'

Even in his worst times, Hudson felt nothing like this. The very fact that he suffered greater hardships made him value life more deeply.

One feeling Hardy and Hudson shared was their love of the remote past, which sent Hudson to lonely barrows on heaths and downs, ancient stones on Cornish moors and to the 'temple of the winds' on Salisbury Plain. At twilight on Beaulieu Heath he felt very near in spirit to the ancient dead, and felt that he was accepted; not an intruder, one of 'the little eager busy people, hateful in their artificial lives', but a primitive of their own tribe.

Stonehenge at the summer solstice gave little chance for musing. The days were gone when only a few shepherds gathered to watch the sunrise. By the end of the nineties, theories about the first ray and the sacrificial stone had caught the popular imagination. On foot, on bicycles and in cars, the crowds began to gather: on 21 June 1908 he was one of 500: 'I had a few good minutes at the ancient temple when the sight of the rude upright stones looking black against the moonlit and star-sprinkled sky produced an expected feeling in me; but the mood could not last; the crowd was too big and noisy...'

These crowds had not yet overrun Cornwall. His book *The Land's End*, published a month earlier, pictures for the most part a remote, close-knit community with a highly individual way of life, based on hard trades, farming, clay-working and fishing. On his first visit, three years before, he left London on a dark November morning, and found himself next day in springlike weather at St Ives. Between the midwinter storms there were days when he saw a peacock butterfly, a wheatear, an adder, and found last summer's flowers, the wild yellow pansy and pink geranium, and then the first vernal squill. He returned again and again, lodging among the rooftop jackdaws of St Ives, in a 'coffin-shaped' house at Zennor and a wind-racked farmhouse near Land's End. He loved the climate, the coast, the wild haunts of fox and raven, the tangled rocky hedges; and the furze with its wintering goldcrests and numerous common wrens, its spring brilliance, and that scent whose 'peculiar richness' he tried to capture—'I should say cocoanut and honey, and we might even liken it to apple tart with clove for scent and flavour.' He took a great liking to these Celtic people, especially on the little inland farms. *The Land's End* shows this; but some aspects of Cornish life and character were strongly attacked in one or two chapters. Students at the Camborne School of Mines amused themselves by shooting seals, which were tolerated by the fishermen. In recent years, seagulls also had come to be protected as the fisherman's friend; but many other birds were persecuted. Bush-beating was still a common winter pastime among men and boys. Kingfishers were destroyed when they took goldfish from a pool in the Morrab Gardens in Penzance. Worst of all was the practice at St Ives of using teagles—baited hooks on threads—to snare famished migrants, golden plover, ring plover and lap-wings, in a spell of snowy weather.

As he intended, the press seized on this aspect of the book. Correspondents from St Ives in turn accused 'that very unnatural naturalist Mr W. H. Hudson' of grossly exaggerating a 'very occasional practice of some of the younger natives' in past days. The Mayor of St Ives added darkly: 'is he booming his book?' Hudson wrote to Roberts, 'The St Ives people are very angry with me . . . I'm very glad they are angry. Perhaps they will now mend their ways a little.' And later:

> I've just received a delightful letter from a gentleman at Camborne, inviting me on behalf of the Literary Society to go and discuss Cornish character with the Cambornites, who will be delighted to meet me face to face . . . The Cambornites have a name for rough-ness: they very nearly killed Will Thorne when *he* went to meet them face to face, and I shall have to ask you to come with your gun to back me up.

Roberts urged him on no account to make himself a target for a 'rough mining population' that felt itself insulted. However, he was soon back in Cornwall, campaigning against raids by French crabbers on gulls' eggs and young.

Some of the natives or residents welcomed his revelations; among them Herbert Thomas, editor of the Penzance newspaper *The Cornishman*, who, with many columns to fill, gave *The Land's End* generous coverage in five successive weeks after its appearance. Admitting that he began to read with a certain bias ('From first to last he evidently meant to "put us in a book", as we put things in a pasty') and objecting, for instance, to the term 'peasant' (one of Hudson's blind spots), he declared that the picture given was a fair one. As for the teagles, they were promptly banned. An MP, Sir Frederick Banbury, was appalled by what Hudson wrote and rushed through an Act within three months.

The RSPB and its activities were steadily expanding. Bird sanctuaries had been set up to protect rare species, with paid watchers in the nesting season, and work had begun on other long-term problems, oil pollution at sea, the deaths of migrants at lighthouses. Hudson on his journeys spent much time persuading county councillors to bring in local by-laws. Often it was uphill work, but there were heartening signs. The goldfinch, for instance, was no longer a declining species; in Dorset, after a county protection order came into force, he found them everywhere. Meanwhile he was helping to launch another campaign, aimed at the young, and particularly at country children.

Long ago at Cookham Dean he had kept an eye on the village boys and their bird's-nesting; noting that, while there was one bad character out to destroy and perhaps to torture, the rest might be open to better ideas. D. H. Lawrence, growing up close to the countryside of the eighties and nineties, and later influenced by Hudson, was to sum up the old attitude to wild life in 'Snake':

> The voice of my education said to me
> He must be killed . . .
>
> And voices in me said, If you were a man
> You would take a stick and break him now, and finish him off . . .

Clearly education needed a new voice. The campaign was backed by suitable literature, and included 'Bird and Tree' essay competitions which encouraged the children towards bird-watching instead of killing and egg-collecting. Hudson took a close interest in all this, and visited village schools to give talks and show lantern slides. The scheme was directed by a gifted woman who joined the Society's staff in 1900. To Hudson her presence soon became, as he said, the best thing in his life.

Linda Gardiner was a born field naturalist and writer, daughter of a provincial newspaper editor. At seventeen she was writing a weekly column on birds for her father's paper, and helping with proof-reading and other editorial work. This early training no doubt helped to develop her talent for 'grasping abstruse and intricate subjects' such as Bird Protection Acts, and summarizing them for the general reader. Removing to London with her sister Marion, a talented artist, she worked in the office of the RSPCA, and continued to write. Between 1888 and 1897 she published several competent crime or mystery novels in the style of the day. Then came something more characteristic: an introduction to botany for little girls, *Sylvia In Flowerland*, a pastiche of the *Alice* books. One illustration has a caption that recalls Hudson in ironic mood: 'There's a man down at the farm who shoots the owls and hawks, and it must be because they kill the rats and mice which he likes to see enjoying themselves in his barns.' Even before they had met, they were allies.

Engaged by the Society as a clerical assistant at a 'very modest' salary, Miss Gardiner soon became the first paid secretary, and, in 1903, editor of their new quarterly journal, *Bird Notes and News*: both posts to which she was ideally suited, and which she was to hold for over thirty years. The journal records that Hudson quickly recognized and fostered her literary abilities, 'as well as finding her an apt and enthusiastic pupil in all subjects connected with Natural History, especially with the study and observation of birds in the open country; she in return rendered him great assistance in the preparation and publication of several of his books. This led to a close friendship between him and the two sisters.' It also led to a long secret love affair with Linda, or Ethelind (her real name) as he liked to call her, perhaps because no one else did so.

For both, as surviving letters show, it was sometimes a tormenting affair. As a rule they could meet only in the office, with other people close by; more rarely in teashops or elsewhere in London; now and then perhaps in the country when she was on holiday. Her letters, addressed to him at a stationer's shop in Bayswater, were evidently kept brief and discreet for fear they might go astray. His own continually reproach her for not writing more often and more openly: 'Write ... and tell me just what your heart tells you' (July 1901). 'I was grateful to you for

190

writing so soon, and more still for writing as I love you to write, fully, freely from the heart.' 'Why should you not tell me everything you would like to, since now you could not be more to me even if I had—in the old English sense of the word—known you?' 'If you ever wish for me I don't know it, and if you do not wish, I cannot know it, since your lips are sealed . . . I don't see that it need be so. Do you wish me to wait patiently in a grey world until life is over? Well, I can't' (1902?). 'It is wrong of you to lie awake and think you must have been mad. Think rather . . . you must have been sane . . . I find time frightfully long; what folly it seems not to see each other a little oftener since we are able to meet now . . .' (28 December 1904).

He assured her tacitly that Emily would not be harmed: 'we are doing wrong to no one so far as I know' (September 1902). But character and upbringing made it hard for her to accept this. 'So still, so reticent, so patient', and so intelligent, she could not help seeing, too, what their happiness might cost. In their middle-class environment, disclosure could have brought scandal and injury not only to themselves but to the bird society which meant so much to them both. The strain is sometimes evident in his concern for her. 'It troubles me', he wrote from the New Forest in September 1902, 'to think of you so much alone in that high-up room [at 3 Hanover Square] during the week, and perhaps really feeling nervous.' At times she suffered from neuralgia, or bad dreams, or there was some cloud between them: 'But let this cloud too pass . . . and be as if it had never been. The pity of it is that while we are both here we should so strangely fail to understand each other. . . . Always and ever yours, W.' (February 1905).

At times he was wretched at her situation: '. . . it seemed to me that I was but a poor one for you to love and lean upon . . . I cannot but remember the disparity in our years and in our physical state' (September 1902). She too had dark moods about the future. He wrote from Cornwall in May 1907, evidently to reassure her: 'When I grow tired it will be of my life, dear, not of you.' And again in that year: 'You have fancied you have seen signs of change—the feeling waning—and you have told yourself that it would be so; some day we should quarrel or slip back into friendship only.' If this change came, he insisted, it would not be of his making, or through a quarrel; but only from his own decline.

> You say you have been angry with me and may be again. I don't mind, dear. . . . All I desire is that when the quarrel or anger comes that you will have it out with me, and not let it feed like a canker on

191

you. One thing more in your letter—the wish to go away from it all
. . . to some undiscoverable country. Well, everyone with a burden
feels that . . .

Escape was not possible. There could be no question of deserting Emily, now growing old and frail. But in a letter to Garnett he wrote with deep bitterness of current sexual mores and 'the law that forbids a man to have more than one wife'. He was thinking perhaps of that 'grand old gaucho estancerio' he had known on the pampas, living in patriarchal independence with as many wives and children as he chose.

Since the most intimate are missing, these letters tend to show more of the stress than the delight of a hidden love affair. But there was also great happiness, and lasting devotion. To Linda Gardiner he remained for over twenty years her 'greatest and dearest friend', depending on her for much practical help, and still writing long letters to her almost to his last day. She never brought herself to destroy the letters, knowing that, as he himself said, a time would come when the secret could no longer harm anyone:

> 'Time, the old god, invests all things with honour and makes them white. '. . . if in a score or fifty years' time others could know this secret of ours, they would say of it—what do you think? They would say that my friendship with you—and more than friendship—was the sweetest and best and most purifying influence I had known, and that because of it I was better as well as infinitely happier.

14

South American Romances

Past, present and future combined to make 1901 the great year of Hudson's prime. His writing had won official recognition, high praise and a modest competence. The bird society was flourishing. His talks to village schools had begun; and this year he met the old shepherd whose memories were to form the basis of his best English book. He knew that his love for Linda Gardiner was returned. That autumn, too, he had other hopes. He was eagerly awaiting a publisher's verdict on *El Ombu*, the story begun in 1890 when, in the excitement of meeting Cunninghame Graham, he had got out his old notebook, still stained by the 'great dust storm' of 1868 and the rain that came down as 'liquid mud'.

This was his first work of fiction to be completed since *A Crystal Age* had appeared and disappeared fourteen years ago. Yet *El Ombu*, and the stories published with it, are by no means a departure from his usual vein. He was a born story-teller. The nature books are in the main a series of true anecdotes, and he was at home with every kind of folk-tale. He had shown this in *The Purple Land*: in recounting, for instance, the marvels seen by a benighted traveller who peers through a crack in a hovel occupied by a repulsive old crone. His country essays show the same narrative power. In 'Rural Rides', first published in December 1901, he glides smoothly from early bicycling adventures to a terrible rural crime (the victim was stung to death by hornets) and a public execution on the Coombe Hill gibbet; then on past other highlights of parish history to an encounter with a blackberrying tramp, who, despite his splendid appearance—over six feet tall, blue-eyed and golden-haired, dressed in tight blue trousers,

193

fancy waistcoat, scarlet tie and black frock-coat—failed to win the dole he clearly expected, or the sympathy Hudson had felt for the man from Lewes gaol: Hudson thought he knew an 'irreclaimable blackguard' when he saw one. *Afoot in England*, in which this essay later appeared, has some of his best stories. In the chapter 'On Going Back' the reader seems to stray with him into the eerie world of M. R. James and *Ghost Stories of an Antiquary*; his only venture in this genre, and a notable one.

Nor did he really need that old transcript, or the stimulus of shared experience, to remind him of South America. The old life was always present to his inward eye and ear. In a notebook kept in 1900 he listed 226 bird species seen in La Plata and Patagonia. Of these he found he could still clearly visualize 215; while, out of 192 whose 'cries, calls, songs and other sounds' had been familiar, he could 'hear' 154. The English countryside brought continual reminders. Pale blue butterflies on the south downs recalled 'the great blue Morpho butterfly of the tropics soaring high in the sunlight'. Flying beech leaves in October were like red tropical butterflies in migration; and the red sails of Cornish fishing boats swayed like butterflies in the pampas reed-beds. The fishing fleet moved out of St Ives harbour at sunset like great birds—stork, wood ibis or flamingo—drifting across a lake. Basking adders, seen through his powerful new glass, became 'kings of the serpent kind'. Cornish field paths were like the social trails of the *vizcacha*, 'worn by the feet of the little animals visiting their neighbours'. As he drowsed on a crag at Land's End, the wash of the sea changed to the sound of wind-blown poplars, bringing such vivid dreams of home and family that he had to rouse himself for fear they might end in delusion and a fall to the rocks below.

El Ombu, the story of another lost home, has a great deal of the poetry and vitality of *The Purple Land*, but far more cruelty. A sequence of dreadful events, murder and battle, torture and revenge, lead on to a climax when the monstrous General Barboza, a man 'like an eagle . . . that great bird that has no weakness and no mercy', is advised to cure a mysterious sickness by bathing in the carcase of a freshly killed bull. From this bloodbath he emerges raving mad, 'yelling and whirling his sword round so that it looked like a shining wheel in the sun'. The ghastly recital is heightened throughout by the quiet background, the ombu tree, the hum of summer insects, the simplicity of the old man telling the story:

194

Tell me, señor, have you ever in your life met with a man who was perhaps poor, or even clothed in rags, and who yet when you had looked at and conversed with him, has caused you to say: Here is one who is like no other man in the world? Perhaps on rising and going out, on some clear morning in the summer, he looked at the sun when it rose, and perceived an angel sitting in it, and as he gazed, something from that being fell upon and passed into and remained with him. Such a man was Valerio. I have known no other like him.

El Ombu—that strange and brutal story, as *The Times Literary Supplement* called it—leaves an impression of bloodshed in brilliant sunlight. In *Marta Riquelme* the emphasis is on darkness and degradation. A. F. Tschiffely in his biography of Cunninghame Graham hints at the grim fate of white women abducted by marauding Indians. Hudson must have heard many such tales; another in this collection, *Niño Diablo*, tells of the rescue of one woman prisoner. Escape and return come too late for the unfortunate Marta. At the end, Hudson uses the legend of the Kakué bird to express a sense of suffering beyond human endurance, experienced both by Marta and her secret lover, the priest who tells the story:

> For even in that moment, when [her] terrible cries were ringing through my heart, waking the echoes of the mountain solitudes, the awful change had come, and she had looked her last with human eyes on earth and man. In another form—that strange form of the Kakué—she had fled out of our sight for ever to hide in those gloomy woods which were henceforth to be her dwelling-place.

The priest is left to contend with his own horrors: the sense that the old gods of the region are still alive, 'awful in majesty and wrath', and stronger than his own faith.

In this narrative, as the *Times* reviewer said, Hudson 'cuts deepest into human nature, and into the nature that is beyond humanity', and displays deep insight into the unhinged mind; insight that appears again in the last part of *Green Mansions*. Yet these stories might never have found a publisher, and *Green Mansions* might have remained unfinished, but for the championship of Edward Garnett, who described their first meeting in September 1901:

> It was my last day as Heinemann's 'reader', and I was clearing up my work when a lad announced 'Mr Hudson!' and looking through the window I saw a tall dark man standing on the leads

outside my little room. Some weeks before I had impressed on Mr William Heinemann that 'El Ombu' was a work of genius and that he must publish it. . . . He had temporized, afraid either to return the MS or to accept it, and now Hudson had come to learn his decision. I went up to Hudson and told him that he had written a masterpiece. Its grave beauty, its tragic sweetness, indeed, had swept me off my feet, as it does now when I read it. Hudson glared at me, astonished, as though he wished to annihilate me . . .

Heinemann's terms did not suit Hudson, but within a few weeks Garnett had persuaded Gerald Duckworth to publish *El Ombu*, and was urging Hudson to write more in this vein. As they became close friends, Garnett would 'tease and banter him; telling him it was a terrible waste of his talents for him to write about little birds hopping about in the trees and not about men and women and stories drawn from his experience or his imagination', to which Hudson would retort that 'he was a field naturalist and had no interest in made-up rubbish . . .' Garnett gave him back his confidence, and under his influence *Green Mansions* was brought out and completed.

The 'green mansions' are the trees in the vast tropical forest of the upper Orinoco. To visit this primitive wilderness has been a cherished dream for the hero Abel, and here he arrives, a political refugee, exiled from city pleasures and then disappointed in a search for gold. One evening, after a day of rain and despondency in an Indian hut, he has an experience like Hudson's in Patagonia: 'I felt purified and had a strange sense of apprehension of a secret innocence and spirituality in nature— a prescience of some bourn, incalculably distant perhaps, to which we are all moving . . .' Dreams of success or riches fade: he wishes only 'to rest for a season at this spot, so remote and lovely and peaceful'. Wandering day after day in a wild tract of woodland, he hears a strange and melodious voice like that of a bird. The Indians are afraid of the place, thinking it haunted by an evil spirit, 'the daughter of the Didi'. This mysterious being at length comes out of hiding to stop Abel from stoning a snake. She is Rima, a beautiful young girl, the last survivor of a lost high-caste race. In the wood everything is under her 'law' and protection. When Abel and Rima fall in love, life seems to offer them a shared paradise; but the Indians are biding their time: 'She, poor child, detested them because they were incessantly at war with the wild animals she loved, her companions; and having no fear of them, for she did not know that they had it in their minds to turn their little poisonous arrows against herself, she was constantly in the wood frustrating them.'

During a separation they find their chance, trapping her in a solitary tree. Fear and superstition hunt her down; only her ashes are left. In revenge, like Mowgli, Abel destroys the Indian village. Hudson is more realistic than Kipling: Abel brings in an enemy tribe to wipe out Rima's killers. But, fleeing back to her wood, he is overwhelmed by what he has done: 'What horrible thing—what calamity that frightened my soul to think of, had fallen on me? The revulsion of feeling, the unspeakable horror, the remorse, was more than I could bear.'

He tries in vain to recapture peace and to console himself with the idea that he and Rima are now one soul— 'like two raindrops side by side, drawing irresistibly nearer, ever nearer: for now they had touched and were not two, but one inseparable drop . . .'

But he feels her spirit reproaching him. At length, haunted by piteous or dreadful phantoms, he is forced to leave and make his way back to civilization, carrying Rima's ashes 'to mix with mine at last' when death shall release him.

For the sake of remoteness, Hudson set his romance, or allegory, in a region he had never seen. Savernake and the New Forest were the deepest woods he knew. But his tropical forest has all the beauty and mystery that childhood imagination had found in the trees and weeds of the home plantation; and, apart from a few creatures—such as the howler monkey and sloth—drawn from his reading, the fauna are his own, described with the passionate detail of *The Naturalist in La Plata*: birds and snakes, the great spider stealing out at dusk—'who knows on what murderous errand!'—the small spider trying to capture a moving shadow, the pale bright moth that falls 'straight and swift into the white blaze beneath': a cruel metaphor.

Morley Roberts had heard about this tale for so long that he could hardly believe it was finished: 'it bore all the marks of the one great story an author never ends or never even begins.' The delay is understandable. Hudson could not easily have brought himself to work out and carry through a theme so intensely subjective, originating not only in memory and conscious experience—the earliest games in the ombu tree, his feeling for nature and for the mysterious 'white and lovely children' of the pampas—but in his deepest inner life: the 'bird-woman' idea, the sense of animism evoked by the moonlit acacias, the mystic experience in Patagonia, and other memories less pleasant to live with. The story of Rima, Roberts saw, is also 'the story of those birds and of that ancient beauty which inevitably perish at the hands of the barbarians, even of those gold-giving and reddened hands of the collectors he hated'. Hudson too had been a collector. Abel's self-hatred and remorse in the second half of the story may well be more than a vivid piece of imaginative writing.

The theme of *Green Mansions* is rooted in the old struggle between Darwin and the Book of Genesis. Abel finds that he cannot go back and live innocently in Eden. There is no such place for man; there is only the law of nature and the law of civilization. At their first encounter, absorbed in watching Rima, Abel is bitten by a snake and expects to die. This proves a false alarm, a 'false coral snake'. But Rima does die, through breaking the same law of nature: she fails to recognize and guard against her enemies. After his murderous act, Abel is overcome by his sense of guilt, the great punisher of civilized man: in this Hudson anticipates Freud. Abel becomes Cain, the guilty fugitive, travelling east away from lost Eden; then a wanderer, 'a new Ahasuerus, cursed by inexpiable crime'. Deprived of religion, he cannot find expiation in 'prayers, austerities, good works', but must learn the harder way of self-forgiveness and self-absolution. This goal, reached years after his return to civilization, marks the end of Abel's pilgimage.

But it is the central part of the story that is most memorable: Abel's surrender to the influence of the wild, and his love for Rima. Critics writing in the *Saturday Review* and *Times Literary Supplement* were probably typical of many subsequent readers, or non-readers. As John Alcorn has shown, the book was in the mainstream of contemporary 'nature novels'; and the *Saturday Review* critic, while paying tribute (now customary) to Hudson's literary gifts, was evidently weary of 'the "plein air" method' and 'the modern facility of effective description, with its wealth of adjectives and its unsparing use of colour'. Not surprisingly, then, the story of Rima could not engage his sympathy, and in the dénouement he saw only a striving after 'the sensational and the miraculous'. The *Times* reviewer, ready to be disarmed by the poetry and natural history, found the tragedy too painful, but felt that in the end 'this idyll leaves an impression of tenderness and charm.' It was left for a third type of reader to discover that *Green Mansions* was not simply another nature novel, or idyll, but an experience: something that—as with other works as disparate as *The Jungle Books*, *Amaryllis at the Fair* or *Moby Dick*—can be felt rather than defined; and whose impact, when widely .shared, gives rise to the kind of vogue sustained by *Green Mansions*, first in Edwardian England, later in America, then to some extent worldwide. This third type had an early spokesman in the critic of the *Daily Chronicle*. After outlining the first chapters as far as the meeting of Abel and Rima, he continued:

> The story which follows we dare not pretend to abridge. It is one of the finest of all love stories; to some it may be the finest; for it is unique . . .
> Some may find the story too long; they are not fit to read it. The book is one of the noblest pieces of self-expression for which fiction has been made a vehicle.

Appreciation could hardly go further. The writer was almost certainly Edward Thomas.

A few days later, in the *Speaker*, Garnett also paid tribute to Hudson's 'peculiar genius', and particularly to the last part of the book: 'The analysis of Abel's rage, revolt, sorrow and stupor is most masterly in its psychological insight, and we know nothing in modern English literature with which it can be compared.'

'The sales of books are less affected by even the best criticism than they are by gossip and discussion, by readers pressing the book on their friends' (Christopher Sykes, in his biography *Evelyn Waugh*). It seems likely that this happened with *Green Mansions*: word passing from Garnett, Thomas and the Mont Blanc coterie to other friends, then to a wider public. One of the circle that included the Garnetts and Edward Clodd was E. Nesbit, the children's writer, who began her *Story of the Amulet* the year after *Green Mansions* appeared. It may be more than coincidence that a raindrop simile strikingly like that quoted above occurs three times in her last chapter, two souls converging at the climax 'as one drop of water mingles with another': an example perhaps of the impact of Hudson's powerful imagery on a receptive mind.

The appeal, or prestige, of *Green Mansions* has continued. Over seventy English and American editions appeared up to 1977, and foreign editions have included translations into Finnish, Japanese and Serbo-Croat. Illustrators have given vivid impressions of the tropical forest; but the central figure of Rima—forest girl, bird-woman or nature spirit—taxes the artist's imaginative powers as it taxed those of Epstein. A film of the late 1950s, made partly in authentic settings south of the Orinoco, encountered the same problem: the *Times* review (headed 'Alas, Poor Hudson!')

describes her as a disaster, 'a fey child of nature communicating with her dead mother, imitating the songs of birds and running about the forest in a kind of nightdress'. Hudson's Rima does all these things, and the assenting reader, sharing the writer's vision, suspends his sense of ridicule; as he must also do for Ophelia and Desdemona.

Green Mansions came out in the spring of 1904; and that autumn a new edition of *The Purple Land* received the acclaim it had missed nineteen years earlier. The *Saturday Review*, with unconscious irony, said the writer was 'one of the most subtle and original who have enriched English letters for some years'. Duckworth was now showing interest in another old manuscript, a children's story of the pampas, and Hudson wanted David Garnett to read it first. The Barrie-like title, *A Little Boy Lost*, may have caused his young friend some apprehension: in 1902 Hudson had sent him *The Little White Bird*, which he disliked so much that he sent it back. Hudson had perhaps glanced briefly at the book beforehand and gathered that it was about a boy named David, also about the birds and children of Kensington Gardens, and the dream of flying—all as much a part of his life as of Barrie's—without noticing the mawkishness that affronted a boy of ten, let alone other aspects that strike the post-Freud reader. The book was written for adults, many of whom found such fantasies not only tolerable but delightful. That Christmas (1904) *Peter Pan* was to captivate a 'highly sophisticated' audience, and a few years later, at *Pinkie and the Fairies*, the stalls would be filled with military men quietly weeping for their lost childhood. (David Garnett, incidentally, was to make his name twenty years on with a fantasy for the adult reader, though in more astringent style.) But *A Little Boy Lost* was meant for children, and the boy's disgust must have put Hudson on his guard. In fact the story has one episode rather in the Barrie manner, where the runaway boy Martin finds a new mother. Otherwise, Martin's adventures with birds, animals, Indians, wild horses and so on are based on true natural history, though related in fairy-tale style. The theme was perhaps suggested by a gaucho legend of the brown cuckoo, said to be a changeling endlessly calling 'Crispin, Crispin', after a lost child. The production was modelled on a recent fine edition of Grimm, illustrated by Arthur Rackham, and Hudson's old friend A. D. McCormick supplied pictures with the Rackham touch.

Twelve-year-old David Garnett, who treasured Hudson's *British Birds*, was of course too old to care for *A Little Boy Lost*, but he refrained from saying so; and the story played its part in Hudson's development. For the first time he had written about the pampas from a child's viewpoint. Ten years later he would do so again.

15

A Shepherd's Life

Silchester, in the wooded triangle between Reading, Newbury and Basingstoke, was one of Hudson's favourite places. New excavations in the deserted Roman city had been going on since 1890; and he liked to wander there, thinking of inhabitants long dead, while observing the wildlife of the leafy thickets covering the walls: badger and owls at night, ring snake and small birds by day. But there was a stronger attraction. At Easter 1901, and again in the following October, he was staying at a house called The Pines on the edge of the common with people named Lawes. James Lawes was a retired shepherd, a tall bent man in his seventies, with large clear hazel eyes in a 'fawn-like' face. Out of doors he walked painfully with a stick: like Hudson, he had suffered all his life from the after-effects of rheumatic fever in his early years, brought on by exposure to wet and cold. They spoke of birds; it appeared that Lawes, unlike many countrymen, was a keen observer of wild-life, and he told Hudson how once, as a boy, he had released a captive meadow pipit while two other boys were fighting over it. He had been out on the downs at the time, looking after his father's flock, which he had helped to do from the age of six: something else the two had in common. For both men it was one of the happiest encounters of a lifetime.

Obviously the old man could not walk far or stand about for long; Hudson went back with him into his house and sat down by the fire to continue their talk. It was to go on for the next nine years, and from it Hudson wrote *A Shepherd's Life*, calling his friend 'Caleb Bawcombe'.

The shepherd's busy wife, who provided comfortable lodgings for the archaeologists on the dig, had little patience at first with all this browsing over old times. She 'talked of this and that, and hinted as politely as she knew that I was in her way. To her practical peasant mind there was no sense in my being there. "He be a stranger to we, and we be strangers to he."' But the intruder was not to be put off, and the old man was as glad to recall the past as Hudson was to listen.

> He was long miles away from his beloved home . . . a disabled man who would never again follow the flock on the hills nor listen to the sounds he loved best to hear—the multitudinous tremulous bleatings of the sheep, the tinklings of numerous bells, the crisp ringing bark of his dog. But his heart was there still, and the images of past scenes were more vivid to him than they can ever be in the minds of those who live in towns and read books.

From now on Hudson was often a lodger there, and through many autumn and winter evenings Caleb would recall events not only of his own lifetime but of his father's, born in 1800: memories of sheep and sheep-dogs, shepherds and farmers, villagers and gipsies, good times and bad. Sheep-dogs were a favourite topic, his own and other men's, each one an individual: Rough, trained as a road dog, who could divide a driven flock 800 strong to make way for the Salisbury coach, 'which was not delayed a minute'; Jack, 'a tarrible good dog', a fierce adder-killer, and Monk, who hunted foxes; Tory, who went on strike, with a tragic result, when his master offended him; playful Badger, who would spend his leisure time 'amusing of hisself' like a child, chasing butterflies or rolling down slopes; Dyke, who was stolen away for a year, and made a joyful midnight return; Tramp, a stray from a circus, identified as 'a Rooshian' by a Crimean veteran; and gentle Watch, who would catch mice and rabbits without hurting them: though Caleb, when talking of this to the farmer, 'probably forgot to mention' that when Watch caught a rabbit he would take it to his master 'as much as to say, Here is a very big sort of field mouse I have caught, rather difficult to manage—perhaps *you* can do something with it?'

Most farm men, while despising the real poacher as 'an idle dissolute fellow', felt free to take whatever came their way for the pot; but the farmers did not fall in with this view. From another head shepherd, Hudson heard about a farmer who complained that his dog had been seen hunting a hare:

The shepherd indignantly asked who had said such a thing.

'Never mind about that,' said the farmer. 'Is it true?'

'It is a lie,' said the shepherd. 'My dog never hunts a hare or aything else. 'Tis my belief the one that said that has got a dog himself that hunts the hares, and he wants to put the blame on someone else.'

'May be so,' said the farmer, unconvinced.

Just then a hare made its appearance, coming across the field directly towards them, and either because they never moved or it did not smell them it came on and on, stopping at intervals to sit for a minute or so on its haunches, then on again until it was within forty yards of where they were standing. The farmer watched it approach and at the same time kept an eye on the dog sitting at their feet and watching the hare too, very steadily. 'Now, shepherd,' said the farmer, 'don't you say one word to the dog and I'll see for myself.' Not a word did he say, and the hare came and sat for some seconds near them, then limped away out of sight, and the dog made not the slightest movement. 'That's all right,' said the farmer, well pleased. 'I know now 'twas a lie I heard about your dog. I've seen for myself and I'll just keep a sharp eye on the man that told me.'

My comment on this story was that the farmer had displayed an almost incredible ignorance of a sheepdog—and a shepherd. 'How would it have been if you had said, "Catch him, Bob," or whatever his name was?' I asked.

He looked at me with a twinkle in his eye and replied, 'I do b'lieve he'd ha' got'n, but he'd never move till I told'n.'

Caleb's father, whom Hudson called 'Isaac Bawcombe', had been the exception: rabbits, hares and partridges were so plentiful on his downland sheep-walk that a grateful sportsman recommended him for a pension from an old charity fund, with a cottage, clothing and 8 shillings a week, all of which he enjoyed for twenty-six years: after working for half a century and bringing up a family on no more than 7 shillings a week. Yet as a young man he had taken to the dangerous sport of deer-stealing. In that bitter winter about 1820, with only barley bread to eat, he would go out at night with his dog, as though to look at the sheep, and return in the small hours to his mother's cottage with a deer, which was quickly cut up and hidden. The deer-stealer risked a term in prison; the sheep-stealer might share the fate of sheep-killing dogs on the pampas: Hudson recalled a time when all his father's dogs were hanged for this crime.

Caleb's wife had got over her first prejudice against Hudson, and would join in her husband's talk; sometimes urging him to recount family matters, or to recall old gossip which he, from innate good feeling, would have passed over. In this way Hudson heard of the time Caleb went to Wilton fair expecting to meet his brother, Shepherd David Bawcombe, only to learn that he had been dead two years; and the story of Caleb's brother-in-law, Tommy Ierat, child of a poor dairymaid who, forsaken by her shepherd lover and turned out by her employers, had found refuge at 'Winterbourne Bishop', Hudson's name for Martin, Caleb's native village; and about the gamekeeper who one morning found a baby on his doorstep, with the message 'Take me in and treat me well, for in this house my father dwell'—to the joy of the keeper's childless wife. She also told the story of another childless family of several brothers, supposed to be under a curse. After a machine-breaking riot in 1831 their father had allowed an innocent man to be convicted of taking part, and transported for life; two years later he received a letter with an Australian postmark, and nothing inside but a transcription from Psalm 109, including the words, 'Let his posterity be cut off; and in the generation following let their name be blotted out.'

This tale set Hudson researching into newspaper files, and questioning the oldest villagers he could trace, about that dark period of rural history. One old woman, 94-year-old Joan Edwards of Fonthill Bishop, recalled 'that miserable and memorable year of 1830' when labourers broke up the thrashing machines; and at nearby Hindon he found a man of eighty-nine who as a small boy had looked out of the schoolhouse window one market day, when the new machines were on view, and had seen 'a great excited crowd', men and cattle and sheep all mixed together, and heard the angry shouts and the sound of smashing machinery. From 89-year-old Malachi he heard too of an unfortunate young man, Johnnie Budd, who was hanged in 1821 for stealing a sheep to feed his starving family. This episode became the story *An Old Thorn*, about a tree with supernatural powers, and the ill luck following irreverent treatment: 'if you hurt it, it will hurt you.' He tells how, after the theft of the sheep, a child playing with others in the village street 'let out that she wasn't hungry, that for three days she had had as much nice meat as she wanted to eat'. So the fatal talk had begun and spread until it reached the constable, sealing poor Johnnie's fate. The law as it stood made no distinction between the systematic thief and the honest man driven to desperation, though in practice many death sentences were commuted to transportation. Yet despite such misery, personal assault was rare. Machine-breaking or rick-burning were the chief crimes for which, at the Salisbury Assizes in 1830, twenty-nine men were sentenced to hanging and five to transportation. The history of this rising by farm labourers, 'the most patient and submissive of men', had yet to be written when Hudson compiled his chapters on 'Old Wiltshire Days' for *A Shepherd's Life*. He describes the scene following that trial at Salisbury, as he heard it from a woman, then in her teens, who had lived all her life in a nearby village:

> It was when the trial was ended, when those who were found guilty and had been sentenced were brought out of the court-house to be taken back to prison, and from all parts of Wiltshire their womenfolk had come to learn their fate, and were gathered, a pale, anxious, weeping crowd, outside the gates. The sentenced men came out looking eagerly at the people until they recognized their own and cried out to them to be of good cheer. ''Tis hanging for me,' one would say, 'but there'll perhaps be a recommendation to mercy, so don't you fret till you know.' Then another: 'Don't go on so, old mother, 'tis only for life I'm sent.' And yet another: 'Don't you cry, old girl, 'tis only fourteen years I've got, and maybe I'll live to see you all again.' And so on, as they filed out past their weeping women on their way to Fisherton Jail, to be taken then to the transports in Portsmouth and Plymouth harbours waiting to convey their living freights to that hell on earth so far from home. Not criminals but good, brave men were these!—Wiltshiremen of that strong, enduring, patient class, who not only as labourers on the land but on many a hard-fought field in many parts of the world, from of old down to our war of a few years ago in Africa, have shown the stuff that was in them! . . . Very few, so far as I can make out, not more than one in five or six, ever returned.

Hudson usually ignored politics, except when Bird Protection Acts were in question. So far as he was anything, Roberts said, he was Conservative; and his distrust of new trends at times found vent in irritable outbursts: 'progress means slaughtering birds and cutting down woods to build beastly rabbit-hutches for people to breed boys to rob nests.' His sympathies were with the under-paid and under-valued farm worker, even while he showed distrust of social reformers and their propagandists, by now active even in remote parts of the countryside. He detested the rule of the squire, the pheasant-preserver and the gamekeeper, as making for subservience and tending to deprive the villagers of their ancient rights of way and firewood rights, also of nuts and rabbits and other time-honoured gleanings. Like Cobbett, he loved the upright independent intelligent countryman and woman who showed initiative and industry:

'Better, to my mind, the severer conditions, the poverty and unmerited sufferings which cannot be relieved, with the greater manliness and self-dependence when the people are left to work out their own destiny.' Especially he liked to hear about some skilled craftsman enjoying life, 'with not only a strong preference for a particular kind of work, but a love of it as compelling as that of an artist for his art': Caleb and other shepherds, 'old Reed of Odstock' who loved thrashing with the flail, 'Old Father Time', happiest when mowing with the scythe, and 'Liddy', whose skill and knowledge with horses took him up in the world from carter's boy to groom in a hunting stable. Hudson could always sympathize too with the individualist, such as Old Joe the Wiltshire coal-carrier, famous for his string of donkeys or 'neddies'; and the gipsy for whom 'it is not so much the wind on the heath, brother, as the fascination of lawlessness, which makes his life an everlasting joy to him.'

At the same time, he was aware that many people were incapable of running their own lives, and thought that, if it came to a choice of evils, they were less likely to be ill-treated by a squire in a great house than by a village tyrant. Caleb himself had once come up against a villainous character, 'Elijah Raven', who, beginning in a small way, made himself a rich man by exploiting his neighbours. Eventually he took over the village benefit club, using his position as secretary for his own ends and to pay off old scores. At length Caleb was forced to sue him in the county court for six weeks' sick benefit which Elijah had refused to pay: 'a brutal case', as the judge said.

Not surprisingly, Hudson had heard a good deal from Caleb about Elijah Raven, and he was later amused to discover that, when he first visited Winterbourne Bishop, he had stayed in 'the two very rooms' where Elijah lived for years. Soon after meeting the old shepherd, he had sought out that remote downland village on the border of south Wiltshire: finding a long winding street of small old cottages, thatched or tiled, and a churchyard shaded by beeches, with a spreading yew tree which still remains. The village was set among wide downs with pewits, magpies and sheep-folds: the sheep were to vanish after Hudson's day, but have now returned. The downs were approached through lanes with wild hedges full of hips and haws, sloes and hazel-nuts, 'a thousand times more nuts than the little dormice require'. He named the village after the winterbourne, the underground stream which after a wet season would gush out in its roadside channel, a boon to the housewife; sometimes, in those days, overflowing and turning the village street into a river, to the delight of the children.

Curiosity had prompted that first visit; his feeling for the pampas brought him back, when he realized that the sense of elation and of homecoming which he experienced there sprang from the likeness of the low downs and wide green spaces to his early home. Like Simonsbath, Wells and Silchester, it became a favourite place. He wrote to Garnett in April 1903:

> The loneliness of this little downland village suits my nerves. We are 3 miles from a telegraph office, 7 miles from a butcher, a doctor and a newspaper, and there is no public house so it is all dark and still after 8 o'clock and everyone goes to bed. The only light is from the stars and the only sound the faint far-off tinkle of sheep-bells.

Forty years later he was still remembered there 'with a sort of amused affection, as a likeable oddity': a useful persona for a country researcher. As in talking to Caleb, he knew that he could rarely learn anything of interest from direct questioning. He had to make himself accepted, to listen quietly, with the patience of the naturalist, and take what came. On at least one occasion, however, a more positive approach did prove rewarding, when he fell into talk with an old dame in a Wiltshire churchyard:

> I went over to the stone she had pointed to and read the inscription to John Toomer and his wife Rebecca. She died first, in March 1877, aged seventy-two; he in July the same year, aged seventy-five.
> 'You knew them, I suppose?'
> 'Yes, they belonged here, both of them.'
> 'Tell me about them.'
> 'There's nothing to tell; he was only a labourer and worked on the same farm all his life.'
> 'Who put a stone over them—their children?'
> 'No, they're all poor and live away. I think it was a lady who lived here; she'd been good to them, and she came and stood here when they put old John in the ground.'
> 'But I want to hear more.'
> 'There's no more, I've said; he was a labourer, and after she died he died.'
> 'Yes? go on.'
> 'How can I go on? There's no more. I knew them so well; they lived in the little thatched cottage over there where the Millards live now.'
> 'Did they fall ill at the same time?'
> 'Oh no, he was as well as could be, still at work, till she died,

then he went on in a strange way. He would come in of an evening and call his wife. "Mother! Mother, where are you?" you'd hear him call. "Mother, be you upstairs? Mother, ain't you coming down for a bit of bread and cheese before you go to bed?" And then in a little while he just died.'

'And you said there was nothing to tell!'

In *An Old Thorn* Hudson writes of showing the tree to an artist friend who found it 'a fine subject for his pencil'. The artist was Bernard Gotch, illustrator of *A Shepherd's Life*: in this respect, one reviewer said, the most fortunate of Hudson's books. With Hudson he visited and sketched many Wiltshire scenes, including Salisbury market; the Lamb Inn, Hindon; Broad Chalke (where Ford had been staying with Maurice Hewlett when he and Hudson watched the rookery); Winterbourne Stoke and many other villages; though not Winterbourne Bishop, which readers would have to track down for themselves. He also pictured old Joan, hale and handsome at ninety-four after a life of toil, mainly in the fields, from the age of ten till she was past eighty-five; besides drawing sheep and sheep-folds, shepherds and their dogs.

Some years earlier, Hudson had persuaded James Lawes to be photographed outside the Silchester cottage; something of an ordeal to the old countryman, as indeed it was to Hudson himself: 'I would sooner have a musket aimed at me than a Kodak.' Hudson told Emily that the 'old boy' had 'got himself up in his best clothes, and stiff hat and polished boots ... I never saw anyone look so unhappy over an operation.' For another photograph, however, 'I made him put on his old cap and my old cloak, and go and stand leaning on a gate ... when he looked like an old shepherd.'

Hudson could not have written of this countryside without including fine pages on natural history; foxes, hedgehogs and shrews, wild flowers, downland birds, and a chapter of good cat stories. His researches took him to Warminster, Wilton and over the border into Dorset, as well as up and down the five river valleys of the chalk country west of Salisbury: Bourne, Avon, Wylye, Nadder and Ebble, among villages whose names many readers might never have heard but for his writings: Chilmark, Fovant, Swallowcliffe, Teffont Evias and Tisbury. In a chapter on the Wylye valley, as beautiful today as when he explored its villages and tree-shaded churchyards, he paid a rare tribute to garden flowers. Greatly disliking the formal summer flower-beds still in vogue, with their red and yellow 'salad arrange-ments', geraniums and 'detested calceolarias', he loved cottage gardens and the old homely blooms, 'so old that they have entered the soul': mixed hollyhocks and lilies, gillyflowers and carnations, sweet williams, larkspurs, 'old woman's nightcap' and especially the marigold, in whose scent he found 'an atmosphere, a sense or suggestion of something immeasurably remote and very beautiful—an event, a place, a dream perhaps...'

But human life and the history of country people form the chief part of *A Shepherd's Life*, and it is Caleb's voice that is most memorable, giving small true touches of a kind seldom recorded; the fact, for instance, that even in sleep he could not forget his flock: 'his dreams are always about sheep.' The book is domi-nated by his personality, and by that spirit and philosophy, found in no other trade, which had come as a revelation to Hudson when, after years in London, he fell in with the shepherds of the Sussex and Wiltshire downs. Their way of life, as Caleb himself realized, linked them with the men of the Old Testament; and the book ends with some impressive words. The old man told Hudson, 'I don't say that I want to have my life again, because 'twould be sinful. We must take what is sent. But if 'twas offered to me and I was told to choose my work, I'd say, Give me my Wiltsheer Downs again and let me be a shepherd there all my life long.'

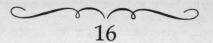

16

The Time Remaining

A Shepherd's Life met with instant appreciation. One reviewer noted the new quality in the writing, 'or rather the concentration and perfection of an old one', and said that the material was 'arranged by invisible means into pictures and studies of man and Nature with a breadth and austerity nowhere to be found in our time, except in this man with a wild, a great feeling for Nature, and yet a sympathy with common men'. Another declared: 'There is no book outside his own, in our time, with which to compare *A Shepherd's Life*, and few at any time. In ease and simplicity it is like *Selborne*, though its delicacy and range of feeling alone make the comparison ridiculous.' (Far too laudatory, Hudson commented.) Arnold Bennett wrote: 'How many men know England—the actual earth and flesh of England—as Mr Hudson knows it? This is his twelfth book, and four or five of the dozen are already classics.'

It was the beginning of a new phase. In literary circles he had become a cult figure, not only for his writings but in himself. To strangers who read his books he was 'the great Mr Hudson'; to close friends their incomparable 'Huddie'. Bernard Shaw, alluding to country things, remarked, 'I'm not a W. H. Hudson.' For that generation he was the archetypal naturalist, and their memoirs were to carry on the legend. William Rothenstein, whose picture of Hudson (1906) hangs in the National Portrait Gallery, wrote: 'His peculiar mysterious charm was indescribable. Something about him tore at one's heart, so lovable he was. Yet he never invited affection: he was a lonely man, with something of the animal about him, walking

away and returning with the nonchalance of an animal, and then
disappearing again.'

Others noted a reserve of power and scorn that was impressive, and qualities of beauty and harmony blending with a
deeper strain of passion and melancholy. His beauty, Violet Hunt
declared, was in his whole being, not only in his face, which in
later years seemed to her

> too small, too beak-like, too much refined to a point. If, as we have
> it, all men suggest likeness to some animal, one might figure him
> some bird pressing forward against a gale; his profile and his hair,
> even, had a wind-blown, backward sweep. It was not an open
> face, the gaze of it was, on the whole, too shrewd, too wilful and
> withdrawn. The eyes were bright and dark, the regard narrowed
> continually in a sort of wild, astute vigilance

—the same vigilance that Richard Curle saw as they watched
wild geese together in Norfolk. He noted too the look of coldness,
'covering may be, a boiling indignation', with which Hudson
examined a dead goose shot by a wildfowler; and the keen glance
like that of a Red Indian while he gazed through the trees at
grebes swimming on a lake, 'as though he could never gaze
enough'.

Such tributes brought the inevitable reaction. 'A grudging old
man with a lively habit of observation' was one posthumous
verdict. Grudging he was not, except in off moments; cantanker-
ous would be nearer the mark, as Roberts's *Portrait* shows. The
need for privacy made him foster a reputation as a recluse; and
the quest for fresh subjects led to a certain ruthlessness. He
would rarely simulate polite interest; and his frankness was
bound at times to be unwelcome. One victim was the mother of
two young girls who had passed the age of childish originality.
When she unwisely asked why he no longer wrote about them,
'he explained simply that they did not now interest him, and was
surprised to find she seemed angry.' Sometimes when invited to
visit a friend he would ask with unconscious rudeness, 'Who will
be there?' Of his experiences in Worthing, Emily's home in later
years, he wrote with ingenuous warmth: 'I have never yet met
anyone in it who has been of any use to me. It is talk, talk, talk, but
never a gleam of an original or fresh remark or view of anything
that does not come out of a book and newspaper.' Neither the fool
nor the bore was suffered gladly; and as bird-watching became
popular, his patience must often have been tried:

> A lady of your acquaintance tells you the result of putting some
> crumbs on a window-sill—the sudden appearance . . . of a quaint
> fairy-like little bird which was not a sparrow, nor a robin, nor any
> of those common ones, but a sparkling lively little creature with a
> crest, all blue above and yellow beneath—very beautiful to look at,
> and fantastic in its actions. A bird she has never seen before . . .
> though all her life has been passed in the country. Was it some rare
> visitor from a distant land . . . ?

His comments on fellow writers and their work were apt to be
salted by personal prejudice. Of the poet Richard le Gallienne he
wrote in disgust: 'He comes to you, as it were, fresh from the
dressing-table, with all the cosmetics, powders and perfumes on
him. One would like to kick him.' *Sons and Lovers* he thought 'A
very good book indeed except in that portion where he relapses
into the old sty—the neck-sucking and wallowing-in-sweating-
flesh': he did not object to the bawdiness of Chaucer or Smollett,
but thought that Lawrence's 'obsession' with sex produced bad
art and untruthful writing. His judgements could be strikingly
apt; as when he advised the young Masefield to write narrative
poems, or remarked of Edward Thomas, then known only as a
prose writer:

> I believe he has taken the wrong path and is wandering lost in the
> vast wilderness. . . . He is essentially a poet, one would say of the
> Celtic variety. . . . I should say that in his nature books and fiction
> he leaves all there's best and greatest in him unexpressed. . . . I
> believe that if Thomas had the courage or the opportunity to follow
> his own genius he could do better things.

This verdict was to be ironically fulfilled when, in the early war
years, Thomas found his short-lived opportunity. Hudson's
sympathy and perceptiveness did not, however, extend at once
to appreciation of the poems. He actually wrote in 1919: 'I had a
thin volume of verses by Edward Thomas sent to me a few days
ago but find his poetic gift was rather a small one.' Against this
astonishing verdict, however, one must place Hudson's admiration for Charles Doughty's massive epic *The Dawn in Britain*,
which had, he admitted, impaired his taste for 'smoother' kinds
of verse.

With increasing years, his patience and tolerance dwindled,
but he was never malicious in a narrow sense. His gaucho companions had taught him from infancy to give and take hard
knocks, and he was still doing so at seventy. As Garnett said, he
enjoyed opposition, 'and his own capriciousness was partly a

device to sting others into declaring themselves'. H. J. Massingham found in him

> an almost Miltonic severity: his dignity and reticence were such as
> men used to associate with the nobleman, and a man so full of
> character, so solitary and aloof and a kingdom to himself, might
> well give the impression of being roughened by prejudice and
> hardly approachable. He did indeed take some knowing . . . some
> navigating his numerous but agreeably salty prejudices. But once
> over the bar and his friend found a personality that was gracious
> and affectionate, if melancholy and a little lacking in humour.

Here, however, Edward Garnett understood him better: 'It was
necessary to have a sense of *his* humour. And certain people
failed to recognize it because it was very deep.'

Women whom he took to, as Garnett saw, felt his immediate
responsiveness; and he was a good deal sought after. On the day
following his death, with the papers full of his praises, Virginia
Woolf wrote: 'I was to have been taken to see Mr Hudson this
winter by Brett, who adored him—I think her sister was in love
with him?—no, I have got it wrong. . . . Anyhow, I wish I had
seen him.' She was no doubt thinking, not of Dorothy Brett's
sister Sylvia Brooke, but of her mother-in-law, who had married
Charles Brooke, the second white Rajah of Sarawak. Margaret
Brooke was a handsome woman, 'queenly' and impressive, who
'could dominate a room with her personality and her magnetic
eyes, and enchant everyone in it'. Strong-willed and resourceful,
she had solved the problem of marrying off her three 'shy and
unapproachable' sons by forming a private orchestra of eligible
young women. Formidable as this sounds, she was also generous
and warm-hearted, revealing a charming simplicity to friends,
and using her wealth and authority in acts of sensitive kindness.
She had befriended Oscar Wilde's wife after the tragedy, and
looked after her until her early death. Her marriage with the
Rajah, 'a cold and indifferent man', had ended on a macabre note:
'he destroyed her pet doves and served them in a pie for supper.'
They lived apart, and she became devoted to Hudson, whom she
met in 1904, and who in his seventies owed a great deal to her
thoughtful care. Their love of music was a strong link; love of
birds another. She kept a brilliant South American macaw that
would sit on her wrist, alarming timid guests: she had rescued it
from dismal captivity in an ironmonger's shop.

In long affectionate letters to this 'well-beloved', Hudson
recaptured the light-hearted intimacy of the *Ebro* letters written to

his family a lifetime ago; signing himself 'William the Miserable' or 'William the Garrulous', and later Dominic, the name of his natal saint, first used by the Spanish neighbours of his childhood. Like them she was a Catholic; and, knowing his dread of death, she would try to impart her own faith in immortality. Though he was, as she said, 'a most spiritually-minded man', his response could be sardonic: 'Thanks also for your long letter about the character of God. The God you feelingly describe is not the God of Nature, he is *your* God—the Ranee of Sarawak's "Giant shadow..."' He especially enjoyed their quarrels, missed her keenly when they were apart, and grumbled when the affairs of her grown-up children kept her from joining him for the winter in Cornwall.

Another friend was Violet Hunt, his early acquaintance, now a well-known writer. Dark, striking and temperamental ('never notable for emotional reticence,' wrote Douglas Goldring, she had 'wept copiously on famous shoulders') and given to dashing off 'fluffy, helpless, sparkling, impulsive letters', she was admired by many distinguished men, including Henry James, Somerset Maugham, H. G. Wells and Hudson himself, for her great personal charm as well as 'her intelligence, her gifts, the wit and acidity of her conversation'. Hudson was especially kind in the period after her break with Ford Madox Ford, with whom she had a long and much-publicized partnership. 'I am sorry you are ill,' he wrote, 'and it disgusts me to hear that Ford is so selfish or unsympathetic or something I don't like in him—greatly as I do like him for other things. I wish I was near to go and hold your hand for him...'

He was also captivated by Alice Rothenstein, the painter's wife, a beautiful and high-spirited young woman who before her marriage had been on the West End stage. Paintings by her father, Walter Knewstub, and her husband, show the bright golden hair which Hudson always greatly admired. In younger days, a friend wrote, he had been very proud of Emily's 'masses of beautiful hair'.

If these attachments again recall Hardy, Emily's experience as the wife of a successful writer unhappily recalls that of the first Mrs Hardy. Since the early 1900s the Hudsons had held a weekly At Home at Tower House; and these occasions were sometimes made painful by her dislike and resentment of the women friends. 'More than once,' said Roberts, 'I sat with her apart from Hudson and some women who waved censers before him, and she moaned a little about the days when he was all her own.' She can hardly have helped remembering how friendless they had been, for instance, in that dark winter at Ravenscourt Park, with the cocoa-nibs simmering, the sick man shivering and trying to write, the critics deriding *The Purple Land*, the postman bringing rejected manuscripts, and herself braving the cold in quest of music pupils. Sadly, in retrospect those were the good days. Obviously a wish to compensate now contributed to the Hudson cult and the outspoken admiration, as it would give rise after his death to the early plan for a memorial. If people had realized Emily's share in the past struggle, they would have seen under her dim and faded aspect, as Roberts saw, 'qualities which truly ennobled her'. As it was, she must have been well aware that some people thought the house and furniture unworthy of him, and held the same opinion of herself. After one of the Wednesday tea-parties, when the atmosphere had been particularly strained, Hudson went to the door with Mrs Rothenstein, who burst into tears and exclaimed passionately, 'Why do you stay here? Why don't you find someone to love, and go away?'—to be silenced by the quiet bitterness of his answer: 'Oh, I've loved you for years. *For years.*'

But with those Emily could like, and who appreciated her, the picture was different. Constance Garnett was evidently one of these. The observant child David Garnett, taken to tea many times at Tower House, saw no querulous encumbrance, but 'a fragile, birdlike, elegant little old lady', and was impressed by the gentleness and affection with which Hudson treated her. 'There was a total absence of the aloof touch of bitterness he so often showed. It was clear that he loved her and wanted to make her happy.'

But there was little happiness ahead for Emily. In the hot summer of 1911 they were both ill, and she never fully recovered. Their relationship was now reversed; it was she who depended on him, becoming so nervous and exacting that she could hardly bear to be left, even for a couple of hours, or to eat a meal if he were not there; and friends had to be asked not to call. In this close confinement, the 'stammering heart' and other ills that he had carried so long became a heavy burden. He could do little work, beyond preparing another collection of his essays from the *Saturday Review*, the *Cornhill* and other periodicals. *Adventures among Birds* contains fine descriptions of the wild geese he had seen wintering on the Norfolk coast. These memories made him try the experiment of leaving Emily for two weeks in October 1912, when he was finishing the book; and at Wells-next-the-Sea he enjoyed the most magnificent spectacle he had ever seen in England—a vast flock of some 4,000 geese streaming across a stainless evening sky and circling down to their resting-place in the marsh.

Again, after Christmas, he hoped to get away for a time to Cornwall; but just as he was setting out Emily went down with bronchitis and neuritis, and soon afterwards he suffered a bad heart attack. So it went on. In June 1913 he managed to take her to Seaford in Sussex; but she continued weak and wretched, over-taken by the losses of old age; her musical talents long gone, her home life going, her eyesight now too poor for reading, she was left with 'no way at all to occupy her time'. Too ill himself to write, walk or cycle, he could only look at the distant downs and remember his old day-long rambles. In August he took her to rooms at Furze Platt, Maidenhead, not far from Cookham Dean; and on fine days he was able to get about a little on his bicycle while she sat in the garden. The RSPB was trying to have one of the local commons made into a protected area, and this gave the place some interest for him. There he met an old countryman, past seventy—as he was himself—who talked of boyhood days when the skies were full of larks: he never saw or heard that bird now, he said. A lark was singing over their heads as he spoke. To Hudson it was a warning that his own splendid sight and hearing might not last for his lifetime. When Edward Garnett wrote suggesting that he should explore the Pembrokeshire coast, he replied on a new despondent note: 'I see no prospect of getting to places I want to visit any more. My health doesn't allow me to hope for anything now.'

That winter both he and Emily grew worse; and the doctor told him that he must 'get rid of all anxiety, live under blue skies and soak myself in sunshine—which seems a large order in West-bourne Park'. A large order it was, but the time had come to carry it out, as far as possible, or resign himself to death. In the spring of 1914 he took Emily to Worthing, in the hope, as he wrote compassionately, of finding somewhere where she could exist without him. Sympathizing with her dread of nursing-homes, he settled her with a companion at The Cottage in Park Road, a guest-house with a large garden. Here she was to live for the next two years. Once more he hoped to reach Cornwall, but the strain of achieving these arrangements proved too much. Back in town he again collapsed, and was rescued by Margaret Brooke, who took him to Grey Friars, her home among the pinewoods near Ascot, to be looked after and treated by a new doctor. 'My wife is going on all right,' he told Garnett: 'she urges me to stay on here where I'm getting every comfort and help and half a dozen servants to look after me.' But the separation must have seemed hard; and he would later be accused of neglect and ingratitude. Emily's feelings became centred in the fear that, if he were to die as the Ranee's guest, he would be given Catholic burial, and she would not even share his grave. They heard from each other almost every day, and in November he was able to visit her at Worthing; but this proved disastrous. He caught cold and had to remain there for the winter, so ill that for two months he could not leave his room. The outlook was bleak; but Emily for a time became much better, cheered by his presence and by the new occupation of knitting for the troops.

It was the first winter of the war. From his window he watched thousands of army recruits losing their city pallor in the sea air. The year before, he had told Edward Garnett: 'I hope to stay on to see the flame of war brighten in this peace-rotten land.' That hope fulfilled, he wrote in February 1915: 'You think it a "cursed war", I think it a blessed war. And it was quite time we had one for our purification . . .' though it might be, he added, 'that in another fifty years the human race will discover some means of saving itself from rotting without this awful remedy of war.'

At that date, as David Garnett has pointed out,

> our young armies were as yet unslaughtered and one of the fairest flowers in them was writing:
>
>> Now God be thanked who has matched us with His hour
>> And caught our youth and wakened us from sleeping
>> To turn as swimmers into cleanness leaping
>> Glad from a world grown old and cold and weary . . .
>
> That wave of emotion, welcoming sacrifice, was shared by the vast majority of English people, and Americans like Hudson and James, who had adopted England as their country, were naturally particularly patriotic . . .

Even those who hated war were caught by the appeal to their patriotism, among them Edward Thomas, whose death in 1917 was the hardest blow of all to Hudson: 'all war and fighting was so hateful to his soul,' he wrote to Margaret Brooke when he heard the news, 'and yet he went because he could do no other, because, as he said, he would never dare to say that he loved England again if he could not fight and die for her.'

He suffered deeply, too, at the loss of Rupert Brooke, Charles Hamilton Sorley and other young men; and as the years and the havoc went on, there were no more expressions of 'views'. Too old and ill for any active part, 'he turned with a shrug and a sigh back to his permanent interests.'

In the summer of 1915 he was again at Grey Friars, watching squirrels, birds and ants in the pinewoods, and making the effort to write. A short piece, 'Little Girls I Have Met', was followed by half a dozen others on the same theme. Like so many of his generation, Hudson found little girls enchanting company in their early years: 'It was said of Lewis Carroll that he ceased to care anything about his little Alices when they had come to the age of ten. Seven is my limit: they are perfect then.' Like Carroll, too, he had not waited to become 'a mild-mannered old gentleman' to enjoy these friendships. Several are described in his boyhood memoir and in The *Purple Land*; and on the *Ebro* voyage his 'very particular little friend' was a child named Honorina Marques, much missed when she left the boat at Lisbon. At Roydon House in the New Forest there had been little Maude, with whom he watched the fledgeling cuckoo and later went bicycling in the forest 'armed with our deadly cameras'. Sent away to school in Southampton, she lost some of her 'child quality and spontaneity': but an eighth birthday was not always the end. One girl was still loved at fourteen 'as much as if she had been my daughter, because of her sweetness and charm and loving disposition, the bright clear temper of her mind and other engaging qualities; and I wished to adopt her—a desire or craving that sometimes attacks a childless man.' From his accounts of her family, it seems likely that this was Maude. In his last book, *A Hind in Richmond Park*, he described their continuing relationship: so close that, when she was in great distress, he thought they were linked by telepathy.

There were many other small friends, from self-possessed London children to little rustics whom he talked to at the village spring or helped to carry home the milk. Not that self-possession was found only in the city. At Selborne, about 1907, he encountered four mischievous little girls who 'suddenly stopped and curtseyed all together in an exaggerated manner': they had been rehearsing for the benefit of the pilgrims. The curtsey was vanishing from the country scene, with other relics of the past; and, while he approved of this where their elders were concerned, he perhaps felt some regret that little village girls no longer learned 'to mimic that pretty drooping motion of the nightingale, the kitty wren and wheatear'.

Whatever their deeper significance, his friendships, like Carroll's, were obviously harmless and delightful, and he enjoyed writing these affectionate sketches; but in doing so he may have had a hidden motive. By 1913, Frank Swinnerton has said, 'the literary world had discovered Freud.' Ten years earlier, when Garnett suggested that he should provide some biographical notes for a publisher, Hudson was quick to scoff: 'of what interest would such things be to any soul on earth!' By now, however, he must have realized that he could not hope to escape the biographer, even the literary gossip writer, after his death; and he felt a deep distaste for the idea that aspects of his private life might become fodder for 'the curiosity of the mean scandal-loving world'. This was his reason for destroying personal papers and any letters he could get hold of; and these accounts of 'dear little friends', apparently so artless, would take the gloss off any attempt at 'revelations' by some writer primed with theory on repressed emotions and subconscious desires.

It was now six years since he had finished *A Shepherd's Life*. It must have seemed impossible that he should ever again feel strong enough to plan and carry out a major book; least of all about his early years, of which he thought he had already related everything worth telling. But a host of memories lay deeper, and might never have come to light if the next winter had not brought 'a marvellous experience': a fortunate conjunction of time, place, physical rest and mental stimulus. In November 1915 he went to Lelant in Cornwall as the Ranee's guest, but on falling ill he insisted on being removed to a convent nursing-home in Hayle; no doubt telling her, as he told Violet Hunt, 'My dear, I don't want to die in your house.' He had been reading Serge Aksakoff's *Childhood*, and the writer's feelings, so like his own—'intense love of his mother, of nature, of all wildness'—at once caught his sympathy; while the picture of Russian landscape, weather and bird-life, of eating wild strawberries and picking mushrooms in the forest, stirred his creative impulse by their sheer contrast with the pampas. These emotions, combined with his weak state, the dim lamplight of his room and the sound of the winter storms outside, seemed to lull him into a kind of waking trance in which he relived his own childhood, feeling himself thousands of miles away in the sun and wind of La Plata. Pencil in hand, he began at once to write down some of these impressions; and the first scrawled notes, patiently added to, cut and shaped over the next three years, grew into the memoir *Far Away and Long Ago*; an achievement of visionary quality which, as he said of Aksakoff's book, owed its truth and freshness to the fact that in 'temper, tastes and passions' he was still the child he had been.

The summer of 1916 saw him back at Tower House, absorbed in this work, looked after by a housekeeper, Mrs Jessie McDougall, and going at weekends to visit Emily. From Lelant he had written wistfully to Cunninghame Graham in South America, 'How I envy you all these wanderings and the adventures you must have had! And now you talk of Venezuela!' He hoped at least to revisit the New Forest, Exmoor and Dartmoor; and there were tempting invitations, one from the old parsonage at Coombe, near New-bury, where he had heard the grim story of the gallows recounted in *Afoot in England*. But these plans had to be dropped. His heart trouble was entering a new and grave phase. Morley Roberts, who had studied cardiology, and who watched unobtrusively over his friend's health, recognized the change and sent him to a specialist. Told that he could not expect ever to be right again, he was given digitalis and instructions on how to use it, and warned of the danger of bronchial attacks. This did not stop him from getting up at night, when the Zeppelins were over London that September, and spending hours on the roof of Tower House. Even in Penzance he evidently had hopes of seeing some action, 'as it is a place where submarines come dodging about, and we can always expect to have a few shells on the town'. But he wanted to stay alive and finish his book; and in later raids, 'when his spirit burnt low and his heart worked badly', he sat in the basement with the kind and friendly housekeeper, or stayed in his own room—now on the first floor—reading children's essays for the RSPB Bird and Tree competitions, passed on by Linda Gardiner.

The strenuous country rambles, the long bicycle rides, the days of bird-watching in all weathers—these had now to be left behind. He would not see 'beloved Simonsbath' again. The best he could hope for in future was to hear the nightingale in Surrey and feed the gulls and jackdaws in Cornwall, as he had done from his hospital room. There were still causes which he could not help taking up; while he was at the convent, he persuaded a young novice not to take the veil, thinking she ought to marry and have

221

children, and frankly telling her so. But he no longer dared to intervene directly in cases of cruelty to birds: in that of a chained owl, for instance, which must have been a painful reminder of the old defeat at Chichester. It seemed better to go on working for all birds and animals rather than 'to die of rage on some miserable cleric's prison lawn'. He meant to leave his money to further the RSPB's educational work; and the long-delayed success of his books in North America now gave him special pleasure. Two young publishers, Blanche and Alfred Knopf, brought out a new edition of *Green Mansions* in 1916, with an enthusiastic foreword by Galsworthy, after several established firms had turned down the idea. It made an 'immense sensation', and there were twenty-two reprintings by 1925; securing Hudson his first large American audience, and incidentally launching the firm of Knopf on its way. J. M. Dent, who had taken over all his books in England, quickly followed this up, arranging American publication of *The Purple Land*, *El Ombu* and *A Crystal Age*. With a 15 per cent royalty, *Green Mansions* brought Hudson a steady £200 a year, and in July 1917 he wrote to Alfred Knopf, 'I am glad of the money and grateful to you for having made the book a success. It has been like bringing a dead thing to life again'. In August 1920 he resigned the Civil List pension he no longer needed. However, he showed less appreciation of his English publisher's share in this new prosperity; writing to Dent, in the mood which Roberts and Garnett knew so well:

> I don't want money for myself as you know; my ideal has been poverty—like St Francis except for the shoes on my feet—and my publishers have always helped me religiously to keep to it. I am grateful to them; but money is needed all the same for certain purposes I have in view and which will be carried out by others.

J. M. Dent did not fail to rise to this:

> You say that your publishers have helped to keep you like St Francis. Still, do not blame the publishers altogether. Please remember the public takes a long time to grow into knowledge of a good book. We have done our best for you and I do feel depressed when you make out that we have bought our book in the cheapest market and always sold it in the dearest ... don't be too cynical about publishers!

And, a few months later:

> I am a little distressed about the way in which you look upon my business connection with you and the work I want to do for you.

> You seem to suspect that I am making a considerable sum of money out of your books ... I cannot help feeling hurt about this ...

Figures enclosed showed that since the takeover Hudson's books had earned only about £600, and Mr Dent went on:

> I don't think you will feel that the profit so made is abnormal. ... I trust that you will believe that my work for you is not a mere piece of 'business' but a really con amore piece of effort that I offer you as a proof of real affection not only for the books themselves but for yourself ...

Cynical or not, Hudson now exacted all he could get from publishers, sold off first editions to collectors and even consented to the publication in book form of *Ralph Herne* and the reissue of *Fan*, knowing how slight was their true value. He also put together a last sheaf of slender papers, *A Traveller in Little Things*, aimed at those who would read anything he had written. Garnett's concern for his hard-won reputation was justified—Virginia Woolf was to comment that 'parts of his books are very good—only others are very bad'—but for the sake of the bird society he was bent on making the most of this late harvest. Yet he could be curiously blind to financial values. Parts of the later manuscripts survived—chapters from *Far Away and Long Ago*, *Dead Man's Plack* and *A Shepherd's Life*, one a complete manuscript, were given to the Rothensteins—but many more were sacrificed to his passion for destroying papers, notebooks and letters.

Meanwhile, through the dark years of the war, the writing of *Far Away and Long Ago* went on. Outwardly his life settled into a quiet rhythm. The winters were passed in Cornish lodgings, the rest of the year in London, with constant visits to Worthing. In 1916 there was a plan for Emily also to spend the winter in Cornwall, but this was abandoned. Cornwall was now his second home, and friends sent him the local news when he was away. Early in 1917, when the Lawrences and their circle were stirring up Zennor, he heard about it from the Vicar, and told Margaret Brooke:

> I think people are a little too ready to run away with the idea that all the cranks and queer people they come across are conspirators. Mr Winkle you remember put on a large sombrero and a cloak so as not to attract attention when going to fight a duel; and so your conspirators disarm suspicion by being eccentric—wearing long hair, going without hats and so on.

No doubt he also wrote in this tolerant strain to others on the spot; but bearded Lawrence in his orange jersey, Frieda in her parti-coloured stockings, had no chance against spy mania and Cornish xenophobia. Though innocent as the rabbits in the field, as Lawrence said, they had to go.

Through that year and most of the next, the memoir was continued. In Penzance, storms swept in from the sea and gulls cried; in London, traffic roared and sparrows chirped in the trees outside Tower House; but he did not hear them. Day after day in his working hours he returned to his vision of the past. He saw the great bird flocks, the whirling thistledown, the spring grass and flowers, the snakes, the moonlit acacias. He heard the summer wind in the poplars, the huge voices of mating birds and toads in late winter, the cries of screamers soaring and circling. He saw his parents with the old childish feelings, and with the new insight of age: he was older now than they. He remembered his brothers and sisters and the laughter of their youth. Dining cautiously, perhaps on a boiled potato, he recalled with amusement those 'past perilous adventures', the hot maizemeal cakes at breakfast and 'the salad of cold sliced potatoes and onions, drenched in oil and vinegar, a glorious dish with cold meat to go to bed on!' Also he painted vivid pictures of the gauchos, of neighbours on the plain, and the streets and water-front of Buenos Aires, evoking a vanished era in the history of his native land.

The book appeared in October 1918, and was hailed as a masterpiece. Refusing to be impressed, he wrote forbearingly to Edward Garnett:

> It is always grateful to me to hear of a friend or individual who has found some pleasure in a book of mine, but nothing do I care for the stuff in the papers and I daresay when you suppose I'm 'overwhelmed' it was 'writ sarkastic'. Good God no! all those twenty or thirty columns of it I've seen so far had not one thought in it all to give me any pleasure.

He no longer had time or energy to spare even for thoughts on the future of Europe; much less for journalistic praise. In this aftermath of the war he told Garnett, 'I want to use whatever time remains to me in doing my own work. The world is a shambles, but I wasn't born to set it right.'

With mental powers still in full flow, he was now absorbed in a huge new subject as well a half a dozen lesser projects. He had begun to write *Dead Man's Plack*, a story of the Saxon King Edgar's murder of his friend, Athelwold, in Harewood Forest: a task he soon found wearisome, with natural history subjects waiting, but which he felt compelled to finish. He was also adding fresh material to the early Cookham Dean essay, to be reprinted as *Birds in Town and Village*; and revising his 200 descriptive passages from *Argentine Ornithology*, renamed *Birds of La Plata*, besides supervising the illustrations. In 1919 *The Book of a Naturalist* appeared, containing all he had written of his abandoned *Book of the Serpent*, condensed into four brilliant chapters; also one of the most important of the shorter pieces, 'Hints to Adder-seekers'. This he had begun years ago as a straightforward country essay, the first part being included by Edward Thomas in his *Book of the Open Air*. But when he returned to it, the subject, so near his heart, took hold of him, and the adder-watching theme developed into a passionate statement of his whole philosophy.

> But what is the seeker to do if, after long searching, he discovers his adder already in retreat, and knows that in two or three seconds it will vanish from his sight? As a rule, the person who sees an adder gliding from him aims a blow at it with his stick *so as not to lose it*. Now to kill your adder *is* to lose it. It is true you will have something to show for it, or something of it which is left in your hands, and which, if you feel disposed, you may put in a glass jar and label *'Vipera berus'*. But this would not be an adder. . . . We can read about the scales and bones in a thousand books. We want to know more about the living thing, even about its common life habits.

'Alas!' he went on, 'it took me a long time to discover the virtue of not killing.' Describing how he once destroyed an adder in a place where children often came, he shows how this act seemed to produce an immediate change in his attitude to living things:

> The curiosity was not diminished, but the feeling that had gone with it for a very long time past was changed to what it had been when I was a sportsman and collector, always killing things. The serpent gliding away before me was nothing but a worm with poison fangs in its head and a dangerous habit of striking at unwary legs—a creature to be crushed with the heel and no more thought about. I had lost something precious, not, I should say, in any ethical sense, seeing that we are in a world where we must kill to live, but valuable in my special case, to me as a field-naturalist. Abstention from killing had made me a better observer and a happier being, on account of the new or different feeling towards animal life which it had engendered. And what was this new feeling—wherein did it differ from the old of my shooting and collecting days, seeing that since childhood I had always had the

same intense interest in all wild life? The power, beauty, and grace of the wild creature, its perfect harmony in nature, the exquisite correspondence between organism, form and faculties, and the environment, with the plasticity and intelligence for the readjustment of the vital machinery, daily, hourly, momentarily, to meet all changes in the conditions, all contingencies; and thus, amidst perpetual mutations and conflict with hostile and destructive forces, to perpetuate a form, a type, a species for thousands and millions of years!—all this was always present to my mind; yet even so it was but a lesser element in the complete feeling. The main thing was the wonderfulness and eternal mystery of life itself; this formative, informing energy—this flame that burns in and shines through the case, the habit, which in lighting another dies, and albeit dying yet endures for ever; and the sense, too, that this flame of life was one, and of my kinship with it in all its appearances, in all organic shapes, however different from the human. Nay, the very fact that the forms were unhuman but served to heighten the interest;—the roe-deer, the leopard and wild horse, the swallow cleaving the air, the butterfly toying with a flower, and the dragon-fly dreaming on the river; the monster whale, the silver flying-fish, and the nautilus with rose and purple tinted sails spread to the wind.

Happily for me the loss of this sense and feeling was but a temporary one, and was recovered in the course of the next two days, which I spent in the woods and on the adjacent boggy heath, finding many adders and snakes, also young birds and various other creatures which I handled and played with, and I could afford once more to laugh at those who laughed at or were annoyed with me on account of my fantastic notions about animals.

But, whatever the average countryman might think of his 'notions', the scientist, as well as the literary critic, was now unlikely to belittle them. A great change was taking place. A few years earlier, one of his readers, Julian Huxley, had published his own observations on bird courtships; and this was, as Huxley later wrote, a turning-point. Field natural history was again becoming scientifically respectable, and Hudson's prestige was at its height.

In one of his *Traveller* sketches he compared the writer's approach to a new subject with that of a reaper who begins by toying with a grain or two in a cornfield, and at length sets seriously to work, but finds after many days' toil that 'the field has widened and now stretches away before you to the far horizon.' His new book, a discourse on the senses—eventually called *A Hind in Richmond Park*—sprang from two small incidents. A

hind which he was feeding with acorns reacted with alarm to a
child's red jacket; another, lying under a tree, kept moving her
'beautiful trumpet ears' to pick up a succession of faint woodland
sounds, reminding him of an old lady with an ear-trumpet whom
he had watched in a village church. From this account of the
listening deer he went on to a long leisurely meditation, discussing ears in primitive man, human reaction to wind, 'the sense of
polarity', telepathy, smells, sense of direction, sounds, bird
voices, music, poetry, colour sense, visual art and many other
subjects; each topic interwoven with observations and anecdotes,
some going back to his earliest notebooks, others sent by correspondents all over the world, and some—like the story of two
homing cats—brought to him as he sat writing in Penzance.

At the end, like Sir Isaac Newton, he sees himself as a child
playing on the shore, all his life-work only the gathering of
'ribbons of seaweed and a few painted shells'. Both modesty and
self-knowledge, as one critic of *A Hind* was to remark, had
inspired everything he wrote:

> It is grievous to think that this is the last book we can have from
> Hudson, especially as it quickens the feeling that he had yet a great
> store of things worth saying. But all that he cared most for, and
> himself too, in his own personal and yet selfless way, he had
> expressed more fully than most writers . . .
> He has looked at everything he met, flowers and birds, children,
> men and women, with the same detached intentness. We call it
> detached because of its control and frankness, but inwardly it was
> passionate.

As in the past, many points were eagerly discussed with
Roberts. He also questioned Sir Arthur Keith, to whom Roberts
introduced him, on racial types ('He's a real Beaker man,' commented Keith, much taken with him); and, when reading in the
Penzance Library about the sense of smell, he wrote asking the
Ranee to pass on anything useful she might have gleaned among
the Malays and Dyaks.

This subscribers' Library, dating back to 1818, with book collections put together by the taste and care of generations of scholars
and students, had been established since 1888 at Morrab House, a
fine building set in gardens close to Hudson's lodgings. It was his
daily club. Here on winter mornings, when London might be
wrapped in freezing fog, he could sit reading in a high sunny
window framed by magnolia boughs, looking down from his
book at sheets of early crocuses and daffodils in the garden

below, or out over feathery sub-tropical foliage to the distant blue of Mounts Bay.

His own books as a rule were locked up at Tower House when he let his flat in the autumn. One year, however, the bookcase was left unlocked. A lady and her two young daughters, calling in reply to his advertisement, were so anxious to secure the rooms that, as they waited on the tattered leather sofa, they took out a rosary and prayed for help. Hudson must have taken in a good deal at a glance. Expecting the usual business interview, they found themselves in absorbing conversation with this tall, kindly, keen-eyed man who seemed at once the friend he soon became. The elder girl was shy and hesitant in her speech; the younger remembered how he waited quietly for her to speak, encouraging her to talk about her favourite poets. The flat was theirs, and he invited them to make use of his books during their stay; adding with a smile that perhaps they should not read *The Golden Bough* as it might disturb their religious faith.

He still enjoyed new contacts as well as seeing old friends—Roberts, the Garnetts, Violet Hunt, Ralph Hodgson, Rabindranath Tagore. The American publisher Alfred Knopf gives an engaging glimpse of one reunion when Hudson had been away six months:

> Blanche and I had him and Edward Garnett, the critic, around to tea at the hotel at which we were staying—the Royal Palace, I think, in Kensington. The two old fellows were so glad to see each other and seemed to have so much to talk about that we soon felt ourselves as an all-but-unnecessary presence. But we were young and good listeners.

He also met Wilfrid Ewart, author of a celebrated war novel, and T. E. Lawrence, then at the height of his fame. The meeting with Lawrence took place in the summer of 1919 when both were sitting to Rothenstein in his studio on Campden Hill.

> I found him arrayed in the most beautiful male dress of the East I have ever seen—a reddish camel-hair mantle or cloak with gold collar over a white gown reaching to the ground, and a white headpiece with 3 silver cords or ropes wound round it. As he is clean-shaven and has a finely sculptured face the dress was most effective. He said it is worn only in Mecca by persons of import-ance, and nowhere but at Mecca. He is a worshipper of Doughty, and a'so told me he had read *The Purple Land* 12 times. While W. R. worked on my portrait I had a grand talk with Col. L. in his remarkable dress and we argued furiously about Science versus Art. But though he was all for art he had a keenly observant mind

228

and could put one into the East and its atmosphere better than any book I know—except Doughty perhaps . . .

'It struck me,' he added, 'that *The Purple Land* was just the sort of book that would appeal to a young adventurer like Lawrence—a sort of Richard Lamb himself.'

This was not his only chance of studying Eastern atmosphere. The next summer he stayed again with Wilfrid Scawen Blunt at Newbuildings Place in Sussex, where his friend, now an invalid, went about in a chair drawn by an Arabian horse. Hudson wrote to Linda Gardiner:

> Whenever Blunt comes out of the house in his Arabian white robe, his favourite robin appears and follows him about, and often flies into the house to look for him. And when we sat at tea jays kept flying impudently by us and coming into the orchard and knocking down heaps of apples . . . after dining we, the guests, would go up to him and sit round his bed, and the endless discussion of Arabian politics would go on for an hour or so. The chief guest was a Mr Philby, a Government official just back from Arabia with much new interesting matter to impart . . .

In Cornwall too he liked to revisit old friends and talk to writers, newspapermen and painters. He lodged at 23 North Parade, Penzance, a hilltop terrace near the Morrab Gardens; he could reach the sea road through a by-lane with ferns and wild flowers growing in the walls. A much younger acquaintance, convalescing there, would watch him walking by the shore on wild days when he himself could not venture out, 'an impressive figure as he battled with the storm and bent to the wind'. Indoors, for the only time in his life, things were arranged to his own taste. When he arrived, the sitting-room had been 'dingy with dark, dirty paper' and crowded with ornaments, a dolorous reminder of the past. Having worked on the landlady until she exclaimed crossly, 'Oh, Mr Hudson, do what you like!' he had the room stripped and painted white, the furniture covered in blue chintz, and a set of coloured plates from *Birds of La Plata* hung over the fireplace.

Emily lingered on at West Tarring, near Worthing, in the care of her companion; often delirious and apparently senile, yet at other times conscious and alert. On New Year's Day 1921 he had grave news of her, and felt he must go at once in case she might still know him; but Roberts and his doctor, certain that the strain would kill him, persuaded him to remain.

A few weeks earlier he had met with an accident which might

well have been fatal. Returning in the dark from a visit to friends, he stepped off one of the town's high pavements and crashed four feet into the roadway. No bones were broken, but he was bruised and badly shaken, and could not sleep. Sitting up by candlelight, he felt his heart 'tumbling all over the place', and thought he would be found dead in the morning. He was soon out again, buying books as Christmas presents for child friends, and, as Roberts saw with affectionate amusement, betraying pleasure at the sight of his own books in the shop. He went on slowly with *A Hind*, and answered letters that came to him daily from many countries. Typical of his courtesy is a letter written a week after the accident, telling a Wiltshire clergyman exactly where to find wild columbines, and explaining in a postscript that his writing is 'worse to read than ever' as his right hand has been hurt.

In March came the news that Emily was sinking. Again his doctor would not let him travel; and on 19 March 1921 she died.

She was buried in Broadwater cemetery at Worthing, where Richard Jefferies lies, and also a friend of Emily's singing days, Sims Reeves. After visiting the place in June he wrote,

> I wished that the grave could have been acquired in that part where Jefferies was buried. It is the loveliest spot, with old stone pines and a wealth of flowers and wild plants. But . . . I must be satisfied to rest, as they call it, in a less attractive spot. However, there is a good pine tree by the grave, and the turtle doves were crooning all the time I stayed there. The whole place seems swarming with birds.

He arranged for the plot to be thickly planted with daisies, and a stone placed there with the text *I will not fail thee*: in deference, as some thought, to Emily's fear that he might be buried elsewhere. 'I shall meet her in that hollow hole,' he wrote, echoing Bishop King of Chichester:

> I will not fail
> To meet thee in that hollow vale.

With Emily gone, he made a new will leaving everything to the RSPB, except for a few bequests: £100 each in gratitude to three of those nearest to him, Linda Gardiner, Morley Roberts and Edward Garnett; and small sums to a young girl who had helped to look after him in Penzance, to Mrs McDougall, his housekeeper in London, and to 'dear little Nesta', the last of his child friends. He directed that the money for the bird society should provide leaflets and pamphlets suitable for village schools, 'each one to be illustrated with a coloured figure of a bird' and 'the writing to be not so much "educational" or "informative" as anecdotal'.

It was all carefully thought out; but in no spirit of resignation. He felt 4 August 1921, his eightieth birthday, to be 'an evil date'. In an essay, 'The Return of the Chiff-Chaff', published that autumn, he expressed all his grief for doomed humanity, for lost family and friends, for his faithful correspondent Mary Ellen, who had died in 1919 in Buenos Aires, and for Emily, 'the last to go', whose death—despite the years of separation—had left him feeling 'very much alone'. He felt bound to dismiss the consolations of those who, like Margaret Brooke, saw death as the door to more complete lives. Like the shepherd James Lawes, he wanted only the life he knew. Over the years he had persistently and wistfully discussed with friends the chances of immortality. The balance of evidence, he felt, was on the side of 'immortality in the race by transmitted influence'; but not of personal survival, except in the memories of others.

Before returning to Penzance he carried out another wholesale burning of letters and papers. He did not expect to see Tower House again. But the following June, after a long slow winter's work at *A Hind in Richmond Park*, he was there once more. The book was almost finished. J. M. Dent had seen the manuscript, which gave him 'great delight and pleasure', and wrote confirming that he would pay £1000 for all rights apart from the American contract. Dent wanted the work completed as soon as possible; but there were other claims on Hudson's strength—friends he must see, a present to be bought for a child in Penzance, appeals for help or advice to be answered. To Linda Gardiner he wrote in August: 'I have lost all hope of ever getting out of London. Illness, illness all the time and a perpetual struggle to finish work.' One service, to Mrs Edward Thomas, he would not leave undone: 'poor young wife and children!' he had written when Thomas died. Now he was asked to write a preface for *Cloud Castle*, a last collection of Thomas's essays; and he sent a message asking Helen Thomas to lunch with him at Whiteleys, a large Bayswater department store where nowadays he often met his friends. She found him waiting there, looking weary and sad, with hollow cheeks and eyes that were startling in their brilliancy:

'Mr Hudson, I am Edward's wife.' After silently taking my hands

231

and gazing into my face with his hawklike eyes, he sat down . . .

When I had composed myself and Hudson had ordered our simple meal, he began to talk in his quiet deep voice, seeking to reassure me and overcome my obvious shyness. When he questioned me about the manner of Edward's death, I lost all self-consciousness in telling him of that strange and dramatic occurrence—my meeting by accident with a man who had been in Edward's battery and had been present at his death. I could see by the expression on Hudson's face that he was deeply moved. He stretched his hand across the little table and said, as his eyes filled with tears: 'Mrs Thomas, I loved your husband as I would have loved a son. I loved him for himself and I admired him as a writer. There was no one like him.'

He asked about the children and about my means. He said: 'I have a complete set of my first editions for you and these you shall have. They will be valuable.' I thanked him. Then he said, 'You know I am ill. I can't talk any longer, it is good that we have met.' We parted in the noisy London street.

Helen Thomas had not spoken only of her own affairs. She told him first of an encounter in Scotland with an egg-collector who was looking out for nests of the snow bunting, and had told her 'dreadful tales' of the greed of other collectors. That evening he sent a long account of this to Linda Gardiner. It was his last letter to her—signed 'Ever yours'—and his last act for the protection of birds.

In the next two days he managed to draft a few pages of the *Cloud Castle* foreword, knowing that his name would help to sell the book. He described how he and Thomas had been drawn together by their love of nature and of poetry, though 'poles apart in the circumstances of our lives, he an Oxford graduate and a literary man by profession; I unschooled and unclassed, born and bred in a semi-barbarous district . . .'

Perhaps he felt less lonely in the face of death as he forged this link with his 'son'; but his instinct, like that of a wild creature, was to die alone. On 17 August Roberts found him in bed, unable to write and in pain. The final chapter of *A Hind* was on his work table at the foot of his bed: 'It's all finished, but not put together and revised. I can't get it done.' They spoke about wild Exmoor: his mind was still following that river. On leaving, Roberts took his hand and held it for a moment. 'He looked so splendid, kind and anxious, and ready, just a little, a very little, to cling not only to life but to one who loved him.' Yet Roberts dared not insist on staying.

The housekeeper got up to make tea for him at four o'clock next morning, knowing he slept little. She thought he was rather dazed, because, as she turned to leave, he shook hands and said 'Goodbye'. Later that morning she sent her little girl up to the room with his letters. The child returned saying that he was asleep, that she had touched him and he did not wake.

He was buried beside Emily. But Roberts, who folded his hands as he lay dead, wrote afterwards:

> I wished to take him out upon the open pampa, with a long wide view beyond the sight of man even on horseback, with the great clear sky above. So I would have digged a grave and put him there to rest in his blanket just as he had fallen asleep, without disturbing his attitude of quiet peace.

Afterword

On a hot windy day in August 1899 Hudson spent hours on Kingston Hill near Lewes in Sussex, watching masses of floating thistledown stars. On 14 August 1979 a Force Eight gale again loosened the down from the few thistles left on the hill: only a patch or two, but enough to bring the goldfinches. As on Hudson's day, the wind was too violent for larks to fly. The view to north and east was still the view he saw: sun and cloud shadows over meadows and ripe wheatfields, walnut trees, yellowwort and scabious, and swallows down in the village feeding their late broods on the swinging telegraph wires, that natural perching-place, as he noticed.

On Easter Saturday 1905 he saw children gathering primroses in Wiltshire to decorate the village churches: 'they might have filled a thousand baskets, without the flowers being missed, so abundant were they in that place.' Seventy years on, only a few primroses were flowering in the hedgerows. Sprays had destroyed them, local people said, some time in the 1950s, before the danger was realized. But on Easter Saturday the churches were again filled with flowers brought, not by the village children, but by their mothers and grandmothers; the primroses no longer wild but grown from seed in their gardens.

Thistle and primrose are symbols of inevitable change, in an island where population has grown since 1901 from under 37 million to 55 million, and with it the need for intensive farming. That massive countryside invader, the motor vehicle, has increased in the same period from 18,000 to 15 million. Hudson, like Kenneth Grahame, was quick to note the aggressiveness of

234

the well-to-do early motorist. Hooted at and choked with dust, he cried in 1908, 'How long will the slaves of England endure this brutality?' But he himself, his walking days over, was glad of the Ranee's stately motor; and the populace joined in as soon as possible. Inevitably, too, the shadow of modern industry has fallen over some of his favourite places—Aldermaston, Fawley on Southampton Water, even the New Forest. Yet, in retracing his footsteps, what so often seems amazing is the lack of change.

At Wells the green woodpecker still calls, a few pairs of 'the Bishop's jacks' build in their old cathedral niches, the sound of bells is carried by easterly winds to the wooded hills. The source of the river Exe, the leafy bird-haunted gardens of Cookham Dean, Martin and its surroundings, the flowers and cottages of the Wylye valley, grey stones and gorse above Zennor, the lime grove at Itchen Abbas, the long grass on Ditchling Beacon, the wild thickets of the west Sussex downs and many other places remain much as he saw them. The same is true of the little twilit churches where he rested from the sun, and churchyards where he scraped away the gravestone lichen to read the old parish names. Clyst Hydon church, set about with stone emblems of once-great families, sun and stars, vine leaves and crown (one of them married a Siamese princess) while the dust of many labourers, wool-combers and shoemakers rests outside; Fovant, Tisbury, Martin where Caleb's father Isaac Bawcombe lies; Bishopstone under the bare chalk hills; Singleton where the huntsman's memorial shook him; Upton Lovell, shaded by tall beeches, the knight in armour sleeping near the altar; Itchen Abbas where he went to the harvest service and criticized the decorations; Boldre with its beautiful tiles and pony-proof stile; those high churches, swept by sea winds, looking down on Blakeney in the east and Penzance in the far west: they have changed perhaps only in one respect, that they are now more valued and more lovingly cared for than ever before. The view of Wilfrid Scawen Blunt's old Squire—

> I like to be as my fathers were
> In the days e'er I was born

—felt by many country people approaching middle age, must be a potent influence in village conservation.

Hudson's voice can still be heard in his old haunts. At Clyst Hydon a notice advertised evening classes on bird-watching. In Kingston village a RSPB poster advised: 'If you see a young bird, please leave it alone. Its parents will return to feed it when you have gone.' One bird man remarked to him in 1892 that in another hundred years there would probably be few birds left. He devoted much of his life to seeing that this did not come true.

His work, of course, is not yet done. Wild life exists as though in a shrinking cornfield with the reaper making its ominous rounds. Hudson sent his followers into the countryside. Today he might urge them to stay away for a time, to let the grass grow and the birds breed and winter in peace.

From its country house in Bedfordshire the RSPB continues to protect and invigilate, to give help and advice for bird casualties, and to produce information and bird-watching opportunities for ever increasing numbers. Membership in the last decade took a great leap from 71,000 to 340,000.

Hudson's portrait hangs in the RSPB headquarters, unnoticed by most of the visiting thousands. No one has done more to promote their pleasure and awareness. 'To enjoy the world for ever was his philosophy'; and he wanted others, and other species, to enjoy it also.

Appendix 1

Hudson's attack on Darwin (1870) and Darwin's reply.
Reprinted from *Letters on the Ornithology of
Buenos Ayres*, edited by David R. Dewar,
Cornell University Press, 1951

(To Dr Philip Lutley Sclater, Secretary of the Zoological Society of London)

Buenos Ayres. Jan 28th 1870.

My dear Sir,

There are four woodpeckers in this country—(B.A.[1]). two of these, the Picus mixtus and the Chrysoptilus chlorozustus,[2] you have seen in my collections; to both these birds the natives have given the vulgar name—*Come-palo*, wood-eater. Both of these species are quite common in the places they frequent, and are occasionally seen in the thickets South of the Rio Salado; but this is the extreme Southern limit of their range, and they prefer the Sayno forrests bordering on the Plata. The chlorozustus is sometimes seen to light on the ground, apparently to feed on worms and ants; its cries are when excited, loud, rapid and shrill, at other times it modulates them to notes exceedingly soft and sorrowful.

The third species—the *Carpintero Blanco* (White-Carpenter-bird) — — affords another illustration of the influence of the riverine wood in introducing new species from the North to this country: for this bird is a native of the Northern States of La Plata, but is occasionally found within a few miles of Buenos Ayres city, though, to my knoledge, never South of it. Probably the divergence from the typical mottled color of the woodpeckers is greatest in this species. I am not acquainted with any of its habits.

The fourth species is the *Carpintero*, — — more widely distributed, and better known than the other members of the genus to

---

[1] Province of Buenos Ayres.   [2] *Proceedings = chlorozostus.*

237

which it belongs. In size it is like the chlorozustus, and also resembles that bird in color, but has not its blood-red crest, or the orange color of the wing shafts: altogether it is an interesting bird in its appearance and habits; it is also in reference to the erroneous account of it in Darwin's great work that makes it worthy of particular attention.

However close an observer that naturalist may be, it was not possible for him to know much of a species from seeing perhaps one or two individuals, in the course of a rapid ride across the pampas. Certainly if he had truly known the habits of the bird, he would not have attempted to adduce from it an argument in favour of his theory of the Origin of Species, as so great a deviation from the truth in this instance might give the opponents of his book a reason for considering other statements in it erroneous or exaggerated. In Chap. IV. of 'Origin of Species' the author speaks of diversified habits, caused by change of habitat and other extraneous sircumstances, and infers that it would be an easy matter for natural selection to step in, and alter an animal's structure so as to make a new species of it, after its habits have been so diversified. He says—(reversing the order of progression from aquatic to terrestial, according to the author of *Vestiges*) 'I can see no difficulty in a race of bears being rendered, by natural selection, more and more aquatic in their structure and habits, with larger and larger mouths, till a creature was formed as monstrous as a whale.'

It may be that animals change by such easy and rapid transitions, and it is perhaps a happy sircumstance for science that Mr Darwin can see no difficulty in it, but the immaginary case of the bear's transformation to a whale must stand alone, as our woodpecker certainly lends no favor to this part of the argument.

The author, after asking, 'if there can be a more striking instance of adaptation given than of a woodpecker in climbing trees and seizing the insects in the chinks of the bark?' speaks of the woodpecker inhabiting the plains of La Plata, 'where not a tree grows', and consequently a woodpecker 'which never climbs a tree!' (Chap. IV p. 169.[3])

The perusal of the passage I have quoted from, to one acquainted with the bird referred to, and its habitat, might induce him to believe that the author purposely wrested the truths of Nature to prove his theory; but as his 'Researches', written before the theory of Natural Selection was conceived—abounds in similar misstatements, when treating of this country, it should rather, I think, be attributed to carelessness.

Besides orchards, groves of willow, poplar etc, which have been planted wherever the plains are settled on, there is also the con-

---

[3] Hudson's references to Chap. IV on this and the preceding page were altered in the *Proceedings* to Chap. VI, and, in the case of his second quotation, the following was added in parenthesis—(*Origin of Species*, 4th ed., vi., pp. 212, 213).

tinuous wood I have already described, growing on the shores of the Plata. South of Salado river, the numbers of wild trees have given a name to a large department of this Province. There is also in the vicinity of Dolores, one hundred and fifty miles South of Buenos Ayres city, a very extensive forrest. All these woods are frequented by the Carpintero, where he may be observed climbing the trees, resting on his stiff and frayed tail feathers, and boring the bark with his bill as other woodpeckers do.

But his favorite resort is to the solitary Ombú, a tree found over a great extent of the plains of Buenos Ayres; this tree attains a considerable size, there is one within fifty paces of the room I am writing in, that has a trunk, measuring, three feet above the ground, thirty feet in circumference. This very tree was, for many years, a breeding place for several Carpinteros, and still exhibits on its trunk and larger branches, scars of old wounds inflicted by their bills. The wood of the ombú is very soft, and the Carpintero invariably bores for breeding where it is green and sound: the hole it forms runs horizontally about nine inches, then slants upward a few inches more, and at the end of this passage a round chamber is excavated to receive the eggs.

The Carpintero frequently lights on the ground, where it is seen to feed on ants and larvae, and is sometimes found several miles distant from any trees; this however is very seldom, and it is on such occasions always apparently on its way to some tree or trees in the distance: it very rarely takes a long flight, but travels by very easy stages. These circumstances have led to its being described as living exclusively on the ground. Outlying the regions abounding in trees, and which I have described as the habitat of the Carpintero, there are vast tracts, in the Southern and Western portions of Buenos Ayres, where in truth, 'not a tree grows', but in these regions the Carpintero is never seen. It is not only the altogether erroneous account of this bird's habits that makes Darwin's mention of it peculiarly unfortunate for him, but also because it is rather an argument against the truth of his hypothesis. Darwin himself describes it as a perfect woodpecker, not only in conformation, but in its coloring, undulatory flight and shrill, obstreperous cries: a bird adapted to a wooded country; it is plain then that natural selection has left it unaltered.

And is it not reasonable to suppose, that if there was such an agent in nature it would have done something for this species, placed in a situation so badly adapted to its structure and habits?

But in truth it has done absolutely nothing: its colors and[4] not dimmed or its loud notes subdued; but even when it traverses the open country it calls about it the enimies from which it has little chance of escape, natural selection not having endowed it, for its safety, with the instinct of concealment so common in the true

[4] *Proceedings* = are.

pampa birds. Its peculiar flight, also, so admirably adapted for gliding through the forrest, here only excites the rapaceous birds to pursuit. In fact, the evidence of this species in a region where conditions seem inimical to its preservation, so far from modifying seems rather to have intensified its characteristics. Compared with the other woodpeckers of this portion of South America, in structure, size, color, voice, flight it is the type of the genus; the habit of occasionally perching on the ground it possesses in common with other species, but it never roosts on the ground, like the true pampa birds, builds a nest, or burrows in banks like the Patagonian parrot, or ventures onto those vast and treeless plains that border on its habitat. Scarcity of provisions and seeking for trees better adapted for breeding, with perhaps other reasons, have probably led to the distribution of this species over a great extent of country.

Twenty years ago, which is as far back as my recollection extends, it was rather a common bird, but has now become so very rare, that for the last four years I have met with only three individuals.

That it should, in time, become extinct or nearly so would not be at all surprising, far less easy would it be to tell what were the favorable circumstances that led in the first place to its increase and general diffusion.

I am sir, very truly yours

William H. Hudson.

Dr P. L. Sclater.

P.S. Of two of the woodpeckers I have described I have not given the Latin names, but think it probable you will be able to tell what species they are. In a former letter I believe I gave the specific name of Poozpira albifrons, albescans. It will often be impossible to ascertain the Latin names of birds I would like to describe, as there is no translation of Burmeister's work and the birds in the B.A.[5] not being labelled.

Dr Burmeister would assist me but is dangerously ill at present. If you know of any book that would be of any use to me in this particular I would like you to give me its title.

yours truly—

W.H.H.

The greater part of this letter was published in the *Proceedings* of the Zoological Society, 1870, Part I (pp. 158–60). In the *Proceedings*, 1870, Part III (pp. 705–6) Darwin wrote:

Note on the Habits of the Pampas Woodpecker (*Colaptes campestris*). By Charles Darwin, FRS

[5] (Editor's note): presumably the Natural History Museum in Buenos Ayres City. This postscript does not appear in the *Proceedings* and is printed here for the first time.

Appendix 1

In the last of Mr. Hudson's valuable articles on the Ornithology of Buenos Ayres, he remarks, with respect to my observations on the *Colaptes campestris*, that it is not possible for a naturalist 'to know much of a species from seeing perhaps one or two individuals in the course of a rapid ride across the Pampas'. My observations were made in Banda Oriental, on the northern bank of the Plata, where, thirty-seven years ago, this bird was common; and during my successive visits, especially near Maldonado, I repeatedly saw many specimens living on the open and undulating plains, at the distance of many miles from a tree. I was confirmed in my belief, that these birds do not frequent trees, by the beaks of some which I shot being muddy, by their tails being but little abraded, and by their alighting on posts or branches of trees (where such grew) horizontally and crosswise, in the manner of ordinary birds, though, as I have stated, they sometimes alighted vertically. When I wrote these notes, I knew nothing of the works of Azara, who lived for many years in Paraguay, and is generally esteemed as an accurate observer. Now Azara calls this birds the Woodpecker of the plains, and remarks that the name is highly appropriate; for, as he asserts, it never visits woods, or climbs up trees, or searches for insects under the bark. He describes its manner of feeding on the open ground, and of alighting, sometimes horizontally and sometimes vertically, on trunks, rocks, &c., exactly as I have done. He states that the legs are longer than those of other species of Woodpeckers. The beak, however, is not so straight and strong, nor the tail-feathers so stiff, as in the typical members of the group. Therefore this species appears to have been to a slight extent modified, in accordance with its less arboreal habits. Azara further states that it builds its nest in holes, excavated in old mud walls or in the banks of streams. I may add that the *Colaptes pitius*, which in Chile represents the Pampas species, likewise frequents dry stony hills, where only a few bushes or trees grow, and may be continually seen feeding on the ground. According to Molina, this *Colaptes* also builds its nest in holes in banks.

Mr Hudson, on the other hand, states that near Buenos Ayres, where there are some woods, the *Colaptes campestris* climbs trees and bores into the bark like other Woodpeckers. He says, 'it is sometimes found several miles distant from any trees. This, however, is rare, and it is on such occasions always apparently on its way to some tree in the distance. It here builds its nest in holes in trees.' I have not the least doubt that Mr Hudson's account is perfectly accurate, and that I have committed an error in stating that this species never climbs trees. But is it not possible that this bird may have somewhat different habits in different districts, and that I may not be quite so inaccurate as Mr Hudson supposes? I cannot doubt, from what I saw in Banda Oriental, that this species there habitually frequents the open plains, and lives exclusively on the food thus obtained. Still less can I doubt the account given by

241

Azara of its general habits of life, and of its manner of nidification. Finally, I trust that Mr Hudson is mistaken when he says that any one acquainted with the habits of this bird might be induced to believe that I 'had purposely wrested the truth in order to prove' my theory. He exonerates me from this charge; but I should be loath to think that there are many naturalists who, without any evidence, would accuse a fellow worker of telling a deliberate falsehood to prove his theory.

Appendix 2

Hudson's letter to *The Times*, 17 October 1893; reprinted as a pamphlet by the Society for the Protection of Birds, 1893

FEATHERED WOMEN

To the Editor of *The Times*

SIR,

In a letter from Professor Newton denouncing the bird-wearing fashion, which appeared in your columns seventeen years ago (28 January 1876), the writer predicted that the continuance of such a mode would inevitably cause the extinction of many of the most beautiful species on the earth. We know that it has continued down to the present time, in spite of prophecies and protests, of ridicule, of all that individuals and associations have been able to do to arrest it. Many of those who have been trying to save the birds have doubtless ere now experienced the feeling which caused Ruskin to throw down his pen in anger and sickness of heart when engaged in writing *Love's Meinie*. Small wonder that he could not proceed with such a work when he looked about him to see all women, even his worshippers, decorated with the remains of slaughtered songsters! I have not the courage to quote here the Cambridge Professor's words, which you, Sir, printed; but his prophecy has not proved a false one. In the American ornithological journals we read the lists of bright-plumaged species which are on the verge of extinction; and besides these, which were lately abundant but are now represented by a few scattered and harried individuals, there are many others fast becoming so rare that they may be considered as practically lost to the avi-fauna of that region. All the world over, where birds have a bright-coloured plumage, the same destructive war has been waged, with a result that may be imagined when we remember that for twenty-five years the fashion has been universal, and that it was estimated

243

nine years ago that twenty to thirty millions of birds were annually imported by this country to supply the home demand.

Since last autumn many of us have been rejoicing in the belief that bird-wearing was at last going out. So marked was the decline that many of the best millinery establishments at the West End and in country towns ceased to supply birds. Another sign of the falling off was the very low prices at which even the finest examples were offered at drapers' and milliners' shops in the poorer and unfashionable districts of London. In some of the thoroughfares where Saturday evening markets are held, I saw trays and baskets full of tropical birds exposed—tanagers, orioles, kingfishers, trogons, humming-birds, etc., from twopence to fourpence-halfpenny per bird. They were indeed cheap—so cheap that even the ragged girl from the neighbouring slum could decorate her battered hat, like any fine lady, with some bright-winged birds of the tropics. The change was attributed to that better feeling so long desired; to the literature which the Selborne, the Bird Protection, and other societies had been industriously disseminating; and to the increased regard for bird life which comes with increased knowledge. Is it possible any longer to cherish such a belief when we see the feathers displayed in the windows of milliners and drapers in London and every country and seaside town at the present moment; when we read in all the ladies' journals that wings are to be 'all the rage' during the coming winter; and when almost every second woman one sees in the streets flaunts an aigrette of heron's plumes on her bonnet? Of these aigrettes, formed of 'ospreys', it may be mentioned that they consist of the slender decomposed dorsal feathers of the white herons or egrets; that they are the bird's nuptial ornaments, consequently are only to be obtained during the breeding season, when the death of the parent bird involves the death by starvation of the young in the nest. For the sake of the few ornamental feathers yielded by each bird killed, the white herons have been entirely exterminated in Florida, their great breeding district in North America, and the massacre has since gone on in South America, Africa, India and Australia—the birds being slaughtered wholesale in the heronries. According to Lord Lilford, in his beautifully illustrated *Birds of the British Islands*, the thoughtless fashion for these feathers has caused the almost entire extermination of more than one species. About the cruelty of killing these birds when they are engaged in incubation and rearing their young, nothing need be said here. Doubtless it is very great, so that men who live, so to speak, in a rougher world, and are harder than women, are sickened at the thought of it; but it is really a very small matter, scarcely worthy of mention, compared with the crime and monstrous outrage of deliberately exterminating species such as the snowy egrets, birds of paradise, and numberless others that are being done to death. For these are not of the commoner

244

types, universally distributed, and mostly of modest colouring, which would not be greatly missed after their vacant places had been occupied by others; the kinds now being destroyed cannot be replaced, not in a thousand years, nor ever; they are Nature's most brilliant living gems and give her greatest lustre. A dead and stuffed bird may be an object of scientific interest to a man; without the life and motion proper to it, it cannot be an object of beauty; but if it were beautiful beyond all other objects, the thought of its cost—of the ruthless war of destruction waged against bird-life, and the irreparable loss to nature—would serve to make it appear ugly to the eye and hateful to look at; and no man who has given any thought to the subject, who has any love of nature in his soul, can see a woman decorated with dead birds, or their wings, or nuptial plumes, without a feeling of repugnance for the wearer, however beautiful or charming she may be.

Why then do women, who have received sufficient enlightenment on this subject during the last few years, still refuse to give up a fashion which degrades them? It is Herbert Spencer's idea that women do not progress side by side with men, that they lag very far behind, and intellectually, especially on the side of the aesthetic faculties, occupy a position about mid-way between the civilized man of our era and the pure savage. There is an illustration in this week's *Punch*, in which one of Mr Du Maurier's vulgar, fat, well-dressed women is seen entering a shop, and to the obsequious shopman's inquiry of 'What can I have the pleasure of serving you with, madam?' the stout lady replies, 'Wings'. The satirist entitles his picture 'A Large Order'. And those who agree with our great philosopher, would regard it as an equally 'large order' to ask that women should have the feeling for nature that men have—that they should be expected to sacrifice the ornament of a pair of bright wings, or a spray of egret's nuptial feathers, merely to preserve the existence of a species of bird. On that large and somewhat delicate question I offer no opinion; and some of our sisters may find comfort in the reflection that Herbert Spencer is not omniscient. What we regard as beyond doubt is that to progress is a law of our being—that we all, men and women, whether abreast, or men first and women far behind, are continually advancing. A slow advance, true, but not to be doubted if we look on ourselves as in very truth descendants of the low-browed prognathous cannibals of the earlier stone ages. Holding such a doctrine, it becomes only reasonable to believe that the time will come when the destructive madness of the present day will be impossible, when a woman will be as much above wearing 'murderous millinery' as she is now, in Europe, above wearing the savage ornaments with which the naked female savage of Venezuela decorates herself, or the necklace of human ears (captured from the enemy) which a Mexican lady is said to have exhibited in a ballroom. But what an impoverished nature and earth future generations will inherit from us! God's footstool, yes, but with all the shining golden threads picked out of its embroidery. Some knowledge will survive among our remote descendants of the wonderful and brilliant forms of bird-life that are now passing away—the unimaginable beauty and grace that they would have known how to appreciate, and with it some knowledge of how it was destroyed in the space of a few decades for the gratification of a detestable vanity. They will, I fancy, think less kindly of their cultured, Ruskin-reading nineteenth-century ancestors, than of those very much more distant progenitors who had some shocking customs, but spoilt nothing. At all events, the old cannibals had no immeasurable past and future to exist in as we have, and no soul-growths to speak of, and did not sin against the light.

I am, Sir, yours obediently,
W. H. HUDSON.
(*The Times*, 17 October, 1893.)

Appendix 3

The search for 'Caleb Bawcombe' of *A Shepherd's Life*

To The Editor of *The Times Literary Supplement*   23 June 1945

Sir—In a memoir of W. H. Hudson it is related that he swore he would never disclose the whereabouts of Winterbourne Bishop, the scene of his book 'A Shepherd's Life.' It is, however, now known to be the village of Martin on the borders of Hampshire, Wiltshire and Dorset. But the identity of the shepherd who inspired his character Caleb Bawcombe has, as far as I know, never been established. By supplementing the biographical details furnished by Hudson with extracts from the Church Registers it is, I think, possible to identify him almost beyond reasonable doubt.

Isaac Bawcombe, father of Caleb, was, we read, an only child (Chap. XII). He was born in 1800 and he and his wife died within a year of each other in 1886 (Chap. IV). Their son, Caleb, was lame for life and his wife, an enterprising woman, temporarily left him to start a little business of her own (Chap. IV). Finally in Chapter XXIII there is a description of a law suit brought against Elijah Raven for the recovery of sick pay from the Village Benefit Club in which Caleb Bawcombe was the principal witness.

Now William Lawes, shepherd, was an only son, born in 1800. In 1823 he married Mary Upjohn, by whom he had four children, the eldest, James, born in 1827. William Lawes died in March, 1886, and his wife in December of the same year. James Lawes is still remembered as having walked with a limp, and his wife as having set up a business on her own. The occupation of both William the father and James the son at the baptisms of their children is invariably that of shepherd. The identification of Caleb Bawcombe with James Lawes is established with certainty by the discovery among the papers in the vestry of an account from a firm of solicitors in Salisbury for six and eightpence for taking an affidavit from James Lawes in the case against Malachi Martin, who corresponds in every particular with Elijah Raven of the book.

James Lawes died and was buried outside the parish, his sons and daughters sought employment elsewhere and the name of Lawes disappeared from the village of Martin some fifty years ago.

E. H. L. POOLE

Martin, Fordingbridge, Hants

To The Editor of *The Times Literary Supplement*   25 August 1945

Sir—I well remember 'Caleb Bawcombe' in the person of 'Old Lawes', living with his wife in a cottage at the Soke near Silchester, where Hudson visited him.

This would I think have been about the year 1900 and those following. Mrs Lawes survived her husband and no doubt their burials could be traced in the register. There was also, I believe, at least one son alive then . . .

Lawes, then very lame, was a most attractive person—as attractive as Caleb, especially when he could be brought to talk of his dog, and his wife a 'character' with a sharp tongue, and a kind heart and a gift for 'malapropisms'. Mill Stephenson lodged with them for several summers, while he was excavating the Roman town at Silchester for the Society of Antiquaries. . . .

W. J. HEMP

The Athenaeum

To The Editor of *The Hants & Dorset Magazine*   (July–Sept. no., 1952)

Sir—Some years ago two letters appeared in *The Times Literary Supplement*, under the heading of 'A Shepherd's Life'. The first, from Mr E. H. L. Poole, of Martin, who, by his researches in the Church Register of that Parish, had identified Hudson's family of shepherds (Bawcombe) with a real family named Lawes . . .

A little later another letter appeared, from Mr W. J. Hemp, the archaeologist, who recalled the period of excavation of the Roman city of Silchester, where he had actually known James Lawes (Caleb Bawcombe) . . .

An interested reader of these letters, and an admirer of Hudson's books, Dr James Fairweather Milne, determined to make further enquiries which might reveal the factual basis of the book. This involved working out, in collaboration with Mr Poole, the Lawes family history. There remained no descendants in Martin, so Dr Milne had to look elsewhere. It may be remembered that in Chapter XIX, Caleb's brother Joseph left his native village for Dorset, and there worked as a shepherd for the rest of his life . . .

Joseph's real name was William Lawes, and the village he came to was Hinton Martell, just off the main Wimborne–Cranborne road. This village was found to have been mentioned by name by

Hudson in a letter to Ford Madox Ford, only recently printed in Douglas Goldring's book *The Last Pre-Raphaelite*. Moreover, Hudson mentioned that he had been there to visit an old shepherd. Not Caleb but Caleb's brother. The enquirer was now on the track of the Bawcombe descendants. Pressing on with this, he discovered old Isaac Bawcombe's great, and great-great-grandchildren alive and flourishing in the same village into which Joseph had walked some eighty years earlier. As a great-great-granddaughter it was an exciting experience to be discovered, and to rediscover a book already known and loved, but now alive with one's own ancestors.

Together we visited old Isaac's grave at Martin, and have since suitably marked his tombstone with a bronze plaque. Then to the task of finding Caleb's last resting place. The search by way of Somerset House took us at last to the churchyard at Mortimer West End, not far from where he lived at Aldermaston Soke. Had he left any descendants? This was not an easy question to settle; but at last came a hotter scent than usual, and we followed it full tilt to land outside a tiny cottage not so very far from those same places. Inside we found Caleb's widowed daughter-in-law, by now an old lady of some eighty years, but rich in memories.

Yes, she could remember Mr Hudson well. . . . This habit of writing down what the old shepherd said did not meet with the approval of Caleb's wife: it puzzled and alarmed her. What did she say, one wonders, when Hudson gave them a copy of the book? And here was the very book to be seen, inscribed by Hudson himself to James Lawes, and a signed photograph as well. How fitting that the closing years of Caleb's life should find him with his own story in his hands, now far removed as he was from his beloved Martin, from the downs, from the sheep, and from his dogs. Here they were all gathered together before him; he had given his story to Hudson, and Hudson had returned it to him fourfold. For Hudson was not writing as a biographer, but as an artist.

(Miss) DAPHNE LAWES
The Manor Farm, Hinton Martell, Wimborne, Dorset

To The Editor of *The Hants & Dorset Magazine* (July–Sept. no., 1953)

Sir— . . . Through an old photograph kindly given me by Mr W. J. Hemp, a photograph taken in Caleb's time, I was readily able to identify the cottage in 1951 where Caleb used to live, and where Hudson was in the habit of visiting him. It is the very last cottage within Hampshire, passing from Aldermaston Soke towards Reading, to the left of the road . . .

Mr Poole's house in Martin is the actual one in which Hudson in his time found lodging. It was then in a derelict state, having been the home of an eccentric old man called Malachi Martin. This is the

Elijah Raven of the book, and Malachi's character, behaviour and appearance were exactly those ascribed to Elijah! . . . I have often been in the room where Hudson, standing upright, nearly touched the ceiling. In the corner is the narrow stairway that led to his bedroom, and as he described in *A Shepherd's Life*, but now in good repair.

In Martin Church is a tablet (restored) commemorating the Talk Charity. This was the charity under which old Isaac Bawcombe (William Lawes) was a beneficiary. . . . Hudson gives the dates and details of the old Bawcombes correctly; the family details are mixed up, even the order of birth etc. The son who went to Dorset (brother to Caleb) like his own father was William Lawes; and he was met as described on the road by a farmer who engaged him, Farmer Burt of Hinton Martell . . .

In Martin, one of Caleb's employers was the farmer Billy Street, himself rather a 'character', as a distant relative, Mr A. G. Street [author of *Farmer's Glory*, (1932)] recalled in conversation with me, though Mr Street was not aware of this link with Hudson's shepherd.

In *W. H. Hudson, A Portrait*, Morley Roberts recorded how he tried to extract from his friend the secret of Winterbourne Bishop, which he always kept close; and how at last Hudson somewhat angrily threw out what were in effect two clues . . . these clues are, in fact, perfectly accurate. There was a Bustard Farm and a Bustard Down nearby, named for the extinct great bird of the Wiltshire Downs; Bustard Farm was to become a monastery . . .

JAMES FAIRWEATHER MILNE

Peterhead, Aberdeenshire

Appendix 4

Hudson's service in the Argentine National Guard, 1859, 1870. Research notes by Herbert F. West, made available by Eric S. Whittle

Excerpt from an article in *La Revista Argentina Libre*, 7 May 1942, entitled 'Some facts about the Hudson family', by José A. Craviotto and César Barrera Nicholson, members of the Council for Historical Studies at Quilmes:

> According to a circular dealing with the reorganisation of the district for the [1859] campaign and signed by Col. Bartolomé Mitre, the then Minister of War for the State of Buenos Aires, the brothers, Daniel and William Hudson, were summoned, as were other citizens of section No. 3, to report at San Vicente and to enlist in the 13th Regiment of the National Guard, and, complying with these orders, they were given registration cards on July 8, 1859. This regiment comprised the Militia of San Vicente, Quilmes and Southern Barrancas, to which was added shortly afterwards the Militia of Lomas de Zamora. In the 1864 and 1865 lists Daniel Hudson is entered as Soldier no. 35 of the first squadron, 2nd company of the regimental Militia. William, however, because of ill health, is registered this same year as no. 76 in the non-active Militia; the following year, as no. 22, he was transferred to the squadron and company of his brother Daniel in the active Militia, but after a short time he was again sent back to the non-active.

Excerpt from an article in the Argentine Review *El Hogar*, 28 August 1942, entitled 'How Henry Hudson was exempted in 1870 from service on the Frontier' by José A. Craviotto and César Barrera Nicholson:

Because of the withdrawal of garrisons from the zones bordering on the Indians, as a result of the war with Paraguay, the Government of the Province of Buenos Aires issued a decree, April 27, 1870, directing the organisation of a military enrollment with a view to filling the defensive needs of the moment. The appropriate order, marked 'very urgent', was received together with 400 registration cards and 40 enrollments on May 3 by Andres Baranda, the Military Commander of the Quilmes district. The instructions specified that, in addition to the sick and physically handicapped, farm overseers, stage-coach drivers and all those responsible for the maintenance of old and infirm parents were to be exempted. The coroner for the Quilmes district, Doctor José Antonio Wilde, began the re-examination of the enlisted men who, because of their physical condition, might be transferred to the non-active Militia. Hudson was no. 4 on the examination list. Dr Wilde's certificate states: The undersigned Doctor of Medicine certifies that Mr [William] Henry Hudson suffers from an organic heart ailment and is subject to frequent rheumatic attacks. Quilmes, May 15, 1870 (signed) J. A. Wilde, Coroner.

Appendix 5

'Doveton' and the 'Ellerbys': *A Shepherd's Life*,
chapters 14–16.
Research by James Laverick

Where is 'Doveton'? I once thought it might be Stockton, but clues in *A Shepherd's Life* did not fit. Hudson says in chapter 12 that 'Caleb Bawcombe' (James Lawes) lived at Doveton in a cottage 'a stone's-throw away' from a river, near a church with beeches and elms growing around, and close to the railway line on which his cat was killed. All this fitted the village of Upton Lovell where I lived; and I found from the 1861 census returns that James Lawes and his wife Emma, née Bush, lived in Scoute Lane, Upton Lovell, from at least 1856 until the end of 1862. He would have passed our home every day on his way to his sheep walks. Four of their children were baptized in St Augustine's church, Upton Lovell. The cottages in Scoute Lane were demolished around 1930–40, and Dutch elm disease took the elms. The beeches are still there, and the green meadows.

The cottage in Scoute Lane belonged to the Ingram family, and it can be presumed that these were the 'Ellerbys' for whom James Lawes worked. Christopher Henry Ingram, probably the 'Mr Ellerby' of the book, married Sarah Patient in 1844. Both the Ingrams and the Patients had been involved in incidents in 1830 which resulted in labourers being sent to the Antipodes. Two men were convicted and transported, on the evidence of Mr Ingram's father, for robbing him of 5s, and nine men were transported for breaking a threshing-machine belonging to Ambrose Patient, Mr Ingram's father-in-law.

Hudson says in chapter 16 that the father of 'Mr Ellerby'

received from Australia, two years later, a long denunciatory passage from Psalm 109, which contains the words: 'Let his posterity be cut off; and in the generation following let their name be blotted out.' In fact, the father died less than a year after the 'riots'. Mr Ingram and his wife lived at Middle Farm, Upton Lovell, and after 17 years of marriage they were childless. Until 1851 neither of his brothers was married. Two sisters had died young. A third sister married and had a son, Richard, on 21 May 1848. She died two days later, and the child died on 15 July 1848, aged eight weeks. There is a memorial to the Ingrams in Upton Lovell church and a tomb in the churchyard.

Notes and References

For Hudson's works, page references are to the Collected Edition, Dent, 1923. Apart from those given below, all references in Part I to Hudson's boyhood experiences are to *Far Away and Long ago. A History of My Early Life*, Dent, 1918. Bird names are those used by Hudson. Modern names, where they are not also given below or in the text, may be found in, for example, *A Guide to the Birds of South America*, Rudolphe Meyer de Schauensee (Curator of Birds, the Academy of Natural Sciences of Philadelphia), Oliver and Boyd, 1970. Place names throughout the book are spelled in the modern way, sometimes differing slightly from Hudson's spelling.

> *page 9*   Epigraph: 'Hints to Adder-Seekers', *The Book of a Naturalist*, Hodder and Stoughton, 1919, ch. 2, pp. 2–3; ibid., p. 20, and *The Book of the Open Air*, ed. Edward Thomas, Hodder and Stoughton, 1907, 'Advice to Adder-Seekers'.

PART I: 1841–1874

Chapter 1: Running Wild

> *page 29, line 2*   The house is situated at Florencio Varela, Quilmes.
>
> *line 8*   parents: Morley Roberts, *W. H. Hudson. A Portrait*, Eveleigh Nash and Grayson, 1924, pp. 20–2; *The Worthing Cavalcade. W. H. Hudson: A Tribute*, ed. Samuel J. Looker, Worthing,

Sussex, 1947, p. 22, reproduces a photograph of the memorial stone to Hudson's parents, originally erected over their grave in the English Cemetery, Buenos Aires.

line 22   purchase of The Twenty-five Ombus: Ezekiel Martinez Estrada, *El Mundo Maravilloso de Guillermo Enrique Hudson*, Fondo de Cultura Economica, Mexico, 1951, p. 9.

line 23   Juan Manuel de Rosas: 1793–1877.

line 24ff.   Herbert Faulkner West, *For a Hudson Biographer*, Westholm Publications, 1958, pp. 33–4, gives the following birth-dates and names (sic): Daniel Augusto, 18 July 1835; Edwin Andrews, 11 January 1837; Caroline Luisa, 21 June 1839; Guillermo Enrique, 4 August 1841; Albert Merriam, 3 August 1843 (all at Quilmes), and Mary Helen, 30 November 1846.

page 30, line 4   surroundings: A. F. Tschiffely, *Don Roberto. The Life and Works of R. B. Cunninghame Graham*, Heinemann, 1937, pp. 432–3.

line 11   woodpeckers: *Birds of la Plata*, vol. II, Dent, 1920.

line 24   William: in letters written to his brother Albert in 1874 Hudson signs himself 'William H. Hudson'. See *William Henry Hudson's Diary Concerning his Voyage from Buenos Aires to Southampton on the 'Ebro'*, Westholm Publications, 1958.

line 37   The location of The Acacias (Las Acacias) is now at Km 74 on Ruta 2, Partido de Coronel Brandsen.

page 31, line 27   night terrors: John Masefield, *The Midnight Folk*, Heinemann, 1927, pp. 11–12; Gwen Raverat, *Period Piece*, Faber and Faber, 1952, ch. 9.

line 28   puma: *The Naturalist in La Plata*, Chapman and Hall, 1892, ch. 2, p. 32.

line 41   first-hand education: *A Shepherd's Life*, Methuen, 1910, ch. 1, p. 5.

page 33, line 4   Hudson apparently never learned to swim: Roberts, *Portrait*, p. 68.

line 6   nearly drowned: *A Hind in Richmond Park*, Dent, 1922, ch. 5, p. 224.

line 32   *Hudson–Garnett Letters*, 134.

page 35, line 17   'perhaps thinking': Edward Thomas, 'Old Man'.

line 21   blue and crimson serpent: this may have been

Dromicus almadensis—a 'very tentative' identification: Mr A. F. Stimson, Reptile Section, British Museum (Natural History).

page 36, lines 5–6   counting the hours: *The Naturalist in La Plata*, ch. 1, p. 20, ch. 17, p. 222.

line 15   November wind: *Idle Days in Patagonia*, Chapman and Hall, 1893, ch. 14, p. 223.

page 37, line 6   Edmund Gosse, his friend: Edmund Gosse, *Father and Son*, Heinemann, 1907, ch. 6; Mrs Frank E. Lemon, 'Recollections of Hudson', *Worthing Tribute*, p. 153.

Chapter 2: Riding Out

page 38, lines 9–13   gaucho riding: A. F. Tschiffely, *Bohemia Junction*, Hodder and Stoughton, 1950, chs. 9, 12.

line 11   spiders' webs: *The Naturalist in La Plata*, ch. 14, pp. 176, 182.

page 39, lines 32–9   *Far Away and Long Ago*, ch. 17, p. 238.

page 40, line 31   rhea: *Rhea americana*.

page 41, line 18   pepsin: *The Naturalist in La Plata*, ch. 4, p. 79.

page 42, line 23   colonists: Charles Darwin, *Journal of Researches into the Geology and Natural History of the Various Countries Visited by HMS 'Beagle'*, Henry Colburn, 1839, ch. 6.

page 43, line 8ff.   grape-vines: *Adventures among Birds*, Hutchinson, 1913, ch. 2, p. 17; St John 2: 1–10.

line 17   potatoes: *The Book of a Naturalist*, ch. 26.

page 46, lines 26–32   *Far Away and Long Ago*, ch. 9, p. 151.

line 35   Edgar Allan Poe, *Annabel Lee* (1849): Roberts, *Portrait*, p. 204.

page 47, line 2   christening: *Far Away and Long Ago*, ch. 7, p. 96; Roberts, *Portrait*, p. 33.

line 13   orchestra: *A Hind in Richmond Park*, ch. 18, p. 301.

line 21   night-watchmen: Hudson's first visit to Buenos Aires was apparently in 1847/8. In 1864 a similar figure was seen in Bond Street, London 'in a slouched hat and long drab coat with cape—the very dress of the old watchmen ... he opened his mouth and cried "Past twelve o'clock!"' Derek Hudson, *Munby, Man of Two Worlds. The Life and Diaries of Arthur J. Munby, 1828–1910*, John Murray, 1972, pp. 191–2.

Chapter 3: Wars and Alliances

page 49, lines 23–4   Parson Woodforde: James Woodforde, *The Diary of a Country Parson, 1758–1802*, Oxford 1924–31, entries for 25 March 1777 and 4 June 1777.

page 50, line 33   Tom Brown: Thomas Hughes, *Tom Brown's Schooldays*, 1857, ch. 8.

page 51, lines 27–32   *Far Away and Long Ago*, ch. 21, p. 291.

page 52, lines 37–42   *Far Away and Long Ago*, ch. 8, p. 130.

page 54, lines 1–14   favourite horse: *The Naturalist in la Plata*, ch. 23, pp. 348–50.

page 55, lines 5–8   'The moving sun-shapes . . .': Thomas Hardy, 'Going and Staying'.

Chapter 4: Finding a Future

page 56, line 14   intelligent people: *Men, Books and Birds. Letters to a Friend*, letters from W. H. Hudson to Morley Roberts, with an introduction and notes by Morley Roberts, Eveleigh Nash and Grayson, 1925, 121.

page 57, line 33   'The Discontented Squirrel': *The Book of a Naturalist*, ch. 6; Dr John Aikin and Mrs Anna Letitia Barbauld, *Evenings at Home*, London, 1792–6. Ruskin also read this story as a child: see *A Peculiar Gift: Nineteenth-century Writings on Books for Children*, ed. Lance Solway, Kestrel, 1976.

page 58, line 30   last book: *A Hind in Richmond Park*, Dent, 1922.

page 60, lines 11–18   *Far Away and Long Ago*, ch. 22, pp. 305–6.

lines 21–33   ibid., ch. 22, pp. 307–8.

line 38   £100 a year: *W. H. Hudson's Letters to R. B. Cunninghame Graham*, ed. Richard Curle, Golden Cockerel Press, 1941, letter of 29 July (about) 1894.

page 61, line 7   Thomas Hardy, 'In the Seventies', quoted by Robert Gittings, *Young Thomas Hardy*, Heinemann, 1975, ch. 11.

line 8   Edward Thomas, *Richard Jefferies, His Life and Work*, Hutchinson, 1908, ch. 3, p. 55.

lines 13–15   letter to *The Times*, 29 September 1956, from Lord Davidson and Mrs Marjorie Mackenzie Potter, former owners of the site of The Twenty-five Ombus ('our uncle used to tell us how young Hudson', etc.)

line 27   *The Book of a Naturalist*, ch. 13.

page 62, line 7   painter: *A Hind in Richmond Park*, Conclusions, pp. 320–1.

line 10   'practising artist': Dr James Fairweather Milne in a letter to the author, 26 April 1950, quoted Mr D. M. Beach, a Salisbury bookseller who had known Hudson well and who recalled him 'as a member of the artist colony at St Ives and as a practising artist'.

line 12   Rollin: Charles Rollin (1661–1741), French writer.

line 21   Edward Gibbon, *History of the Decline and Fall of the Roman Empire*, London, 1776–88.

lines 35–42   *Far Away and Long Ago*, ch. 17, p. 242.

page 63, lines 2–7   ibid., ch. 17, p. 243.

line 8   trees: Hudson wrote of a tree with supernatural powers in *An Old Thorn*, Dent, 1920.

line 16   Gilbert White, *The Natural History and Antiquities of Selborne*, B. White, 1789.

line 19   Mary Russell Mitford, *Our Village*, London, 1824, pp. 1–2.

line 23   diary: *The Naturalist in La Plata*, ch. 3, p. 60.

page 63, line 39   Hurdis: *Nature in Downland*, Longmans Green, 1900, ch. 1, pp. 8–13.

page 64, line 13   James Thomson, *The Seasons* (1726–30), 'Autumn', lines 1091–3.

lines 33–41   *The Seasons*, 'Winter', lines 7–16.

page 65, lines 4–14   *The Seasons*, 'Spring', lines 620–30.

lines 18–22   *The Seasons*, 'Autumn', lines 866–70.

lines 27–8   Robert Bloomfield, *The Farmer's Boy*, London, 1800.

lines 30–6   *Afoot in England*, Hutchinson, 1909, ch. 24, 'Troston'.

page 66, line 11   'the spinsters . . .': Shakespeare, *Twelfth Night*, Act II, Scene IV.

line 17   dive-dapper: Shakespeare, *Venus and Adonis*, stanza 15; *A Shepherd's Life*, ch. 15, p. 180; 94-year-old Joan Edwards of Fonthill Bishop, Wiltshire, called the moorhen 'di-dapper'. Hudson comments: 'it comes no doubt from dive-dapper, an old English vernacular name (found in Shakespeare) of the dabchick or little grebe'.

line 18   nine men's morris: Shakespeare, *A Midsummer Night's Dream*, Act II, Scene 2; *A Shepherd's Life*, ch. 5, p. 66.

line 20   Bloomfield: memoir by E. W. Brayley, *The Farmer's Boy*, 1806 edn.

Chapter 5: Facing Death

page 67, line 5   Thomas Carlyle, *The French Revolution. A History*, James Fraser, 1837.

lines 19–20 Estrada, *El Mundo Maravilloso de G. E. Hudson*, pp. 21–2.

line 21 reading: John William Draper, *The History of the Intellectual Development of Europe*, Bohn, 1852, 'Christianity and Civilization'.

line 26 unhandy: Roberts, *Portrait*, pp. 66–7, 256.

page 69, line 16 wasps: *The Book of a Naturalist*, ch. 18, pp. 201–2.

lines 36–7 Richard Baxter, *The Saints' Everlasting Rest, or A Treatise of the Blessed State of the Saints in their enjoyment of God in Glory*, 1650. Readers of George Eliot's *The Mill on the Floss* will remember that Aunt Glegg resorted to this 'on special occasions' (Book I, ch. 12).

line 42 hope of everlasting damnation: this emotive quip had its origins in a judgement given by the Lord Chancellor, Lord Westbury (1800–73), when two clerical writers successfully appealed against a conviction of heresy. The charge, 'denying the plenary inspiration of the Holy Scriptures', arose from a book they published in 1860, the year after the appearance of the *Origin of Species*. An ensuing 'suggested epitaph' for the Lord Chancellor ended:

> In the Judicial Committee of the Privy Council
> He dismissed Hell with costs,
> And took away from the orthodox members of the Church of England
> Their last hope of everlasting damnation.

See Thomas Arthur Nash, *Life of Richard Lord Westbury*, Bentley, 1888, vol. II, pp. 73–8.

page 70, lines 5–6 Charles Darwin, *The Origin of Species by Means of Natural Selection, or the Preservation of Favoured Races in the Struggle for Life*, John Murray, 1859.

line 11 Genesis 1: 1. Exodus 20: 11.

line 11 J. Aspin, *A Complete System of Chronology or, Universal History Abridged*, A. Whellier, 1812, p. 14.

line 12 James Ussher, *Annales Veteris et Novi Testamenti*, London, 1650, 1654.

lines 31–2 reaction to *The Origin of Species*: *The Book Of A Naturalist*, ch. 18, p. 202 (first published in the *Speaker*, 24 June 1905); *Far Away and Long Ago*, ch. 24, pp. 343–4.

page 71, lines 3–4	'tough reading': Walter Karp, *Charles Darwin and the Origin of Species*, Cassell, 1969, p. 102.
lines 11–14	Darwin, *Origin of Species*, ch. 1, p. 36.
lines 15–16	Mrs Humphry Ward, *Robert Elsmere*, Smith Elder, 1888, Book II, ch. 12.
line 16	*153 Letters from W. H. Hudson*, ed. with an introduction and notes by Edward Garnett, Nonesuch Press, 1923, 50.
line 26	'as a naturalist': Edmund Selous in his Introduction to Charles Waterton's *Wanderings in South America* (Everyman edn, Dent, 1925, p. xv) points out that before Darwin's book appeared 'the relation of structure to habit was not clearly perceived ... the stilt had to struggle through life under the "enormous defects" of legs much too long and a neck much too short for it, (and) the avocet was plagued with a beak that had maliciously been bent the wrong way ....'
lines 27–32	Karp, *Charles Darwin and the Origin of Species*, p. 99, in a quoted letter from Darwin to his wife.
page 72, line 6	heart attacks: Roberts, Portrait, pp. 208–9, 245.
line 18	threat of blindness: *Hudson–Garnett Letters*, 31; Hudson suffered from 'neuralgia of the eyes' in later life: *Hudson–Cunninghame Grahame Letters*, letter of 16 March 1897.

Chapter 6: Hunting Birds

page 73, lines 6–7	Roberts, *Portrait*, p. 19.
page 74, line 1	permission to unsaddle: *The Purple Land*, ch. 3, p. 30.
lines 5–14	*The Purple Land*, ch. 4, pp. 40–1.
lines 16–18	Darwin, *Journal* (Voyage of the *Beagle*), entry for 11 May 1833.
line 24	loan of horse. A. F. Tschiffely, *Don Roberto. The Life and Works of R. B. Cunninghame-Graham, 1852–1936*, Heinemann, 1937, ch. 5, p. 103.
line 41	Lamb's adventures: *Hudson–Cunninghame Graham Letters*, letter of 25 August 1898.
page 75, line 8	fire: Tschiffely, *Don Roberto*, ch. 3, p. 62.
lines 10–15	armadillo meat, etc.: 'On the Habits of the Vizcacha', ZSL *Proceedings*, 19 November 1872.
lines 16–20	fireflies, cicadas, owls: *The Purple Land*, ch. 23, p. 280; reeds, grasses: *The Naturalist in La Plata*, ch. 1, pp. 9–10; tuco-tucos: ibid., p. 14; wild dogs: ibid., p. 15; marsh birds: ibid., p. 20.
line 22	tether: Tschiffely, *Don Roberto*, ch. 5, p. 103.

line 24	Indians: *The Naturalist in La Plata*, ch. 23, p. 354; Roberts, *Portrait*, pp. 247–8.
line 24	cattle: *The Purple Land*, ch. 12, pp. 124–6; Tschiffely, *Don Roberto*, p. 51.
lines 25–6	talons: *Idle Days in Patagonia*, ch. 12, p. 177.
line 26	quagmires: ibid., ch. 5, p. 60.
line 28	snake: ibid., ch. 2, p. 24.
lines 30–5	Tschiffely, *Don Roberto*, ch. 3, p. 51.
line 36	accidents: *Hudson–Garnett Letters*, 23.
line 40	Richard Jefferies, *The Story of My Heart*, Longmans, Green, 1883, ch. 7.
page 76, line 2	riding at night: *The Naturalist in La Plata*, ch. 23, pp. 358–9; Roberts, *Portrait*, p. 45.
line 11	Bruce Chatwin in *In Patagonia*, Cape, 1977, ch. 3, describes a visit to 'the best Natural History Museum in South America' at La Plata, with 'the birds of La Plata stuffed beside a portrait of W. H. Hudson'.
line 19	Baird: John S. Billings, *Memoir of Spencer Fullerton Baird (1823–1887)*, 1889, Smithsonian Institution archives. Professor Baird was Secretary to the Institution from 1878 to 1887. The writer records that as a young man he would walk 'from forty to fifty miles a day for two weeks in succession', and the change to desk work affected his heart, causing his death at the age of sixty-four.
lines 35–41	Letter of 27 December 1865, Smithsonian Institution archives.
page 77, line 12	handwriting: Hudson's writing, sometimes indecipherable in later years, was evidently difficult enough as a rule to be a family joke by 1874 (see p. 103): but all these 'professional' letters are beautifully written and still perfectly legible.
line 12	letter: letters quoted here from Hudson to Professor Baird, and Professor Baird's replies (September 1866 to October 1869) are in the Smithsonian Institution archives. This correspondence, up to 1868, is quoted by R. Gordon Wasson and Edwin Way Teale in 'W. H. Hudson's Lost Years', *Times Literary Supplement*, 5 April 1947.
line 16ff.	letter of 5 September 1866, Smithsonian Institution archives.
page 79, lines 16–18	bird-skins: information made available to the author by Mr Phillip S. Hughes, the Smithsonian Institution.

line 22	military service: Hudson was 'soldier No. 22': Estrada, *El Mundo Maravilloso*, p. 57.
line 24	geese: ZSL *Proceedings*, 21 March 1871.
page 81, line 6	long illness: Señora Violeta Shinya Hudson was told of this by her grandmother, Hudson's sister Mary Ellen.
page 82, lines 9–15	Letter of 5 September 1869, Smithsonian Institution archives.
line 32	Daniel's ranch: *The Naturalist in La Plata*, ch. 7, p. 120; *Birds and Man*, ch. 11, p. 177; Roberts, *Portrait*, p. 247.

Chapter 7: Writing to England

page 84, line 6	Philip Lutley Sclater (1829–1913), Secretary to the Zoological Society of London, 1859–1902; Osbert Salvin (1835–1898).
line 11	report: ZSL *Proceedings*, 13 February 1868. Reports on two further lists, ZSL *Proceedings*, 11 March and 9 December 1869.
line 19	Hudson's letters to Dr Sclater are printed in *Letters on the Ornithology of Buenos Aires*, ed. David R. Dewar, Cornell University Press, 1951.
line 25f.	Hudson's letter of 30 April 1869: ZSL *Proceedings*, 24 June 1869.
page 86, lines 3–6	Gilbert White, *The Natural History of Selborne*, Letter LX.
line 9	first essay: ZSL *Proceedings*, 10 February 1870.
page 87, line 37	notebook for 1870: ZSL *Proceedings*, 16 November 1875.
page 89, lines 7–15	'However close an observer . . .': ZSL *Proceedings*, 24 March 1870 (see Appendix 1 for full text).
lines 17–23, 35–42	ibid.
page 90, line 3	ZSL *Proceedings*, 1 November 1870 (Appendix 1).
line 6	a rapid ride: Darwin rode from Bahia Blanca to Buenos Aires, and on to Santa Fé, between 17 August and 2 October, 1833 (*Journal*).
line 11	Azara: see note, page 133, line 29.
line 22	Hudson's letter of 19 May 1870: ZSL *Proceedings*, 15 November 1870.
lines 24–30	Joseph John Murphy, *Habit and Intelligence, in Their Connexion with the Laws of Matter and Force*, London, 1869, p. 225.
page 91, line 5	Murphy, *Habit and Intelligence*, 2nd edn, 'revised and mostly rewritten', 1879, ch. 11, p. 129.
line 6	woodpecker: Darwin, *The Origin of Species*, 6th

edn, 'with additions and corrections', vol. I, pp. 220–1.

line 9 Molothrus bonariensis: ibid., pp. 334–5.

line 14 Lamarckian: Jean-Baptiste de Lamarck (1744–1829), an early evolutionist, believed that conscious effort preceded structural change in species, while Darwinian theory held that variation was followed by adaptive habits. Hudson's views in later life are discussed in *Men, Books and Birds*, 126, 151 and 153, with Roberts's comments.

line 17 gaucho: *The Naturalist in La Plata*, ch. 23, pp. 347–8.

line 26 storm: letter dated 11 April 1870, ZSL *Proceedings*, 23 June 1870.

line 39 spiders: ZSL *Proceedings*, 23 June 1870.

page 92, lines 2–3 Glossy Ibis: ZSL *Proceedings, 6 December 1870*.

page 93, lines 1–6 Patagonian migrants: ZSL *Proceedings*, 21 March 1871; ibid., 2 May 1871.

line 9 Letter to Professor Baird dated 22 March 1870, Smithsonian Institution archives.

line 14 'Struthio darwini': Struthioniformes (the ostrich family). Hudson was referring to *Rhea darwinii*: Gould, 1837: 'another name for what is now called *Pterocnemia pennata* (Orbigny, 1834). It had to be abandoned when it was realized that *pennata* had priority by three years. The change to *Pterocnemia* reflects a change in classification, separating the Lesser Rhea into a different genus.' This information was made available to the author by Mr I. C. J. Galbraith, Head of the Sub-department of Ornithology, British Museum (Natural History).

line 29 hosts: see *Worthing Tribute*, p. 17, for one of these.

line 31 Stone Age relics: *Idle Days in Patagonia*, ch. 3, pp. 34–9; Roberts, Portrait, pp. 205–6. Hudson's name is not recorded as the original collector of the specimens in the Pitt Rivers Museum, presumably because it was not known to the owner. The Pitt Rivers collection went to Oxford University in 1883. This was the work of General Augustus Henry Lane Fox Pitt Rivers, archaeologist and collector (1827–1900).

page 94, lines 28–9 accident with revolver: *Idle Days in Patagonia*, ch. 2, pp. 21–2, 27–8. No more is heard of this bullet: apparently it was successfully removed by a surgeon at the mission.

line 38 Patagonian parrots: *Idle Days in Patagonia*, ch. 9, pp. 125–6. The Burrowing Parrot is now *Cyanoliseus patagonus*.

page 95, lines 3–11 lesser rhea: 'On the Birds of the Rio Negro of Patagonia', *ZSL Proceedings*, 16 April 1872.

line 16 flamingo: *Idle Days in Patagonia*, ch. 5, pp. 59–61.

line 28 owl: ibid., ch. 12, pp. 175–7.

page 96, lines 1–10 ZSL *Proceedings*, 16 April 1872.

line 19 CMZS: Hudson was made a Fellow of the Society in 1898.

line 23 Swallows: *ZSL Proceedings*, 7 May 1872; 'Further Observations on the Swallows of Buenos Ayres', *ZSL Proceedings*, 19 November 1872.

line 38 Further papers: on the Churinche (*Proceedings*, 5 November 1872); the Vizcacha (ibid., 19 November 1872); the Argentine Pipit (ibid., 2 December 1873); *Molothrus* species of Buenos Aires (ibid., 3 March 1874); the Burrowing Owl (ibid., 19 May 1874); Argentine Herons (ibid., 16 November 1875); the Argentine Spoonbill (ibid., 4 January 1876); Argentine Rails (ibid., 18 January 1876).

page 97, line 2 fare: Royal Mail Lines Ltd, records.

line 4 estate: Estrada, *El Mundo Maravilloso*, p. 21.

line 10 reminiscences: *El Ombu*, Duckworth, 1902, appendix, p. 54.

line 27 Hudson voice: *Far Away and Long Ago*, ch. 19, pp. 263–4.

line 29 Daniel: see note to p. 82, line 32.

line 30 Edwin: Introduction to *Birds of La Plata*, p. xiii, and West, *For a Hudson Biographer*.

line 31 Caroline Louisa and Albert: ibid.

line 32 National College: *Hudson–Cunninghame Graham Letters*, letter of 12 July 1890.

line 35 a hidden quality: *Far Away and Long Ago*, ch. 19, pp. 263–4.

lines 37–8 passed from one to another: *Ebro Diary*, letter from Southampton, dated 8 May 1874.

line 38 nieces' visits (1903 and 1908): letter to Linda Gardiner, 10 August 1903 and research notes by Mr Masao Tsuda, made available to the author by Mr Robert Hamilton.

lines 39–41 for The Twenty-five Ombus today, see note, page 299, lines 28–9.

page 98, lines 5–6	'Of all the people I have ever known . . .': *Far Away and Long Ago*, ch. 24, p. 328; *Men, Books and Birds*, 58.

PART II: 1874–1901

Chapter 8: Coming Home

page 101, lines 1–7	*Afoot in England*, ch. 23, pp. 264–5, 'Following a River'.
line 8	natal city: *Men, Books and Birds*, 91.
line 11	voyage: *Ebro Diary*.
page 102, lines 8–9	Kaka-lani-pandorga-quelanota: Dr Jorge Casares suggests that this was a family expression.
lines 29–31	arrival: Roberts, *Portrait*, pp. 27–8, 258; *A Hind in Richmond Park*, ch. 5, p. 63.
line 33	Pardo: *Hudson–Cunninghame Graham Letters*, letter for 2 August (about) 1895.
line 38	*Ebro* arrival, voyage, freight and cargo: *The Times*, 4 May 1874.
line 39	Winchester: *Hampshire Days*, Longmans Green, 1903, ch. 12, p. 245.
line 42	Burns: Robert Burns, 'To a Mountain Daisy' (1786).
p. 103, line 7	driving into the country: *Ebro Diary*; Roberts, *Portrait*, pp. 258–9; *A Hind in Richmond Park*, ch. 5, p. 62.
line 12	cottage: the Dictator Rosas came to England after his fall from power.
line 21	Tennyson: *Nature in Downland*, ch. 15, pp. 266–7.
line 26	name of Hudson: P. H. Reaney, *The Origin of English Surnames*, Routledge, 1967; C. M. Matthews, *English Surnames*, Weidenfeld and Nicolson, 1966.
line 41ff.	'I put up at a City hotel . . .': *Birds in London*, Longmans Green, 1898, ch. 5, pp. 56–8. Hudson no doubt remembered an account of a rookery in *Evenings at Home* (see note, page 57, line 33).
p. 104, line 32	Charlotte Brontë's first London exploration: Charlotte Brontë, *Villette*, Smith Elder, 1853, ch. 6; Elizabeth Gaskell, *The Life of Charlotte Brontë*, Smith Elder, 1857, vol. II, ch. 2.
line 34	*The Seasons*: Charlotte Brontë quotes Thomson's *Seasons*, 'Autumn', lines 862–5, in the opening pages of *Jane Eyre*.
lines 35–7	Thomson, *Seasons*, 'Summer', lines 1457–61.
page 105, lines 2–3	naturalization: *Men, Books and Birds*, 6 and n.

Notes and References: Chapter 9

lines 4–5	Sclater: Roberts, *Portrait*, pp. 137–8.
line 7	Malmesbury: *Men, Books and Birds*, 45.
line 11	train: Hudson mentions train travel in Argentina only in *Ralph Herne*, though some 800 miles of railway lines had been constructed in the 1860s. The local station on the Buenos Aires Great Southern Railway near The Twenty-five Ombus, formerly called Conchitas station, was renamed Guillermo Enrique Hudson station in 1930. See photograph reproduced in *Worthing Tribute*, p. 65.
lines 18–25	*Afoot in England*, ch. 14, 'The Return of the Native', pp. 173–7.
lines 31–9	*A Traveller in Little Things*, Dent, 1921, 'Apple Blossoms and a Lost Village'.
page 106, line 2	an orchard village: information made available to the author by Miss E. Baker-Clarke.
line 13ff.	River Exe: *Afoot in England*, ch. 23, p. 265, 'Following a River'.
line 28	Stonehenge: ibid., ch. 21, 'Stonehenge', pp. 236–9; *Hudson–Garnett Letters*, 84.
page 107, line 2	Gilbert White's note: White, *Selborne*, Letter XXI.
lines 8–19	*Birds and Man*, Longmans Green, 1901, ch. 15, 'Selborne', 1896.
line 30	Scotland and Ireland: Roberts, *Portrait*, p. 21. Hudson refers to the west of Ireland in *The Land's End*, Hutchinson, 1908.
line 32	the Malonys: Roberts, *Portrait*, p. 258.
line 33	Poland family: information made available to the author by Mr D. H. Aaron, in a letter dated 27 September 1950.
line 36	reader's ticket: British Museum archives.
line 38	Miss Wingrave: *Kelly's Directory*, 1874–7. The 1873 entry gives Mrs Wingrave.
page 108, line 1	his name: ibid., 1878.

Chapter 9: Staying On

page 109, line 1	destiny: Roberts, *Portrait*, p. 59.
line 4	memorial site: Tschiffely, *Don Roberto*, ch. 18, p. 403.
line 9	Robert Gittings, *Young Thomas Hardy*, Heinemann, 1975, ch. 7.
lines 14–15	David Elliston Allen, *The Naturalist in Britain. A Social History*, Allen Lane, 1976, ch. 9.
line 26	indoor naturalist: Roberts, *Portrait*, p. 242.
line 27ff.	visit to John Gould (1804–81): ibid., pp. 29–30.

page 110, line 3   Gould: J. G. Millais, *The Life and Letters of Sir John Everett Millais*, Methuen, 1899, vol. II, pp. 169–70.

line 3ff.   humming-bird collection: *Idle Days in Patagonia*, ch. 12, p. 171. The British Museum (Natural History) acquired an exhibition of mounted humming-birds in glass cases, which Gould prepared and showed at the Zoo in 1851, at the time of the Great Exhibition. About half a dozen of these cases survive, with the birds in reasonable condition, and are stored at South Kensington. Gould made several presentations, chiefly of humming-birds, to the Museum between 1827 and 1872, and his remaining private collection was purchased after his death in 1881. Many of his specimens, mostly in good condition, are in the research collection of humming-birds. This information was made available to the author by Mr I. C. J. Galbraith, Head of the Sub-department of Ornithology. J. G. Millais gives the price of the final sale as over £5,000. A collection of forty-nine illustrated Gould volumes, including his *Family of Humming-birds*, fetched £181, 819 at a New York sale in 1980 (*Daily Telegraph*, 14 April 1980).

line 18   Lear: Lynn Barber, *The Heyday of Natural History*, Cape, 1980, ch. 6, p. 94.

line 38ff.   field-collecting: Robert Swinhoe, for instance, was in the Consular Service in China. Other reports refer to collecting by army officers, a member of the Indian Civil Service, a geologist and a Queensland planter who had caught a live full-grown Australian cassowary, and was anxious to present it to the Society.

page 111, line 10ff.   Royal School of Mines Regulations of Admission, 1874–5 and 1875–6, and Courses: Imperial College, London, archives.

lines 13–14   *The Correspondence of Marx and Engels, 1846–95*, trans. Dona Torr, London, 1934, Letter 59, p. 141.

line 22   little girls: *A Traveller in Little Things*, 'Little Girls I Have Met' and other essays on child friends; see also *Ebro Diary*, 29 April 1874.

line 27   Richard Jefferies: Edward Thomas, *Richard Jefferies*, ch. 8, 9.

line 30   Waters: Roberts, *Portrait*, pp. 28–9.

page 112, line 5   rooks: *Birds in London*, ch. 5.

Notes and References: Chapter 9

line 6   Tower: ibid., ch. 2, pp. 20–1; ch. 8, pp. 101–2.

line 7   wood pigeons: ibid., ch. 6, pp. 65–8, 74; ch. 8; pp. 97–9.

lines 9–11   writing methods: Roberts, *Portrait*, pp. 132, 309.

line 29   Merryweather: Ernest Augustus Merryweather, *Some Notes on the Family of Merryweather*, 1958.

line 32   Merriam family: Roberts, *Portrait*, pp. 20, 230; Charles Henry Pope, *Merriam Genealogy in England and America*, Boston, 1906.

lines 35–6   Alfred Lord Tennyson, *Maud*, Part I, xii. i.

page 113, line 13   Anna Sewell, *Black Beauty*, Tillyer, 1877, Part I, ch. 19.

page 114, line 14   willow wren: *Birds and Man*, ch. 6, p. 102.

lines 17–18   commission: *Birds in London*, ch. 1, p. 6.

line 30   nights: ibid., ch. 7, p. 78.

line 33   Emily's voice: letter to Violet Hunt, dated 4 April 1921. *Worthing Tribute*, p. 117.

line 39   J. H. Wingrave: elder brother? Louise Hanmer Bassett: see note, page 115, line 17.

page 115, line 1   John Hanmer Wingrave is listed in the *Imperial Calendar* as holding the following posts in the Excise Office: Assistant to General Business Accountant, 1834–7; General Accountant for Scotland, 1838; Principal Accountant, 1845–50, when he presumably retired with the grade of Accountant General. A Joseph Wingrave, John Wingrave Junior, F. C. Wingrave and Joseph George Wingrave are also listed. Emily Wingrave's family home was at Eldon Lodge, 3 Eldon Place, Upper Kennington Lane, Lambeth, South London (St Catherine's House, birth certificate, 1839; Kelly's Directory, 1846–8); later at Belvedere House, Ham, near Richmond, Surrey (St Catherine's House, marriage certificate, 1860; P.O. London Suburban Guide, 1861).

line 5   profession: In the 1881 Census return for 11 Leinster Square Hudson is described as 'Writer for periodicals/Journalist' and Emily Hudson as 'Boarding House Keeper'. Three boarders and three servants are listed.

line 9   school: 1871 Census.

line 17   Emily Hudson's age: 1841 Census. The return for Eldon Lodge shows: James [sic] Wingrave, 40, of independent means; Sarah [Mrs John Hanmer Wingrave, née Goatley], 30; John, 13;

Emily, 11; Catherine, 9; Alfred, 7; and an unnamed infant daughter, possibly Louise Hanmer, a witness at the Hudson's wedding. Emily, and their father, were witnesses at her wedding to Alfred Bassett on 12 May 1860 at Petersham, near Richmond, Surrey, when her age was given as 21. A birth certificate for an unnamed daughter, born on 17 October 1839, may be hers; though she would not have been 21 until October 1860. No Wingrave baptisms for the period have been traced in Lambeth.

line 18   late in life: Roberts, *Portrait*, p. 267.

line 19   Emily Hudson: ibid., pp. 41, 55–7, 59–61, 268; *Worthing Tribute*, p. 42, 153.

line 27   it is permissible: *The Purple Land*, ch. 25, p. 304.

line 29   Michael Collie, *George Gissing*, Dawson, 1977, p. 31.

line 41ff.   'It is kindness that counts': letter to Violet Hunt, dated 4 April 1921; *Worthing Tribute*, p. 117.

page 116, line 5   Emily: Roberts, *Portrait*, pp. 55–7.

line 21ff.   description of Hudson: Roberts, *Portrait*, pp. 35–9.

line 26   nose broken: David Garnett, Introduction, *The Purple Land*, Dent, 1951, p. viii.

page 117, lines 5–6   heart trouble: Roberts, *Portrait*, pp. 110–15.

line 7   Roberts: *Portrait*, p. 44; Collie, *Gissing*, p. 26.

lines 19–20   'The Settler's Recompense', *Merry England*, September 1883.

line 23   *Idle Days in Patagonia*, ch. 6.

page 118, line 14   Hackney Marshes: *Birds in London*, ch. 11, pp. 146–53.

lines 16–17   Richmond Park: ibid., ch. 13, pp. 190–3.

line 17   Highgate: ibid., ch. 10, pp. 132–3.

line 19   out of sight: ibid., ch. 13, pp. 190–3.

line 21   sparrows: *Ebro Diary*, letter dated 5 May 1874; *Birds in London*, ch. 1, pp. 6, 8.

lines 29–30   *The London Sparrow, Merry England*, July 1883. Collected Edition, *A Little Boy Lost, Together with the Poems of W. H. Hudson*, Dent, 1923.

page 119, lines 30—1   'In the Wilderness', *Merry England*, June 1884.

line 37   'Gwendoline', ibid., June 1885.

page 120, lines 10–12   giving up verse: *Hudson–Cunninghame Graham Letters*, letter of 5 July 1908.

line 22   'Pelino Viera's Confession', *Cornhill Magazine*, October 1883. Collected Edition, *El Ombu*, etc., Dent, 1923.

line 41 'Tom Rainger', *Home Chimes*, 9 August 1884. Collected Edition *Dead Man's Plack, An Old Thorn and Miscellanea*, Dent, 1923.

page 121, line 11 *Ralph Herne, Youth*, 4 January 1888–14 March 1888. Collected Edition, *El Ombu*, etc., Dent, 1923; see Roberts, *Portrait*, p. 194.

line 24 *Fan: the Story of a Young Girl's Life*, by 'Henry Harford', Chapman and Hall, 1892.

line 31 'the British eye': *Idle Days in Patagonia*, ch. 12, pp. 188–190.

line 33 George Gissing, *The Unclassed*, Chapman and Hall, 1884.

lines 38–9 Hudson and Gissing: Roberts, *Portrait*, pp. 51–2; *Men, Books and Birds*, letter 100.

line 41ff. Gissing's love of the countryside: Collie, *Gissing*, pp. 19, 78. His father, Thomas Waller Gissing, wrote *The Ferns and Fern allies of Wakefield and its neighbourhood*, illustrated by J. E. Sowerby, Wakefield, 1862, and *Materials for a Flora of Wakefield and its neighbourhood*, Huddersfield, 1867.

page 122, lines 4–6 Gissing's London walks: Collie, *Gissing*, pp. 63–4; Hudson's London walks: Roberts, *Portrait*, pp. 36–7.

line 12 Gissing, *Born in Exile*, A. and C. Black, 1892.

line 19 workhouse: Roberts, *Portrait*, p. 52. Gissing wrote to Edward Clodd on 7 November 1899: 'there is a curious blending of respect and contempt in the publishers' mind towards me, and I should like to see which sentiment will prevail ... if the contempt, one must relinquish ambitions ... and so attain a certain tranquillity—even if it be that of the workhouse. I was always envious of workhouse folk; they are the most independent of all.' Quoted by Virginia Woolf, 'The Novels of George Gissing', *The Times Literary Supplement*, 11 January 1912; see *Gissing: the Critical Heritage*, ed. Pierre Coustillas and Colin Partridge, Routledge, 1972, p. 529.

line 21 hunger: Gissing, *The Whirlpool*, Lawrence and Bullen, 1897, Part III, ch. 1.

line 26 boarding-house failure: Roberts, *Portrait*, p. 53.

line 29 Tower House: the 1881 Census shows three occupants—Thomas E. Whitcombe (police sergeant), his wife and his mother-in-law.

page 123, lines 9–10 'It was Christmas Day in the workhouse':

George R. Sims, *Ballads and Poems*, Fuller, 1883.

line 14   oakum-picking: two of Hudson's friends, R. B. Cunninghame Graham and Wilfrid Scawen Blunt, became enthusiastic oakum-pickers while serving prison sentences for political activities. See Tschiffely, *Don Roberto*, pp. 224ff.; Elizabeth Longford, *A Pilgrimage of Passion. The Life of Wilfrid Scawen Blunt*, Weidenfeld and Nicolson, 1979, ch. 13, p. 256.

line 17   demonstrations: *The Journal of Beatrix Potter*, trs. Leslie Linder, Warne, 1966, entries for 8–17 February 1886.

lines 21–2   The Charity Organization Society: Charles Lock Mowat, *The Charity Organization Society, 1869–1913*, Methuen, 1961, ch. 6.

line 23   Poor Law: Sidney and Beatrice Webb, *English Poor Law History*, Longmans Green, 1929, Part II, vol. I, ch. 4, p. 379; Michael E. Rose, *The English Poor Law, 1780–1930*, David and Charles, 1971, Part Four, 67; the Chamberlain Circular, 1886, ibid., Part Four, 77A.

line 27   Hudson wrote to the Royal Literary Fund on behalf of Algernon Gissing (4 January 1904) and Paul Fountain (31 March 1909).

line 31   sparrows: *The Naturalist in La Plata*, pp. 83–4.

line 35   Ravenscourt Park: *Birds in London*, pp. 121–2.

page 124, line 3   darkling thrush: Thomas Hardy, 'The Darkling Thrush' (1900).

lines 9–15   *Men, Books and Birds*, 20.

line 16   'The notice which you have been pleased to take of my labours, had it been early, had been kind; but it has been delayed till I am indifferent, and cannot enjoy it; till I am solitary, and cannot impart it; till I am known, and do not want it . . .' Dr Johnson, letter to Lord Chesterfield, 7 February 1755. See Roberts, *Portrait*, p. 128; *Men, Books and Birds*, 130.

lines 33–41   *The Purple Land that England Lost*, Sampson Low, 1885, ch. 3, p. 37.

page 125, lines 6–9   ibid., ch. 17, p. 198.

lines 18–26   ibid., ch. 21, pp. 261–2.

line 34   first novel: Collie, *Gissing*, pp. 50–1; Gittings, *Young Thomas Hardy*, ch. 13; Andrew Birkin, *J. M. Barrie and the Lost Boys*, Constable, 1979, ch. 2.

line 40ff.   *The Times*, 10, 11 November 1925. Law Reports headed 'W. H. Hudson's First Book'. The original publishers, Sampson, Low, Marston and Co., unsuccessfully sought an injunction against J. M. Dent and Co. and Gerald Duckworth and Co. for alleged infringement of copyright in reissuing the book (as *The Purple Land*). Counsel said that there had been 'an agreement for sharing profits', dated June 1885. The firm lost £30 when the book was remaindered in 1890. A copy of this edition was said to be worth £25 at the time of this action (1925).

page 126, lines 25–9   *Athenaeum*, 26 December 1885.

lines 31–5   *Graphic*, 2 January 1886.

line 37   *London Figaro*, 9 January 1886.

line 40   *The Times*, 2 November 1885 (*King Solomon's Mines*): the reviewer comments, 'Mr Haggard has made much the same kind of successful *coup* as Mr Stevenson in his *Treasure Island*.'

page 127, line 2   reader's report: Peter Beresford Ellis, *H. Rider Haggard: A Voice from the Infinite*, Routledge, 1978, ch. 5.

line 4   *Spectator*, 26 November 1904.

line 12   Professor Keane's review: *Men, Books and Birds*, 133.

line 29   Edwin: Hudson's Introduction to *Birds of La Plata*, Dent, 1920.

Chapter 10: Looking Back

p. 129, line 2   beloved Southampton: letter from Hudson to Mrs Phillips, 31 August 1892, Manchester Central Library collection.

line 14   Emily and Tower House: Roberts, *Portrait*, pp. 54, 60; Kelly's Directory, 1874–82. It seems that the house went first to Sarah Wingrave, Emily's widowed mother, who died there (intestate) on 23 May 1873 (death certificate). See note, p. 107, line 38.

line 19   Derek Hudson, *Munby*, p. 322: 4 February 1873.

line 24   Tower House: 1871 Census.

p. 130, line 9   horses: information made available to the author by Miss Ida Weston, lifelong resident of St Luke's Mews.

line 10   plaque: *The Times*, 30 June 1938: 'The plaque, designed by Señor Luis Perlotti, the Argentine sculptor, is the gift of the Society of Hudson's Friends at Quilmes, near Buenos Aires, where Hudson was born, and it depicts the cottage

which he described in *Far Away and Long Ago*.'
The plaque was unveiled by Señor G. Uriburu
of the Argentine Embassy on 29 June.

line 13   description of Tower House: Roberts, *Portrait*,
pp. 54–5, 59–61; *Worthing Tribute*, pp. 97–8;
William Rothenstein, *Men and Memories,
1872–1938*, ed. Mary Lago, Chatto and Windus, 1978 (abridged edn), pp. 138, 144; Violet
Hunt, *The Flurried Years*, Hurst and Blackett,
1926, pp. 272, 283, and *Worthing Tribute*,
p. 109.

line 31   mortgage: Roberts, *Portrait*, pp. 54–5. In
Kelly's Directory Hudson's name is listed at 40
St Luke's Road from 1878–82, followed by that
of a Peter Warburton (1883–5) and Chas. Geo.
Walker (1886–7). It would seem that the house
was let up to the mid-1880s: see note, page 122,
line 29.

line 34   new regime: Roberts, *Portrait*, p. 55.

line 39   attacks: *Hudson–Cunninghame Graham Letters*,
21 April 1890.

p. 131, line 2   trains: *Birds in London*, ch. 6, p. 67.

line 3   noises: *Hudson–Garnett Letters*, 43.

line 8   Emily Hudson and Roberts: Roberts, *Portrait*,
pp. 56–9.

line 36   writing: John Galsworthy, Foreword to *Far
Away and Long Ago*, Everyman edn, 1939, p. x.

line 37   jottings: Roberts, *Portrait*, p. 309.

line 42   Clare's words: John Clare, Essay on Landscape, quoted by Anne and J. W. Tibble,
Introduction, *John Clare, Selected Poems*, Dent,
1965, p. v.

page 132, line 6   *A Crystal Age*, Fisher Unwin, 1887.

line 14   *Academy*, 14 May 1887.

lines 16–17   Hilaire Belloc: at a luncheon in Soho in the
early 1900s, where the company included
Hudson, Garnett, Belloc and Chesterton, 'it
came out by accident that the book which
[Belloc] has read more times than any other
book, and likes best, is *A Crystal Age*. I was
surprised to hear it, and he was amazed to hear
that I had written it.' Letter to Mrs Hubbard,
dated only '18th', Manchester Central Library
collection. Belloc's review, *Morning Post*, 8
October 1906 (2nd edition): see *Men, Books and
Birds*, 37.

line 20   Butler: ibid., 126, Roberts's note.

lines 20–1   Samuel Butler, *Erewhon*, Trubner, 1872.

line 36   motor car: *Hudson–Garnett Letters*, 69; *Afoot in England*, ch. 23, p. 263.

lines 36–7   William Morris, *News from Nowhere*, Reeves and Turner, 1891.

line 40   central theme: *Hudson–Garnett Letters*, Letter 123.

page 133, line 1   Tickner Edwardes, *The Lore of the Honey-bee*, Methuen, 1908, Introduction.

line 19   'The Vicar of Bray': *A Crystal Age*, ch. 9, pp. 99–100.

line 22   antipathies: ibid., ch. 19, p. 228.

lines 27–8   *Argentine Ornithology*, Porter, vol. I, 1888; vol. II, 1889.

line 29   Felix de Azara (1746–1811), *Apuntamientos Para la Historia Natural de los Paxaros del Paraguay y Rio de la Plata* (Notes for the natural history of the birds of Paraguay and the River Plate), 3 vols., Madrid, 1802–5. New edn: *La Obra Ornithologica de Azara. Apuntamientos*, etc. *Commentada y actualizada tor Jose A. Pereyra*, Montevideo, Biblioteca Americana, 1945. 'Don Felix de Azara (was) a Spanish gentleman, an officer of the Real Armada, sent on a special mission for the purpose of establishing the frontiers between the Spanish and Portuguese colonies in South America. He spent twenty years there working at the construction of plans. During the greater part of this time he lived in the midst of the virgin forest, engaged in noting down his observations on the fauna.' Dr Jorge Casares in a paper on Hudson, read at the 7th International Ornithological Congress, Amsterdam, June 1930.

page 134, line 21   C. E. Montague, *A Writer's Notes on his Trade*, Chatto and Windus, 1930, 'Doing without Workmanship'.

lines 24–7   Robert Burns, 'Auld Lang Syne'.

line 34   Royal Society donation: P. L. Sclater, Preface to *Argentine Ornithology*, vol. I.

page 135, line 4   Richard Jefferies, *Amaryllis at the Fair*, Sampson Low, 1887.

line 15   Sussex book: *Nature in Downland*. Jefferies wrote a number of Sussex essays, e.g. 'The Southdown Shepherd', *Nature Near London*, Chatto and Windus, 1883.

lines 21–37   *Afoot in England*, ch. 5, pp. 33–4.

line 42   *Nature*, 18 October 1888.

line 43   *Saturday Review*, 28 April 1888.

page 136, lines 12–21   *Hampshire Days*, ch. 8, p. 160.
       lines 25–6   *The Naturalist in La Plata*, ch. 14, 'Facts and Thoughts about Spiders'.
page 137, lines 15–20   *The Naturalist in La Plata*, ch. 14, p. 191.
       line 26   'Brer Rabbit': *The Naturalist in La Plata*, ch. 4, p. 73.
       line 33   'wrestler frog': *The Naturalist in La Plata*, ch. 4, pp. 76–8. 'Probably a member of the New World frog family Leptodactylidae, possibly of the genus Leptodactylus ... Frogs and toads are often notoriously unselective in their choice of mate and have been found grasping hold of twigs, pieces of stick, fish, etc.' Information made available to the author by Mr B. T. Clarke, Department of Zoology, British Museum (Natural History). A reviewer also pointed this out: *Land and Water*, 30 April 1892.
       line 41   *Idle Days in Patagonia*, Chapman and Hall, 1893.
       line 42   *The Tempest*: Hudson's reading at the British Museum would certainly have included parts of Antonio Pigafetta's *Voyage* relating to Patagonia, possibly one of the travel accounts that influenced the writing of *The Tempest*. See Chatwin, *In Patagonia*, ch. 49. He would also have read *Caliban on Setebos* by Browning, his favourite contemporary poet. See letter to Mrs Emma Hubbard, 29 November 1896, RSPB collection. Setebos was a god of the Patagonian Indians.
page 138, lines 23–4   Herman Melville, *Moby Dick*, London, 1851 (as *The Whale*).
       line 30   Darwin, *Journal*, ch. 21.
       line 41   the peace of God: Chatwin, *In Patagonia*, ch. 6.
       line 42ff.   Charles Montagu Doughty, *Travels in Arabia Deserta*, Cambridge University Press, 1888.
page 139, line 4   D. H. Lawrence and Hudson: John Alcorn, *The Nature Novel* from Hardy to Lawrence, Macmillan, 1977, ch. 3, p. 51; ch. 4, p. 70.
       line 6   Patagonia today: see Paul Theroux, *The Old Patagonian Express*, Hamish Hamilton, 1979.
       line 15   Lydekker: *Adventures among Birds*, Hutchinson, 1913, ch. 4, 'Great Bird Gatherings'. Richard Lydekker (1849–1915) wrote many zoological works and catalogued fossil specimens in the British Museum and other museums. V. Sackville-West had a similar experience, being assured by an Argentine in the 1930s that Hudson's account of watching

rheas from his pony (*Far Away and Long Ago*, ch. 6) could not be true, as the birds would instantly depart on seeing a mounted boy or man. Hudson was writing of their behaviour with a small child in 1849. See *The Listener*, 23 June 1938.

line 30   bird-life 1947: Louis J. Halle, 'Hudson's Pampas Today', *Audubon Magazine*, July–August 1948.

line 34ff.   bird-life today: information made available to the author by Señora Alicia Jurado.

page 140, line 5   crested screamers: *The Naturalist in La Plata*, ch. 17, 'The Crested Screamer', pp. 223–4.

lines 10–13   *Far Away and Long Ago*, ch. 20, p. 278.

Chapter 11: Protecting Birds

page 141, lines 1–2   J. G. Millais, Sir John Everett Millais, vol. II, pp. 169–73.

line 18   a dead bird: *Birds and Man*, ch. 14, p. 223, quoting St George Mivart (1827–1900), author of *Birds, the Elements of Ornithology*, Porter, 1892.

line 21   Gould's collections: J. G. Millais, *Sir John Everett Millais*, vol. II, p. 169.

lines 22–6   Phyllis Barclay-Smith, 'The Trade in Bird Plumage', *The UFAW Courier*, Autumn 1951, quoting descriptions by Alfred Russel Wallace, *The Malay Archipelago*, London, 1869.

page 142, lines 2–3   Dartford warbler: *Birds and Man*, ch. 12.

line 13   collectors: *Birds in a Village*, Chapman and Hall, 1893, 'Exotic Birds for Britain'; *Birds and Man*, ch. 12, 'The Dartford Warbler. How to Save Our Rare Birds'; John Sheail, *Nature in Trust*, The History of Nature Conservation in Britain, Blackie, 1976, ch. 1, pp. 5–11, ch. 2, pp. 22–36.

line 25   Dartford warbler: *Birds and Man*, ch. 12: see D. A. Orton, 'Dartford Warblers and the Dunkirk Spirit', *The Field*, 16 July 1980, for recent population figures.

line 30   orioles: *Lost British Birds*, SPB, 1894.

line 32   hobby, etc.: *Hampshire Days*, ch. 2, p. 31.

line 39   seashores: Gosse, *Father and Son*, ch. 6.

line 41   plants: Emsworth and district natural history society reports in the 1880s; Sheail, *Nature in Trust*, pp. 5–6.

line 41   sportsmen: Osgood Mackenzie, *A Hundred Years in the Highlands*, 1842–1922, Arnold, 1921; Bles, 1956; Sheail, *Nature in Trust*, pp. 3–4.

page 143, line 4   gamekeepers: The Barn Owl, SPB, 1895, Collected Edition, *Miscellanea*.

lines 6–7   seabird shooting: Sheail, *Nature in Trust*, pp. 4–5; *Letter to Clergymen*, SPB, 1895; *Birds in a Village*, Appendix.

line 14   Thames shooting: *Birds in London*, ch. 8, p. 105.

lines 15–16   bush-beating: Flora Thompson, *Lark Rise to Candleford*, Oxford, 1939–43, ch. 9; A. L. Rowse, *A Cornish Childhood*, Cape, 1942, ch. 11.

line 17   teagles: *The Land's End*, ch. 14, pp. 199–201, 205.

line 18   villagers: *Hudson–Garnett Letters*, 54.

line 20   nightingales: *Nature in Downland*, ch. 15, pp. 267–8.

line 22   parks: *Birds in London*, ch. 10, pp. 126–7; ch. 14, p. 202.

line 24   rooks: ibid., ch. 5, pp. 56–61.

line 29   chaffinch fanciers: ibid., ch. 11, pp. 143–5.

line 35   bird-catchers: Jefferies, *Nature Near London*, 'Flocks of Birds', and *The Gamekeeper at Home*, Smith Elder, 1878, ch. 7.

page 144, line 1   hawks: *The Gamekeeper at Home*, ch. 2.

line 3   white owl: *Nature in Downland*, ch. 14. pp. 255–8.

line 7   excuses: Flora Thompson, *Lark Rise*, ch. 9; Hughes, *Tom Brown's Schooldays*, Part II, ch. 4; Report of the Second Annual Meeting of the SPB, 22 February 1894.

line 12ff.   White, *Selborne*, Letter LXXXV.

line 19   glass cases: Birds and Man, ch. 14.

line 20   The Barn Owl, SPB.

line 26   Sheail, *Nature in Trust*, pp. 9–10.

line 28   Maria Edgeworth, 'The Rabbit', *Rosamond*, Routledge, 1821.

line 33   John Clare, 'The Robin' (1809).

line 39   wildlife sanctuary: Selous, Introduction, Waterton's *Wanderings in South America*, 1925, p. xxi.

line 42   ornithologists: Elliston Allen, *The Naturalist in Britain*, ch. 5.

page 145, line 2   Anna Sewell's aunt: Anne Wright. Her lectures, to boys in a reformatory, were published as *What Is a Bird?*, Jarrold, 1857. See Susan Chitty, *The Woman Who wrote Black Beauty*, Hodder and Stoughton, 1971, p. 79.

line 5ff.   *Dearest Mama: Letters Between Queen Victoria and the Crown Princess of Prussia, 1861–1864*, ed.

Roger Fulford, Evans, 1968: letter dated 8 August 1863.

line 16 grebes: Richard Perry, *Wildlife in Britain and Ireland*, Croom Helm, 1978, p. 184.

line 17 goldfinches: Eleanor Vere C. Boyle, letter to *The Times*, 25 December 1885.

line 17 robins: SPB 6th Annual Report, 1896.

lines 21–2 Newton's speech: Sheail, Nature in Trust, p. 5.

line 28 sequel: SPB 3rd Annual Report, 1892/3, p. 9.

line 39 *Osprey; or Egrets and Aigrettes*, SPB, 1891. Collected Edition, *Miscellanea*.

page 146, line 25 F. O. Morris; *The Times*, 18 December 1885. The Rev. Francis Orpen Morris (1810–93) was an anti-vivisectionist, a bird protectionist and a prolific author, his works including *British Birds*, 6 vols, London, 1851–7. Obituary, *Land and Water*, 18 February 1893.

line 30 'Alas!': letter from Eleanor Vere C. Boyle, *The Times*, 25 December 1885.

line 38 Mrs Eliza Phillips (1823–1916): obituary, *Bird Notes and News*, 7, 1916.

lines 40–1 Fur, Fin and Feather: 'Fin' was presumably included in protest against the display of anglers' trophies in glass cases.

page 147, line 5 Hannah Poland (Mrs Lemel), d. 1942: obituary, *Bird Notes and News*, 20, 1942. Hudson in an article 'Our Wild Birds' in *The Speaker*, 27 February 1904, writes that the SPB in its early days was 'conducted by a brave young girl'.

line 14 Catherine Victoria Hall, d. 1924: obituary, *Bird Notes and News*, 11, 1924/5.

line 17 Winifred, Duchess of Portland, DBE, d. 1954: obituary, *ibid.*, 26, 1954.

page 147, line 23 Croydon: Agnes Maud Davies, *A Book with Seven Seals, A Victorian Childhood*, Cayme Press, 1928, Chatto and Windus, 1974, ch. 13.

line 24 nightingale and cuckoo: *Croydon Chronicle*, 11 May 1889.

line 26 Mrs Frank E. Lemon, 'Recollections of Hudson', *Worthing Tribute*, pp. 151–4.

line 35 professional gull-hunter: SPB 1st Annual Report, October 1891, quoting *The Times*, 5 September 1891.

line 38 trade propaganda: SPB 6th Annual Report, 1896.

page 148, line 1ff. *Osprey* pamphlet.

line 18	*Punch*, 14 May 1892 (cartoon by Linley Sambourne).
line 22ff.	*The Times*, 17 October 1893, reprinted as SPB pamphlet 'Feathered Women', 1893 (Appendix 2).
line 41	painted sparrows: SPB 4th Annual Report, 1894.
page 149, line 9	Macedonian cry: *Letter to Clergymen: the Trade in Birds' Feathers*, Letter from Hudson to *The Times*, 25 December 1895, reprinted as SPB pamphlet, 1895. Collected Edition, *Miscellanea*.
line 10ff.	Hudson's comment: ibid.
line 13	struggle: *Bird Notes and News*, 19, 1941; 20, 1943.
line 19	The Importation of Plumage Act 1921 came into force in April 1922.
line 23	feather boa: This did, however, reappear with evening dresses.
line 25	The original Pip, Squeak and Wilfred cartoons (writers B. J. Lamb, Don Freeman; artist A. B. Payne) appeared in the *Daily Mirror*, 1919 to 1940.
line 28	Phyllis Barclay-Smith, 'The Trade in Bird Plumage', *UFAW Courier*, Autumn 1951.
line 36	imagination: Roberts, *Portrait*, p. 86.
line 38	divorce from nature: G. M. Trevelyan, *English Social History*, Longmans Green, 1944, ch, 18, p. 579.
page 150, line 3ff.	*Birds and Man*, ch. 12, pp. 192.
line 22	*Enquire Within Upon Everything*, Madgwick Houlston, par. 1943 (1909 edn), 'Care of Skylarks'.
line 25	libel: *Birds and Man*, ch. 1, p. 5.
line 26	kingfishers: ibid., p. 11.
line 27	peregrines, etc.: ibid., ch. 14, pp. 222–3.
line 28	the phrase 'murderous millinery' was coined by Henry S. Salt: SPB 2nd Annual Report, 1892.
line 28	collections: a typical nineteenth-century collection may be seen in Wells Museum, Somerset.
line 29	collectors' heirs: *Birds and Man*, ch. 12, pp. 197–8.
line 40	hotel-keepers: *Birds in a Village*, Chapman and Hall, 1893, Appendix.
line 43	rural policeman: *Bird Notes and News*, 8, 1904.
page 151, line 3	British-killed: Sheail, *Nature in Trust*, p. 27.
line 6	postman: *Bird Notes and News*, 11, 1905.
line 10	larks case, brought by the RSPCA: ibid., June

1908. On appeal, the Lord Chief Justice said the magistrate ought to have taken the case further.

line 14	men of standing: *Birds and Man*, ch. 12, p. 202.
line 16	liberty of the subject: ibid., p. 203.
line 18	linnet-catchers: *Birds in a Village*, pp. 67–71.
line 42	pole-traps: *The Barn Owl*, SPB.

Chapter 12: Coming Through

page 153, line 2	*Nature*, 14 April 1892.
line 11	*Natural Science*, April 1892.
line 13ff.	*Daily Chronicle*, 26 March 1892; *Land and Water*, 30 April 1892; *National Observer*, 14 May 1892; *Athenaeum*, 11 June 1892; *Nineteenth Century*, May 1893.
line 15	*Quarterly Review*, October 1892.
line 17	*Morning Post* (undated cutting in Hudson's press-cutting book, RSPB collection).
line 18	*Saturday Review*, 2 April 1892.
line 25	Mr Listless: Thomas Love Peacock, *Nightmare Abbey*, Hookham and others, 1818.
page 154, line 4	reviewer: *The Spectator*, 5 August 1893.
line 9	Dr Johnson, letter to Boswell, 10 April 1778.
line 25ff.	G. M. Trevelyan, *Grey of Fallodon, The Life of Sir Edward Grey, afterwards Viscount Grey of Fallodon*, Longmans Green, 1937, pp. 56–8.
line 33	Richard Burdon Haldane (1856–1928), later 1st Viscount Haldane.
line 40	Grey's blindness: *Men, Books and Birds*, 107.
page 155, line 3	Hudson's obituary of Dorothy Grey: *The Speaker*, 3 March 1906.
line 5	Robert Bontine Cunninghame Grahame (1852–1936).
line 14	Bloody Sunday: Tschiffely, *Don Roberto*, pp. 214–30.
line 21	life in South America: ibid., chs. 3–6.
line 25	'A Naturalist on the Pampas', *Nineteenth Century*, February 1890.
line 26	*Hudson–Cunninghame Graham Letters*: first letter, dated 10 March 1890.
line 34	Indians: Tschiffely, *Don Roberto*, pp. 243–54.
line 34	albatrosses: *Hudson–Cunninghame Graham Letters*, 31 December 1900.
line 36	horse-brand: *Hudson–Cunninghame Graham Letters*, 21 April 1890; see Tschiffely, *Don Roberto*, p. 47.
page 156, line 2	*The Purple Land*: *Hudson–Cunninghame Graham Letters*, 15 April 1890.

line 9   romance: Roberts, *Portrait*, pp. 98–9.

line 12   Pampa: Tschiffely, *Don Roberto*, pp. 180–1.

line 16   boyhood favourite: *Hudson–Cunninghame Graham Letters*, 29 July 1907 or 1908.

line 18   ibid., Richard Curle, p. 11.

line 19   Tschiffely, *Don Roberto*, p. 351.

lines 22–6   See Margaret Brooke, Ranee of Sarawak, *Good Morning and Good Night* [reminiscences], Constable, 1934, pp. 279–80.

line 32   Blunt in Buenos Aires: Elizabeth Longford, *A Pilgrimage of Passion*, ch. 3.

line 36   Bohemians: *Hudson–Cunninghame Graham Letters*, 1 January 1904.

line 38   Roberts, *Portrait*, p. 63.

page 157, line 6   *The Earth Mother*, Downey, 1896; *Hudson–Cunninghame Graham Letters*, 29 March 1896.

line 17   Shoreham: Roberts, *Portrait*, pp. 63–9, 293.

line 40   *Naturalist* reprinted: Payne, *Bibliography*, p. 34.

page 158, lines 12–16   Cuckoos and nightingales still frequent the Thames Valley, though apparently fewer than in Hudson's day. A 1980 Census reported 104 singing nightingales in Berkshire and 72 in Buckinghamshire. Information supplied to the author by Mr Ian Dawson, RSPB Librarian, and Mr P. Standley, County Bird Recorder for Berkshire.

line 27ff.   *Birds in Town and Village*, p. 19.

line 36   *National Observer*, 5 August 1893. In a letter to Mrs Hubbard, 5 August 1900, RSPB collection, Hudson refers to the former editor, W. E. Henley, as 'a savage slashing critic'.

page 159, line 10   Newton: *Men, Books and Birds*, 166.

line 15   *Birds in a Village* review, *The Graphic*, 5 August 1893.

line 18   *Nature*, 31 August 1893.

line 23   ibid., 23 March 1893.

line 26   ibid., 30 August 1900.

line 29   *Saturday Review*, 23 September 1893.

line 39   press-cutting book: RSPB collection.

line 41   *Academy*, 26 August 1893.

page 160, line 4   commissioned: '*British Birds* written to order and no rights retained', entry in list of 'Books produced', Hudson's notebook, 1900, RSPB collection. Hudson's researches in 1894 took him to Surrey in April, to hear blackcaps and whitethroats, and in July to Norfolk, Flamborough and the Farne Islands. Letters to Mrs

Hubbard, 18 April 1894 and 13 July 1894, Manchester Central Library collection. In August he visited Ireland. See note, page 164, line 9.

line 36   golden Christian wrennie: *The Land's End*, ch. 8, p. 90.

page 161, line 16   payments: Longmans archives, Reading University.

line 18   R. B. Lodge: Elliston Allen, *The Naturalist in Britain*, ch. 12.

line 26ff.   Hudson's photographs: *Hudson–Cunninghame Graham Letters*, 25 May 1901(?); *Hudson–Garnett Letters*, 21; *Men, Books and Birds*, 12, note.

line 34   reviewer quoted (on jays): *Birds and Man*, ch. 4, pp. 79–81.

line 39   George Montagu, in his *Ornithological Dictionary*, J. White, 1802, says that jays are 'never gregarious'.

page 162, line 1   *Nature*, 21 May 1896.

line 1   *Popular Science*, May 1896.

line 6ff.   letter to the author from Mr Colin Watson.

line 13   spring 1897: *Men, Books and Birds*, 1.

line 41   sprats: *Birds in London*, ch. 8, p. 107. Letter from Hudson to the *Observer*, 16 January 1921.

page 163, line 30   *Nature*, 23 June 1898.

line 34   payments: Hudson's notebook, RSPB collection; Longmans archives, Reading University.

line 40   £100 a year: *Hudson–Cunninghame Graham Letters*, 29 July (about) 1894.

line 42   lodging at £1 a week: letter to Emily Hudson, 22 April 1903, Manchester Central Library collection.

page 164, line 3   Dartford warbler: *British Birds*; *Birds and Man*, ch. 12.

line 6   invitation to Dublin: letter from Robert S. Ball, Observatory, Co. Dublin, 30 April 1892, RSPB collection.

line 9   Co. Wicklow visit: *Birds and Man*, ch. 2, pp. 47–9; letter to *The Times* from Linda Gardiner. 11 August 1938.

line 10   missel-thrushes: *British Birds*.

line 13   spring travels: letter to Mrs Emma Hubbard, 18 May 1895, RSPB collection. Mrs Hubbard (1828–1905) was one of Hudson's earliest friends in England, a professional indexer of scientific works and a talented artist. See Roberts, *Portrait*, pp. 51, 278 and *Men, Books and Birds*, 24; obituary, *The Times*, 6 June 1905.

line 19   migrants: *Birds and Man*, ch. 5. The wooded hill where Hudson heard the migrants is now National Trust property.

line 20   woodpeckers: ibid., ch. 3, pp. 52–3.

line 23   Thames valley walks; Stratford, Winchcombe, Tewkesbury visits: letter to Mrs Hubbard, 24 October 1895, RSPB collection.

line 27   owls: *Birds and Man*, ch. 9.

line 29   Savernake Forest: Letter to Mrs Hubbard, 12 April 1896, RSPB collection; *Birds and Man*, ch. 4.

line 33   Selborne: ibid., ch. 15.

line 33   Alice Holt, Wolmer Forest: letter to Mrs Hubbard, 25 June 1896, RSPB collection.

line 34   Cookham Dean: Roberts, *Portrait*, p. 242; *Men, Books and Birds*, 2, note.

line 36   Beaulieu: *Hudson–Cunninghame   Graham Letters*, 17 June 1897.

line 38   Norfolk: letter to Mrs Hubbard, 6 August 1897, RSPB collection.

page 165, line 1   home: *Afoot in England*, ch. 6, p. 68; *Birds and Man*, ch. 9, pp. 145–6; *Afoot in England*, ch. 5, p. 54; *Hudson–Garnett Letters*, 43.

line 9   first visit to Wells: *Afoot in England*, Introduction, pp. 5–8.

line 10   bells of St Cuthbert's, Wells: Roberts, *Portrait*, pp. 236–8.

line 17   second visit to Wells: *Afoot in England*, ch. 13, pp. 165–9.

line 22ff.   Dorothy Sayers, *The Nine Tailors*, Gollancz, 1934: 'Through the brazen crash and clatter there went one high note ... that was like a sword in the brain ... his failing wits urged him, "I must get out ..."' Janet Hitchman in *Such a Strange Lady, An Introduction to Dorothy L. Sayers*, New English Library, 1975, says that Miss Sayers did not go into a bell-chamber during a peal until two years after the book was published (ch. 7), and that her plots were often suggested by items she had read (ch. 8).

line 27   'scared': Roberts, *Portrait*, pp. 68–9.

line 30   bathes: *Men, Books and Birds*, 35.

line 31   walks: ibid., 16.

line 33   nights on the roof: *Birds in London*, ch. 8, p. 96.

line 37   companion: *Afoot in England*, Introduction, p. 8; ch. 3, p. 25; Roberts, *Portrait*, p. 157; *Worthing Tribute*, p. 117.

line 40ff.	April 1900: *Men, Books and Birds*, 5; letter from Hudson to Mrs Hubbard, dated 'Good Friday', RSPB collection.
page 166, line 3ff.	Easter 1901: *Afoot in England*, ch. 6; letter from Hudson to Mrs Hubbard, dated 7 April 1901; Dennis Shrubsall, *Hampshire: The County Magazine*, Jan. 1980, 'Round and about Silchester with W. H. Hudson.'
line 14ff.	church: *Afoot in England*, Introduction, pp. 9–11; letter from Hudson to Mrs Phillips, dated 26 March 1894, RSPB collection, written from 'The Olde School, Ockley', describing their discovery of Oakwood church and the story of its origin; Rev. O. Stanway, *The Story of Okewood Church*, 1940. It is still in a wood, approached by ancient bridle-paths.
line 19	cottage quarters: *Afoot in England*, ch. 3, p. 26.
line 23	Emily: ibid., pp. 25–6; Roberts, *Portrait*, p. 56.
line 30	hotels: ibid., pp. 77–8.
line 37	Cookham Dean: *Men, Books and Birds*, 2, note.
page 167, line 1	Edward Thomas, *Light and Twilight*, Duckworth, 1911, 'Hawthornden'.
line 6	badgers: *Birds in Town and Village*, Dent, 1919, pp. 8–9.
line 12	curtsey: *A Shepherd's Life*, ch. 4, pp. 57–62.
line 17	spare room: *Afoot in England*, ch. 3, pp. 27–30.
line 24	elemental pleasures: ibid., ch. 5, pp. 46–7.
line 28ff.	ibid., ch. 10, pp. 124–6.
line 40	cottager: *Afoot in England*, ch. 22, pp. 251–4.
page 168, line 6	Selborne native: *Hampshire Days*, ch. 10, pp. 205–8.
line 13	Ford, *Mightier than the Sword*, Allen and Unwin, 1938, extract reprinted in *Memories and Impressions of Ford Madox Ford*, ed. Michael Killigrew, Bodley Head, 1971, Penguin, 1979, pp. 267–8. Ford probably saw Hudson in a carter's kitchen, not a shepherd's: *Hudson–Garnett Letters*, 25; *A Shepherd's Life*, ch. 23, p. 295.
line 19	*Hudson–Cunninghame Graham Letters*, 16 March (1897).
lines 22–3	2 Corinthians 6:14; Aesop, 'The Raven and the Swan', etc.
line 26	Mrs Bontine: Jean Cunninghame Graham (Lady Polwarth), lecture on R. B. Cunninghame Graham to the Anglo-Argentine Society, 24 January 1979.

line 30ff.	Coulson Kernahan, 'W. H. Hudson as I Knew Him', *The Nature Lover*, May 1934.
page 169, line 9	*A Conversation with Louise Chandler Moulton.* Reprinted from *The Coming Age, A Magazine with a Mission*, Boston, February 1899.
line 13	Hunt, *The Flurried Years*, p. 29. The writer (1862–1942), daughter of a landscape painter, Alfred William Hunt, remembered this first meeting with Hudson as taking place when he was 'starving in Southwick Crescent'; at that time, however (about 1884), Violet Hunt would have been in her early twenties.
line 21	*Swallow Flights*, 1877; London, 1893.
line 26	*On Liberating Caged Birds*, RSPB, 1914.
line 29ff.	Coulson Kernahan, 'W. H. Hudson as I knew him', *The Nature Lover*, May 1934.
line 42ff.	*Hudson–Cunninghame Graham Letters*, 16 March 1897.
page 170, line 9	Edward Clodd (1840–1930), a friend of Roberts and Hudson, wrote many books for the general reader on scientific subjects, including one on animism.
line 10	Rothenstein's generosity: William Rothenstein, *Men and Memories*, 1978 edn, Introduction by Mary Lago, pp. 18–19; Alice Lady Rothenstein, in an interview with the author in July 1953, recalled that he strongly supported this plan.
line 11	Hudson's pension: G. M. Trevelyan, *Grey of Fallodon*, p. 39n.; *Men, Books and Birds*, 4, note.
line 17	naturalization papers: *Men, Books and Birds*, 6, note.
line 24	date of naturalization: Roberts, *Portrait*, p. 46.
line 26	Civil List pension: House of Commons Accounts and Papers. Civil List Pensions, 1901–2. 9 August 1901.
line 26	sixtieth birthday: Emily alone of his friends would have known he was sixty, from their marriage entry.
line 30	a good ten years: Letter to Mrs Hubbard, 24 October 1895, RSPB collection.

PART III: 1899–1922

Chapter 13: High Summer

page 173, line 10	ring-snake: *Men, Books and Birds*, 55.
line 24	'ur-grass': *Nature in Downland*, ch. 3, p. 47. Crested Hair Grass, *Koeleria cristata*: Rev. F. H. Arnold, *Sussex Flora*, Simpkin Marshall, 1887, p. 127.
page 174, line 4ff.	*Nature in Downland*, ch. 5, p. 69.
line 14	reviewer: *Pall Mall*, 25 June 1900.
line 26	pre-natal suggestion: *Nature in Downland*, ch. 5, pp. 80–2.
line 36	Hudson's notebook, RSPB collection.
line 42	Clyst Hydon parish record, 4 February 1726: baptism, Mary Drewe, daughter of John, woolcomber, and Joan: 'the mother of this child having been put into a fright at ye sight of a man who had only one hand, upon May day last at Cullompton Fair, the child who was born on St Paul's day Jan. 25th had only one hand, its left Arm being wanting from ye Elbow'.
page 175, line 34	Chichester: *Nature in Downland*, ch. 14. The city's population in January 1981 was 22,250, with thirty-two churches and chapels and forty-seven public houses.
page 176, line 5	owl: ibid., ch. 14, pp. 255–8; letters to Mrs Phillips, 22 and 27 January 1900, RSPB collection.
line 12ff.	return visit: letter to Margaret Ranee of Sarawak, 25 September 1917(?), Humanities Research Center, the University of Texas at Austin.
line 25ff.	*Nature in Downland*, ch. 5, pp. 86–7.
page 177, line 5ff.	ibid., ch. 7, pp. 130–1.
line 19	omission of species: *St James's Gazette*, 20 June 1900; *Nature*, 30 August 1900.
line 22	unless there be: *Good Words*, August 1900.
line 33	Trevelyan, *Grey of Fallodon*, p. 18n.
page 178, line 4	sickles, oxen: *Nature in Downland*, ch. 3, p. 30.
line 5	farmhouse: *The Land's End*, ch. 9, pp. 108–9.
line 11	well: *Hudson–Garnett Letters*, 25.
line 13	speech: *A Shepherd's Life, passim*.
line 16	owls and crickets: *Birds and Man*, ch. 9, pp. 150–2.
line 20	boys: *Nature in Downland*, ch. 15, pp. 261–3; *A Shepherd's Life*, ch. 1, pp. 4–5.
line 25	*Afoot in England*, ch. 24, 'Troston'; letter to Mrs

Phillips, 17 September 1904, RSPB collection.
line 29   Hurdis: *Nature in Downland*, ch. 1, pp. 8–13.
line 31   Gibbon: *Men, Books and Birds*, 5.
line 35   Roydon House: letter to Mrs Hubbard, 31 December 1899 RSPB collection; *Hampshire Days*, ch. 1.
line 41   'Hints to Adder-Seekers', *The Book of a Naturalist*, ch. 2.
page 179, line 5   cuckoo: *Hampshire Days*, ch. 1, pp. 13–23.
line 10   fishing cottage: *Hudson–Cunninghame Graham Letters*, 26 July (1900); *Hudson–Garnett Letters*, 9; *Hampshire Days*, ch. 12–14. Trevelyan, *Grey of Fallodon*, pp. 46–51. The cottage was burned down in February 1923.
line 18   on horseback: *Men, Books and Birds*, 7.
line 19   Cobbett: *Afoot in England*, ch. 9, p. 110.
line 20   bicycling: ibid., pp. 97–8.
line 22   birds: ibid., pp. 98, 119–20.
line 27   bicycle: David Garnett, *Great Friends*, Macmillan, 1979, p. 28.
line 28   hills: e.g., *Men, Books and Birds*, 23.
line 33   stoat, woodpecker, grass snake: *Afoot in England*, ch. 9, pp. 97–8.
page 180, line 19ff.   *Hampshire Days*, ch. 14, pp. 301–2.
page 181, line 2   hornblower: ibid., ch. 10, pp. 217–19.
line 12   effect of *Hampshire Days*: Anthony Rye, *Gilbert White and His Selborne*, Kimber, 1970, p. 194. The mark is now a granite post.
line 17   requests: *Men, Books and Birds*, 17, 20.
line 19   payments: Hudson's notebook, RSPB collection.
line 23   pension: Roberts, *Portrait*, p. 140.
line 26   *Hudson–Cunninghame Graham Letters*, 28 August 1906.
line 31ff.   Rothenstein, *Men and Memories*, 1978 edn, pp. 154–5.
page 182, line 3   out of touch: *Hudson–Cunninghame Graham Letters*, 17 April 1894.
line 6   letters from Mary Ellen (Mrs Denholme): ibid., 21 October 1910, 7 January 1914; research notes by Mr Masao Tsuda, made available to the author by Mr Robert Hamilton. Mr Tsuda records that Mary Ellen's daughters taught in a grammar school at Cordova. One summer her only son was drowned and six of her daughters died of typhus. With her surviving daughter, Laura, she returned to Buenos Aires where she kept a boarding house for American students.

On coming to England, Laura and her husband were met at Southampton by Hudson and stayed for three weeks at Tower House. Hudson 'was always reminiscing of his days in Argentine. . . . Later, Mr Shinya told me, he recalled many things that he was asked at that time (on reading) Hudson's *Far Away and Long Ago.*' Their daughter, Senora Violeta Shinya Hudson, became Director of the Hudson Museum, Buenos Aires. See note to p. 97, line 38, and note on page 299, lines 32–5.

line 10 niece's visit, 1903: Letter to Linda Gardiner, 10 August 1903, RSPB collection. Hudson's brother Daniel had two daughters, Edwin one daughter, and Albert four (West, *For a Hudson Biographer*).

line 18 desert: *Hudson–Cunninghame Graham Letters*, 10 March 1890.

line 19 lodge: ibid., 28 November (about) 1897.

line 21 Wantage: *Hudson–Garnett Letters*, 66.

line 23 Emily: Roberts, *Portrait*, p. 60; letter to Linda Gardiner, undated (apparently spring 1902), RSPB collection.

line 26 Kent, Sussex, Norfolk: Rothenstein, *Men and Memories*, 1978 edn, p. 154; *Hudson–Garnett Letters*, 87; *Afoot in England*, ch. 5.

line 33 Walter de la Mare, letter to the author, 3 June 1955.

line 38 de la Mare's situation: *Letters from Edward Thomas to Gordon Bottomley*, ed. R. George Thomas, Oxford, 1968, 8n.

line 40 Edward Thomas: Mrs Helen Thomas, in notes supplied to the author, 1950.

page 183, line 2 Hudson: *Thomas–Bottomley Letters*, 79.

line 3 'Edward Thomas's Letters to W. H. Hudson', ed. James Guthrie, *London Mercury*, August 1920.

line 14 everlasting worry: letter to Emily Hudson, 18 June 1900, Manchester Central Library collection.

line 17 Colonel Coulson: letter to Linda Gardiner (about November 1905), RSPB collection. This speaker is mentioned in the Report of the SPB 2nd Annual Meeting, 22 February 1894.

line 18 club dinners: 'Edward Thomas's Letters to W. H. Hudson'.

line 21	'Jacob Tonson' (Bennett), *New Age*, 24 November 1910.
line 24	no banquets: but Ford in his *English Review* years, 1908–10, 'enjoyed giving dinner parties for Henry James or Arnold Bennett, Thomas Hardy or W. H. Hudson'. Frank MacShane, *The Life and Work of Ford Madox Ford*, Routledge, 1965, p. 85.
line 29	hawk: letter to the author from Naomi Royde-Smith (Mrs Ernest Milton), 4 May 1953.
line 34ff.	Edward Garnett, Introduction, *Hudson–Garnett Letters*, pp. 1–2.
line 38	Mont Blanc restaurant: Douglas Goldring, *The Last Pre-Raphaelite, A Record of the Life and Writings of Ford Madox Ford*, Macdonald, 1948, p. 132.
page 184, line 4	Ford on Hudson: Douglas Goldring, *South Lodge. Reminiscences of Violet Hunt, Ford Madox Ford and the 'English Review'*, Constable, 1943, ch. 4.
line 6	Conrad, Ford, James: Ford, *Return to Yesterday*, Gollancz, 1931; Liveright, New York, 1972, pp. 26–7.
line 7	painters: *Men, Books and Birds*, 19, 28 et seq.
line 8	Wilsford: ibid., 47.
line 10	earth-worms: *The Book of a Naturalist*, ch. 29, 'Concerning Lawns and Earthworms'.
line 10	Woburn: *Men, Books and Birds*, 11.
line 16	lodgings: Goldring, *The Last Pre-Raphaelite*, pp. 119–24.
line 18	rookery: Ford, *Return to Yesterday*, Liveright 1972 edn, pp. 28, 283–4.
line 20	Ford and Hudson's voice: Roberts, *Portrait*, p. 199.
line 21	Martin visit, a healer: Ford, *Memories and Impressions*, 1979 edn, pp. 267–8.
line 24	a wasted day: *Nature in Downland*, ch. 15, p. 275.
line 26	bird's nesting boys: *Birds in Town and Village*, p. 55; *The Land's End*, ch. 17, p. 261.
line 27	kingfisher: *Hampshire Days*, ch. 14, pp. 295–6.
line 28	hunting instincts: ibid., ch. 1, p. 5.
line 29	child collectors: ibid., ch. 8, p. 155.
line 31	nature study: Elliston Allen, *The Naturalist in Britain*, ch. 10.
line 33	British Museum gentleman: *Hudson–Cunninghame Graham Letters*, 22 July 1902.
line 39	David Garnett, *Great Friends*, pp. 28–9.

page 185, line 5 Hudson–Garnett Letters, 38.

line 10 nightjars: David Garnett, *The Golden Echo,* Chatto and Windus, 1953, p. 67; *Great Friends,* pp. 29–30; Introduction to *The Purple Land,* 1951, p. ix.

line 14ff. ibid., p. viii.

line 26 raincoat: Hunt, *The Flurried Years,* p. 30.

line 31 Rothenstein, *Men and Memories,* 1978 edn, p. 144.

line 33 his interests: Edward Garnett, Introduction, *Hudson–Garnett Letters,* p. 6.

line 35 Galsworthy, *The Man of Property,* Heinemann, 1906, ch. 2.

line 37 Henry James, 'Owen Wingrave', included in *The Private Life* (stories), Osgood and McIlvaine, 1893.

line 39 *Afoot in England,* ch. 23, p. 268. Ford, *Return to Yesterday,* 1972 edn, pp. 222–3, describes his delight on discovering de la Mare's 'Epitaph', one of the poet's first publications, in the *Pall Mall Magazine.*

page 186, line 9 Mrs Moulton: *One Rare Fair Woman: Thomas Hardy's Letters to Florence Henniker, 1893–1922,* ed. Evelyn Hardy and F. B. Pinion, London, 1972, Letter 6, 30 June 1893.

line 13 *Hudson–Cunninghame Graham Letters,* 16 March (1897): Hudson refers to *The Return of the Native* as Hardy's best work.

line 14 *Afoot in England,* ch. 14, 'The Return of the Native'.

line 15 Hardy on Hudson: Vere H. Collins, *Talks with Thomas Hardy at Max Gate, 1920–1922,* Duckworth, 1928, 1978, pp. 69–70.

line 19ff. proposed visit to Hardy: *Men, Books and Birds,* 19; *Hudson–Garnett Letters,* 30.

line 32 ibid., 31.

line 37 Hudson's qualities: Edward Garnett, Introduction, *Hudson–Garnett Letters,* p. 2.

page 187, lines 4–5, 7ff. Hardy, 'Afterwards'; 'To the Moon'.

line 15 value life: Hudson ends *Far Away and Long Ago:* 'in my worst times, when I was compelled to exist shut out from Nature in London for long periods, sick and poor and friendless, I could yet always feel that it was infinitely better to be than not to be.'

line 19 Cornish stones: *The Land's End,* ch. 4, p. 40.

line 20 Beaulieu: *Hampshire Days,* ch. 2, p. 46–52.

line 25 *Afoot in England,* ch. 21, 'Stonehenge'. On 21

	June 1978, seventy years after Hudson's visit, the crowd numbered about 5,000.
line 35	*The Land's End*, Hutchinson, 1908.
page 188, line 17	seal-shooting: ibid., ch. 16, pp. 246–7.
line 19	bird persecution: chs. 14, 15.
line 21	kingfishers: ibid., ch. 12, p. 160.
line 27	*Cornish Telegraph*, 28 May 1908.
line 31ff.	*Men, Books and Birds*, 46, 48.
line 38	Thorne: ibid., 48n.: General Secretary of the National Union of General Workers.
line 41	on no account: Roberts, *Portrait*, p. 155.
page 189, line 2	crabbers: *Men, Books and Birds*, 50.
line 5	articles on *The Land's End*: *The Cornishman*, 11, 18, 25 June, 2, 9 July 1908.
line 12	ban on teagles: Sheail, *Nature in Trust*, pp. 5, 29.
line 14	RSPB: Hudson, 'Our Wild Birds', *The Speaker*, 27 February 1904. Hudson reports that the Society is now issuing its annual report of 52 pages, and counting the subscribing members in thousands, with many distinguished patrons, and is about to become 'Royal'.
line 15	sanctuaries and watchers: *Birds and Man*, ch. 12, pp. 199–200; Sheail, *Nature in Trust*, pp. 28, 44.
line 17	oil, lighthouses: ibid., pp. 15–19; P. J. Conder, 'Protecting Birds at Lighthouses', *Bird Notes and News*, 29, 1960.
line 19ff.	county councillors, goldfinches: *Hudson–Garnett Letters*, 28, 31.
line 26	boys: *Birds in Town and Village*, pp. 14–15, 55–7.
line 29	influence of Hudson on Lawrence: John Alcorn, *The Nature Novel from Hardy to Lawrence*, Macmillan, 1977, p. 70.
line 32ff.	D. H. Lawrence, 'Snake', 1920.
line 36	education campaign: *Bird Notes and News*, 19, 1941; 20, 1943.
line 41	lantern lecture: letter to Emily Hudson from Silchester, 18 December 1901, Manchester Central Library collection. *Hudson–Garnett Letters* 21 (20 November 1902). Earlier he had rushed into the school 'in a passion after seeing boys persecuting birds'. Letter to Mrs Phillips, 4 October 1901, Manchester Central Library collection.
page 190, line 3	Linda Gardiner, 1861–1941, worked for the (R)SPB from 1900 to 1936, for thirty-five years

as secretary, and as editor of *Bird Notes and News* from 1903 to 1940. Her father, W. S. Gardiner, edited the *Darlington and Stockton Times* and the *Hampshire Observer*. Three of her novels in the British Library are *His Heritage*, Kegan Paul, 1888; *The Sound of a Voice*, Hurst and Blackett, and *Mrs Wylde*, Jarrold, both 1897. She also wrote, as Ida Linn Gerard, *Caught and Other Tales* (five romantic stories), *Observer* office, Winchester, 1881. An article, 'How to Run a Band of Hope', *Girl's Own Paper*, 1895, shows humour as well as practical sense. *Sylvia in Flowerland*, Seeley, 1899, is dedicated to the naturalist Sir John Lubbock. Obituaries: *The Times*, 6 March 1941; *Bird Notes and News*, 19, 1941.

line 34   Letters to Linda Gardiner, RSPB collection. Some are undated, including the last quoted; *Hudson–Garnett Letters*, 69 may allude to a meeting in Suffolk.

page 192, line 6   sexual mores: ibid., 123.

line 15   dearest friend: letter from Linda Gardiner to a RSPB correspondent, Miss Berrill, 16 April 1924. She adds that Hudson's death has left a great blank in her life, and that he was a much finer character than Roberts's *Portrait* shows.

Chapter 14: South American Romances

page 193, line 8   publisher's verdict: *Hudson–Garnett Letters*, 1–3. *El Ombu*, with *Story of a Piebald Horse, Nino Diablo, Marta Riquelme*, Duckworth, 1902.

line 11   storm: Appendix to *El Ombu*, p. 54.

line 18   *The Purple Land*, ch. 19, pp. 223–6. Cf. 'The Old Witch of Joyce Country', Monica Cosens, *Tales and Legends of Ireland*, Harrap, 1925.

line 21   *Afoot in England*, ch. 9, 'Rural Rides': *Saturday Review*, 28 December 1901.

page 194 line 6   *Afoot in England*, ch. 2, 'On Going Back'. White, *Selborne*, Letter, XVII, writes of ladies who kept a pet toad; cf. 'On Going Back'.

line 7   Dr M. R. James, *Ghost Stories of an Antiquary*, Arnold, 1904.

line 11   notebook, RSPB collection.

line 12   South American birds: *Birds and Man*, ch. 1, pp. 23–7.

line 16   blue butterflies: *Nature in Downland*, ch. 4, p. 61.

line 19	red butterflies: ibid., ch. 15, pp. 273–4.
line 21	fishing fleet: *The Land's End*, ch. 1, pp. 9–10.
line 23	adders: *Hampshire Days*, ch. 4, p. 81.
line 23	new glass: letter from Hudson to Mrs Hubbard, 5 October 1898, RSPB collection.
line 24	paths: *The Land's End*, ch. 3, pp. 27–8.
line 28	dreams: ibid., ch. 6, pp. 63–6.
page 195, line 1ff.	*El Ombu*, ch. 4, p. 20.
line 10	*Times Literary Supplement*, 25 April 1902.
line 13	Tschiffely, *Don Roberto*, p. 132.
line 22ff.	*Marta Riquelme*, ch. 4, p. 166.
line 40ff.	Edward Garnett, Introduction, *Hudson–Garnett Letters*, p. 1.
page 196, line 9	terms: ibid., 1.
line 12	'tease and banter': David Garnett, Introduction, *The Purple Land*, 1951 edn, p. ix.
page 197, line 34	the one great story: Roberts, *Portrait*, p. 99.
line 39	children of the pampas: ibid., p. 132.
page 198, line 4	collectors: ibid.
line 12	false coral snake: Louis J. Halle, 'On Re-reading *Green Mansions*', *The Land*, Winter 1947–8, reprinted in Knopf's 1959 edition.
line 26	*Saturday Review*, 2 April 1904.
line 26	*The Times Literary Supplement*, 4 March 1904.
line 28	Alcorn, *The Nature Novel from Hardy to Lawrence*.
line 42	Rudyard Kipling, *The Jungle Books*, Macmillan, 1894/5.
line 42	Jefferies, *Amaryllis at the Fair*.
line 42	Melville, *Moby Dick*.
page 199, line 2	vogue: Alcorn, *The Nature Novel*, pp. 65, 117.
line 5ff.	*Daily Chronicle*, 1 March 1904.
line 14	Edward Thomas's reviews: R. G. Thomas, *Letters from Edward Thomas to Gordon Bottomley*, 11n.
line 15	Edward Garnett, signed review, *The Speaker*, 5 March 1904.
line 22	Christopher Sykes, *Evelyn Waugh, A Biography*, Collins, 1975, ch. 5.
line 26	Doris Langley Moore, *E. Nesbit, A Biography*, Benn, 1933, ch. 12; an invitation to E. Nesbit from H. G. Wells, dated 13 August 1905, mentions Clodd and the Garnetts as his guests.
line 27	E. Nesbit, *The Story of the Amulet*, Fisher Unwin, 1906.
line 34	editions of *Green Mansions*: Payne, *Bibliography*, pp. 79–94.
line 36	illustrators: Keith Henderson, Duckworth,

1926 edn, shows Rima as a kind of elfin Wendy; Horacio Butler, Knopf, New York, 1943, shows a stately nymph garlanded with flowers; Edward Arthur Wilson, Limited Editions Club, New York, 1935—perhaps the most successful—a shadowy elemental.

line 42   film review: *The Times*, 15 September 1959: the writer makes it clear that the actress playing Rima, Audrey Hepburn, was not responsible for the disaster.

page 200, line 9   *Saturday Review*, 3 December 1904.

line 12   *Hudson–Garnett Letters*, 38.

line 16   David Garnett, *The Golden Echo*, p. 68; James Barrie, *The Little White Bird*, Hodder and Stoughton, 1902.

line 25   Peter Pan: *J. M. Barrie and the Lost Boys*, ch. 8.

line 26   *Pinkie and the Fairies*: W. Graham Robertson, *Time Was*, Hamish Hamilton, 1931, p. 321.

line 29   David Garnett, *Lady into Fox*, Chatto and Windus, 1922.

line 33   mother: *A Little Boy Lost*, Duckworth, 1905, ch. 11.

line 36   Crispin legend: *Birds of La Plata*, vol. II, pp. 24–6.

line 38ff.   *Hudson–Garnett Letters*, 42.

Chapter 15: A Shepherd's Life

page 202, line 7   Easter 1901: Dennis Shrubsall, 'Round and about Silchester with W. H. Hudson', *Hampshire: The County Magazine*, January 1980.

line 8   October 1901: *Hudson–Garnett Letters*, 1.

page 203, line 9ff.   *A Shepherd's Life*, ch. 25, p. 332.

page 204, line 1ff.   ibid., ch. 8, pp. 92–3.

page 206, line 9ff.   ibid., ch. 18, pp. 228–9.

line 30   politics: Roberts, *Portrait*, pp. 85–6, 124, 284–5.

page 207, line 33   first visit to Martin: letters to Mrs Phillips, 12 and 20 April 1903, RSPB collection.

page 208, line 6   home-coming: *A Shepherd's Life*, ch. 3; *Hudson–Garnett Letters*, 43.

line 10ff.   ibid., 25.

line 16   likeable oddity: letter, *The Times*, 10 December 1965. In 1942 the writer had lived in Harris's Farm, Martin, where Hudson lodged.

line 23ff.   *A Shepherd's Life*, ch. 4, pp. 61–2.

page 209, line 6   artist: *An Old Thorn*, ch. 1, p. 105. The thorn tree, drawn by Gotch for Hudson's story, was cut down some years ago but is now growing

again. Information made available to author by
Mr G. Bernard Berry.

line 9   reviewer: *Morning Post*, 26 September 1910.

line 11   Broad Chalke: Ford, *Return to Yesterday*, 1972
edn, pp. 283–4.

line 15   Joan: *A Shepherd's Life*, first edn, 1910, p. 231.

line 20   photograph: letter to Emily Hudson, 18
December 1901, Manchester Central Library
collection.

line 35   village names: *The Times*, 20 May 1925. The
Prime Minister, Stanley Baldwin, spoke of
Wiltshire village names in his speech at the
unveiling of the Hudson Memorial on 19 May.

page 210, line 1   salad arrangements: 'Elizabeth' von Arnim,
The Solitary Summer, Macmillan, 1899, p. 13.

line 6   marigold scent: *A Shepherd's Life*, ch. 13. pp.
150–1. It is not clear whether Hudson means
the calendula or one of the *Tagetes*, both having
a strong, distinctive scent. Ford, *Memories and
Impressions*, 1979 edn, p. 268, writes that in
Hudson's lodging at Martin 'there were always
orange flowers in an earthenware mug on the
table, the flower that is just a weed in English
gardens . . .' This sounds like the calendula.
Hudson had known English garden flowers on
the pampas, including marigolds: *The Purple
Land*, ch. 17, p. 183.

Chapter 16: The Time Remaining

page 211, line 2   new quality: *Saturday Review*, 22 October 1910.

line 12   Hudson's comment: *Hudson–Garnett Letters*,
73. 'Jacob Tonson' (Bennett), *New Age*, 24
November 1910.

line 18   the great Mr Hudson: letter to Margaret
Brooke, 25 September 1917(?) Humanities
Research Center, University of Texas at
Austin.

line 19   Huddie: Roberts, *Portrait*, p. 202; Hunt, *Worthing Tribute*, p. 102.

line 19   Shaw: S. Winsten, *Days with Bernard Shaw*,
Hutchinson, 1948, p. 44.

line 24ff.   'His peculiar mysterious charm...': Rothenstein, *Men and Memories*, 1978 edn, p. 144.

page 212, line 7ff.   Hunt, *The Flurried Years*, p. 278; *Worthing Tribute*, p. 106.

line 14   Richard Curle, 'W. H. Hudson', *Fortnightly
Review*, 2 October 1922.

line 22   posthumous verdict: Alan Porter, *Spectator
Literary Supplement*, 5 April 1924.

line 25	recluse: Edward Garnett, Introduction, *Hudson–Garnett Letters*, p. 3.
line 29	two young girls: Roberts, *Portrait*, p. 282.
line 33	'Who . . .': ibid., p. 37.
line 34	Worthing: *Men, Books and Birds*, 108.
page 213, line 1ff.	*Adventures among Birds*, ch. 1, p. 3.
line 10	le Gallienne: letter from Hudson to Mrs Phillips, 15 August 1895, Manchester Central Library collection. John Buchan's father, the Rev. John Buchan, took a rather similar view: Anna Buchan (O. Douglas), *Unforgettable, Unforgotten*, Hodder and Stoughton, 1945, pp. 83–4.
line 13	*Sons and Lovers: Hudson–Garnett Letters*, 90.
line 16	Chaucer, Smollett: ibid., 116.
line 19	Masefield: *Hudson–Cunninghame Graham Letters*, 5 August 1920.
line 22ff.	*Hudson–Garnett Letters*, 94.
line 37	Doughty: ibid., Introduction, pp. 8–9.
line 42	opposition: ibid., Introduction, pp. 5–6.
page 214, line 3ff.	H. J. Massingham, *Untrodden Ways*, Unwin, 1923, pp. 12–13.
line 12	humour: Edward Garnett, Introduction, *Hudson–Garnett Letters*, p. 6.
line 14	women: ibid., p. 3.
line 17ff.	*Letters of Virginia Woolf*, vol. II, ed. Nigel Nicolson and Joanne Trautmann, Hogarth Press, 1976, p. 549.
line 22	Margaret, Ranee of Sarawak: Sylvia Brooke, *Queen of the Head Hunters*, Sidgwick and Jackson, 1970, pp. 27–8.
line 30	Ranee's kindness: Dorothy Whipple, *Random Commentary*, Michael Joseph, 1966, pp. 46–7.
line 31	Oscar Wilde's wife: Vyvyan Holland, *Son of Oscar Wilde*, Hart-Davis, 1954, chs. 2, 4.
line 32	Ranee's marriage: Sylvia Brooke, *Queen of the Head Hunters*, p. 28.
line 36	met Hudson: letter from Hudson to Mrs Phillips, 23 June 1904, RSPB collection.
line 38	macaw: Sylvia Brooke, *Queen of the Head Hunters*, p. 27; Margaret Brooke, 'The Emperor of the Parrots', *Impromptus*, Arnold, 1923.
line 41	Letters from Hudson to Margaret Brooke, the Humanities Research Center, University of Texas at Austin.
page 215, line 6	spiritually-minded: Charles Hall, 'My Acquaintance with Hudson', *Worthing Tribute*, p. 77.

line 8	character of God: letter to Margaret, Ranee of Sarawak, 3 May (1917).
line 14	Violet Hunt: Douglas Goldring, *South Lodge*, ch. 4.
line 24ff.	'I am sorry you are ill . . .': letter from Hudson to Violet Hunt, *Worthing Tribute*, p. 117.
line 29	Alice Rothenstein: John Rothenstein, *Summer's Lease*, Hamish Hamilton, 1965, ch. 1; portrait by Walter Knewstub; William Rothenstein, *Men and Memories*, 1978 edn, illustrations 4, 7.
line 34	Emily Hudson's hair: Mrs Frank E. Lemon, 'Recollections of Hudson', *Worthing Tribute*, p. 153.
line 41ff.	'More than once . . .' Roberts, *Portrait*, p. 268.
page 216, line 3	Ravenscourt Park: *Birds in London*, ch. 9, pp. 121–2; Roberts, *Portrait*, p. 53.
line 4	cocoa-nibs: *Hudson–Garnett Letters*, 33.
line 12	Emily's qualities: Roberts, *Portrait*, p. 268.
line 14	furniture: Violet Hunt, 'Memories of Hudson', *Worthing Tribute*, pp. 103, 109. Roberts, *Portrait*, p. 83.
line 15	Wednesday tea-parties: ibid.
line 17	information made available to the author by Alice, Lady Rothenstein.
line 22	Emily Hudson: David Garnett, Introduction, *The Purple Land*, 1951 edn, p. vii; *Great Friends*, p. 31.
line 32	illness: Edward Garnett, Introduction, *Hudson–Garnett Letters*, p. 9, and Letters 78–81, 86.
line 41	wild geese: *Adventures Among Birds*, Hutchinson, 1913, ch. 26, 27.
page 217, line 1	Norfolk visit: *Men, Books and Birds*, 56.
line 9	illnesses: *Hudson–Garnett Letters*, 84, 85.
line 11	Seaford visit: ibid., 87, 88.
line 17	Furze Platt: ibid., 89, and *Men, Books and Birds*, 58.
line 21	*A Traveller in Little Things*, Dent, 1921, 'The Old Man's Delusion'.
line 27	Pembrokeshire: *Hudson–Garnett Letters*, 89.
line 32	'get rid of all anxiety': *Hudson–Garnett Letters*, 91.
line 36	Worthing: ibid., 100–2.
line 37	plan for Emily: *Men, Books and Birds*, 61.
page 218, line 2	Hudson at Grey Friars: *Hudson–Garnett Letters*, 103. Alan Porter, *Spectator Literary Supplement*, 5 April 1924, refers to 'his treatment of his wife, who worked for him devotedly and whom he neglected without afterthought'.

line 8   Emily's fear: anon, 'Hudson at Worthing', *Worthing Tribute*, p. 135.

line 12   illness at Worthing: *Men, Books and Birds*, 64, 65; *Hudson–Garnett Letters*, 104.

line 14   Emily's health: *Men, Books and Birds*, 65–7, 69.

line 16   knitting: ibid., 65, 69.

line 18   recruits: *Men, Books and Birds*, 66.

line 19   'I hope to stay . . .': *Hudson–Garnett Letters*, 90, 105.

line 27ff. David Garnett, letter to *The Times*, 1 June 1956.

line 38   Edward Thomas: *Men, Books and Birds*, 88; *Hudson–Garnett Letters*, 120.

line 39   letter to Margaret, Ranee of Sarawak, April 1917, Humanities Research Center, University of Texas at Austin.

page 219, line 3 Rupert Brooke, *Men, Books and Birds*, 98.

line 6   'he turned . . .': Edward Garnett, Introduction, *Hudson–Garnett Letters*, p. 9.

line 8   Grey Friars: *Men, Books and Birds*, 67, 68.

line 9   pinewoods: *The Book of a Naturalist*, ch. 1. 'Life in a Pine Wood'.

line 10   *A Traveller in Little Things*, ch. 17–23.

line 18   little girls: *Far Away and Long Ago*, ch. 9, 10; *The Purple Land*, ch. 14.

line 19   Honorina: *Ebro Diary*, 29 April 1874.

line 21   Maude: letter to Mrs Hubbard, 5 December 1902, RSPB collection.

line 23   cameras: *Hudson–Cunninghame Graham Letters*, 25 May 1901(?).

line 26   fourteen-year-old girl: *A Hind in Richmond Park*, ch. 4, pp. 42–5.

line 41   *Traveller*, ch. 15, 'The Vanishing Curtsey'.

page 220, line 8 Frank Swinnerton, *Sunday Telegraph*, 26 August 1979.

line 10   biographical notes: *Hudson–Garnett Letters*, 28.

line 11   Hudson on Freud: Roberts, *Portrait*, p. 212.

line 16   'the curiosity': *Hudson–Garnett Letters*, Introduction, p. 7.

line 26   *Far Away and Long Ago*, ch. 1, pp. 2–5.

line 30   illness: *Hudson–Garnett Letters*, 107.

line 32   Hunt, *The Flurried Years*, p. 279; *Worthing Tribute*, p. 107.

line 33   Sergei Aksakoff, *Years of Childhood*, trans. J. D. Duff, Arnold, 1916. (Edward Garnett may have sent Hudson an early review copy.)

page 221, line 10 Worthing visits: *Men, Books and Birds*, 77.

line 11   'How I envy you . . .': *Hudson–Cunninghame Graham Letters*, 2 November 1915.

line 14   travel plans: *Men, Books and Birds*, 77.

line 17   heart trouble: ibid., 76, 77; *Hudson–Garnett Letters*, 111, 112.

line 24   Zeppelins: *Men, Books and Birds*, 78; Roberts, *Portrait*, p. 127; letter to Margaret, Ranee of Sarawak (undated), Humanities Research Center, University of Texas at Austin.

line 26   Penzance: ibid.

line 29   later raids: ibid., letters of 25 September and 3(?) October (1917); Roberts, *Portrait*, p. 126.

line 38   nightingale: *Men, Books and Birds*, 97.

line 39   feeding birds: ibid., 72.

line 42   novice: ibid., 82, and Roberts, *Portrait*, pp. 160–1.

page 222, line 3   chained owl: ibid., pp. 109–10.

line 7   success in America: *Letters of Ford Madox Ford*, ed. Richard M. Ludwig, 1965, p. 248.

line 18   £200 a year: Roberts, *Portrait*, p. 231.

line 19   letter to Knopf quoted: Payne, *Bibliography*, p. 83.

line 22   resigned pension: *The Times*, 25 August 1920.

line 26ff.   correspondence between Hudson and J. M. Dent: J. M. Dent and Sons' archives, letters dated 8 March 1922, 11 (?) March 1922, 23 June 1922.

page 223, line 18   Virginia Woolf's comment: *Letters of Virginia Woolf*, vol. II, p. 549.

line 22   manuscripts: William Rothenstein, *Men and Memories*, 1978 edn, p. 184 and note 2, p. 222.

line 25   destroying papers: *Men, Books and Birds*, 155; Roberts, *Portrait*, pp. 193, 198; Introduction, *Hudson–Garnett Letters*, p. 7.

line 31   ibid., 113: 'My wife . . . thinks she would like to go to Cornwall for the winter too, so I shall have to arrange that as well.'

line 37ff.   letter to Margaret, Ranee of Sarawak, 3 May (1917), Humanities Research Center, University of Texas at Austin.

page 224, line 4   'though innocent': D. H. Lawrence, *Selected Letters*, ed. Richard Aldington, Heinemann, 1950, 53, 12 October 1917.

line 18   potato: *The Book of a Naturalist*, ch. 26; Hunt, *The Flurried Years*, p. 269.

line 28ff.   *Hudson–Garnett Letters*, 132.

line 36   'I want to use . . .': ibid., 133.

line 41   the writing of *Dead Man's Plack*, Dent, 1920: *Men, Books and Birds*, 138.

page 225, line 16ff.	'Hints to Adder-Seekers', *The Book of a Naturalist*, ch. 2, pp. 19–20.
line 30ff.	ibid., pp. 21–3.
page 226, line 36	turning-point: Sir Julian Huxley, *Memoirs*, vol. I, Allen and Unwin, 1970, p. 85. In *Birdwatching and Bird Behaviour*, Chatto and Windus, 1930, pp. 8–9, Julian Huxley names Hudson and Edmund Selous as 'two of the most indefatigable bird-watchers—as distinct from ornithologists—the world has had in recent times'. Hudson's works are recommended 'as a further introduction to the subject'. For Hudson on Huxley, see *Men, Books and Birds*, 82.
page 227, line 19ff.	*Times Literary Supplement*, 16 November 1922.
line 29	Keith: Roberts, *Portrait*, pp. 214–15, and *Men, Books and Birds*, 103.
line 34	Malays and Dyaks: letter to Margaret, Ranee of Sarawak, dated 'Shortest day of the Year', Humanities Research Center, University of Texas at Austin.
line 35	Cyril Noall, *The Penzance Library*, 1818–1968, Penzance, 1968.
page 228, line 3	books locked up: *Men, Books and Birds*, 169.
line 4	flat: Violet Hunt, *Worthing Tribute*, p. 106, says that Tower House now had 'three flats and basement for a housekeeper', and *Hudson–Garnett Letters*, 110.
line 13	the younger sister: Marcella Knight, later Marcella M. Carver, author of *A Positivist Life. A personal memoir of my father William Knight (1845–1901)*, Brookside Press, 1976.
line 23ff.	Alfred A. Knopf, Preface to *Green Mansions*, New York, 1959 edn.
line 29	meeting with Wilfrid Ewart, author of *Way of Revelation*, Putnam, 1921; Hunt, *Worthing Tribute*, p. 101.
line 33ff.	*Men, Books and Birds*, 125.
page 229, line 11ff.	letter to Linda Gardiner, from 8 Bedford Row, Worthing, 22 July 1920, Manchester Central Library collection. See also *Hudson–Cunninghame Graham Letters*, 5 August 1920. His fellow guest was St John Philby.
line 26	an impressive figure: Charles A. Hall, 'My Acquaintance with Hudson', *Worthing Tribute*, p. 76. For Hudson on Hall, see *Men, Books and Birds*, 122.
line 29	Penzance sitting-room: Roberts, *Portrait*, pp. 219–20.

line 36	Emily Hudson: ibid., pp. 262, 265.
line 42	accident: ibid., p. 218.
page 230, line 9	his own books: ibid., p. 222.
line 13	columbines: letter to Mr Guy Rawlence, December 1920.
line 16	Emily Hudson's death: *Men, Books and Birds*, 154, 155. St Catherine's House record gives her age as 85. According to the 1841 Census return, she was 91 or 92. See note, page 115, line 17.
line 21ff.	*Men, Books and Birds*, 160.
line 30	Emily's fear: *Worthing Tribute*, p. 135.
line 31	'I shall meet her . . .': Roberts, *Portrait*, p. 274.
line 33ff.	Henry King (1592–1669), Bishop of Chichester, 'Exequy on his Wife'.
line 35	Hudson's will, RSPB collection.
page 231, line 6	an evil date: *Men, Books and Birds*, 162.
line 7	'The Return of the Chiff-Chaff', *A Traveller in Little Things*, published September 1921.
line 10	Mary Ellen's death: West, *For a Hudson Biographer*; Roberts, *Portrait*, p. 21.
line 16	discussion on immortality: Charles A. Hall, *Worthing Tribute*, p. 76.
line 21	did not expect to see Tower House again: *Hudson–Garnett Letters*, 151.
line 25	*Hind*: letter from J. M. Dent. 23 June 1922.
line 26	Hudson gave £1,000 to the RSPB education scheme at this time. The residue of his estate, left to the RSPB, totalled nearly £6,000: RSPB records.
line 34	poor young wife: letter to Margaret, Ranee of Sarawak, April 1917, Humanities Research Center, University of Texas at Austin.
line 41ff.	Helen Thomas, 'A Memory of W. H. Hudson', *The Times*, 27 August 1965; *Men, Books and Birds*, 183, postscript.
page 232, line 22	letter to Linda Gardiner, dated 'Wednesday Evening' (16 August 1922), Manchester Central Library collection.
line 26	*Cloud Castle* and other papers, by Edward Thomas, with a Foreword by W. H. Hudson, Duckworth, 1922.
line 34	to die alone: *Men, Books and Birds*, 161.
line 35	final chapter: Roberts, *Portrait*, p. 313; Payne, *Bibliography*, p. 152.
line 37	Exmoor: Roberts, *Portrait*, pp. 314–15.
line 43	housekeeper: ibid., p. 316; Hunt, *Worthing Tribute*, pp. 106–12.

page 233, line 8ff.   Roberts, *Portrait*, p. 317.

Morley Roberts covered Hudson's coffin with heather from Exmoor (Violet Hunt, *Worthing Tribute*, p. 111). He and other friends (*Portrait*, p. 158) drafted the inscription for his grave: 'He loved birds and green places and the wind on the heath, and saw the brightness of the skirts of God.' The last phrase, by the American poet William Cullen Bryant (1794–1878) ends the first essay in *Birds and Man*.

The artist Arnold Forster, of the Eagle's Nest, Zennor, another friend, had a rock on the tor above Zennor carved with the words 'W. H. Hudson often sat here'. A wildlife sanctuary to Hudson's memory was dedicated by Frances, Countess of Warwick on 21 June 1923 at Stone Hall, Easton Park, Essex. The Hyde Park memorial was unveiled on 19 May 1925, and the Tower House plaque on 29 June 1938.

On 4 August 1941 a bronze plaque was unveiled in Buenos Aires, in the presence of the British and United States ambassadors, to mark the centenary of his birth. (*The Times*, 5 August 1941). Lord Davidson and Mrs Marjorie Mackenzie Potter, the owners, presented Hudson's birthplace, with twelve acres of land, to the Province of Buenos Aires in 1956. (*The Times*, 26 and 29 September 1956.) This is now a Museum and Park for Culture and Ecology. The Director of the Museum in recent years has been Hudson's great-niece, Señora Violeta Shinya Hudson, Mary Ellen's granddaughter.

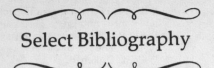

Select Bibliography

See W. H. Hudson. *A Bibliography*, John R. Payne, Dawson, 1977.

First editions of Hudson's books

1885. *The Purple Land that England Lost*, Sampson Low. See below, 1904.
1887. *A Crystal Age*, T. Fisher Unwin.
1888. *Argentine Ornithology*, (with P. L. Sclater), vol. I, R. H. Porter.
1889. *Argentine Ornithology*, vol. II, R. H. Porter. See below, *Birds of La Plata*, 1920.
1892. *The Naturalist in La Plata*, Chapman and Hall.
     Fan, The Story of a Young Girl's Life (under the pseudonym 'Henry Harford'), Chapman and Hall.
1893. *Idle Days in Patagonia*, Chapman and Hall.
     Birds in a Village, Chapman and Hall.
1895. *British Birds*, Longmans Green.
1898. *Birds in London*, Longmans Green.
1900. *Nature in Downland*, Longmans Green.
1901. *Birds and Man*, Longmans Green.
1902. *El Ombu*, Duckworth.
1903. *Hampshire Days*, Longmans Green.
1904. *The Purple Land*, Duckworth.
     Green Mansions: A Romance of the Tropical Forest, Duckworth.
1905. *A Little Boy Lost*, Duckworth.
1908. *The Land's End*, Hutchinson.
1909. *Afoot in England*, Hutchinson.
1910. *A Shepherd's Life: Impressions of the South Wiltshire Downs*, Methuen.
1913. *Adventures among Birds*, Hutchinson.
1918. *Far Away and Long Ago: A History of My Early Life*, Dent.
1919. *Birds in Town and Village*, Dent. *Birds in a Village*, above, 1893, largely rewritten and extended.
     The Book of a Naturalist, Hodder and Stoughton.
1920. *Dead Man's Plack* and *An Old Thorn*, Dent.
     Birds of La Plata, 2 vols. Dent. Hudson's contribution to *Argentine Ornithology*, above, 1888.

1921. *A Traveller in Little Things*, Dent.
1922. *A Hind in Richmond Park*, Dent.

Prefaces by Hudson

To *The Great Deserts and Forests of North America*, Paul Fountain, Longmans Green, 1901.
To *Cloud Castle and Other Papers*, Edward Thomas, Duckworth, 1922.

Pamphlets and monographs

These were mainly on behalf of the (Royal) Society for the Protection of Birds, whose publications were serially numbered.
1891. *Osprey* or *Egrets and Aigrettes*, SPB, 3.
1893. *Feathered Women*, SPB, 10. Reprint of a letter to *The Times*. See Appendix 2.
1893. *Bird-catching*, SPB, 12.
1894. *Lost British Birds*, SPB, 14. This pamphlet, together with notes left by Hudson, was edited by Linda Gardiner and published under the title *Rare, Vanishing and Lost British Birds*, Dent, 1923.
1895. *The Barn Owl*, introduction to a reprint of Charles Waterton's essay, SPB, 19.
Letter to Clergymen, Ministers and Others, SPB, 25.
1897. *Pipits*, SPB, 21.
1898. *The Trade in Birds' Feathers*, SPB, 28.
1904. *A Linnet for Sixpence*, SPB, 50.
1911. *A Thrush that Never Lived*, RSPB, 67.
1914. *On Liberating Caged Birds*, RSPB, 73.
1918. *Ruff and a Linnet*, Humanitarian League.
1921. *A Tired Traveller*, RSPB, 78.
1922. *Seagulls in London*. Privately printed by Clement K. Shorter. Reprint of a letter to the *Observer*, 16 January 1921.

Letters

153 Letters from W. H. Hudson, ed. with an introduction and notes by Edward Garnett, Nonesuch Press, 1923.
Men, Books and Birds. Letters to a Friend. Letters from W. H. Hudson to Morley Roberts, with notes, some letters and an introduction by Morley Roberts, Nash and Grayson, 1925.
W. H. Hudson's Letters to R. B. Cunninghame Graham, ed. with an introduction by Richard Curle, Golden Cockerel Press, 1941.
Letters to Professor Spencer Fullerton Baird, Smithsonian Institution, Washington, 1866–1870. Smithsonian Institution archives. Extracts from these letters, 1866–8, appear in 'W. H. Hudson's Lost Years', by R. Gordon Wasson and Edwin Way Teale, *The Times Literary Supplement*, 5 April 1947.

Select Bibliography

Letters on the Ornithology of Buenos Ayres, ed. David R. Dewar, with a foreword by Herbert F. West. Published by permission of the Zoological Society of London, Cornell University Press, 1951.

William Henry Hudson's Diary Concerning his Voyage from Buenos Aires to Southampton on the 'Ebro', from 1 April 1874 to 3 May 1874. Written to his brother Albert Merriam Hudson. With notes by Dr Jorge Casares of Buenos Aires, Westholm Publications, New Hampshire, Hanover, 1958.

Letters to Mrs George Hubbard, Mrs Edward Phillips, Mr and Mrs Frank E. Lemon and other correspondents, Manchester Central Library collection, RSPB Library collection.

Letters to Miss Linda Gardiner, 1901–1922, Manchester Central Library collection. 184 Letters from Hudson to Margaret Brooke, Ranee of Sarawak, 1912–21, Humanities Research Center, University of Texas at Austin.

Letters to Edward Garnett and other correspondents, Lockwood Memorial Library collection, State University of New York at Buffalo.

Birds of a Feather. Unpublished letters of W. H. Hudson. Edited and introduced by Dennis Shrubsall. Moonraker, 1981.

Biography and Criticism

W. H. Hudson. A Portrait, Morley Roberts, Eveleigh Nash and Grayson, 1924.

William Henry Hudson y su Amor a los Pajaros, Dr Jorge Casares, Establecimiento Gráfico Tomás Palumbo, Buenos Aires, Madrid, 1930.

Semblanza de Hudson, Dr Fernando Pozzo, Instituto de Conferencias del Banco Municipal, Buenos Aires, 1940.

W. H. Hudson. The Vision of Earth, Robert Hamilton, Dent, 1946.

The Worthing Cavalcade. William Henry Hudson. A Tribute by Various Writers, ed. by Samuel J. Looker. Worthing Art Development Scheme, Worthing, Sussex, 1947.

El Mundo Maravilloso de Guillermo Enrique Hudson, Ezequiel Martinez Estrada, Fonda de Cultura Economica, Mexico, Buenos Aires, 1951.

From Pampas to Hedgerows and Downs. A Study of W. H. Hudson, Richard E. Haymaker, New York, Bookman Associates, 1954.

For a Hudson Biographer, Herbert Faulkner West, Westholm Publications, Hanover, New Hampshire, 1958.

Las Huellas de Guillermo Enrique Hudson, Masao Tsuda, Editora e Impresora, Buenos Aires, 1963.

Vida y Obra de W. H. Hudson, Alicia Jurado, Argentina Fondo Naçional de las Artes, Coleccion Ensayos, Buenos Aires, 1971.

W. H. Hudson, Writer and Naturalist, Dennis Shrubsall, Compton Press, 1978.

Edward Thomas's Letters to W. H. Hudson, ed. James Guthrie, *The London Mercury*, August 1920.

Viscount Grey of Fallodon, 'An appreciation of W. H. Hudson', Foreword to *Dead Man's Plack, An Old Thorn and Miscellanea*, Dent, Collected Edition, 1923.

306

Eric Fitch Daglish, Foreword, *Nature In Downland*, Dent, 1932, Open-Air Library edition.

Ernest Rhys, Introduction, *A Shepherd's Life*, Dent, 1936, Everyman edition.

John Galsworthy, Foreword, *Far Away and Long Ago*, Dent, 1939, Everyman edition.

David Garnett, Introduction, *The Purple Land*, Dent, 1951.

'W. H. Hudson', Alan Porter, *Spectator Literary Supplement*, 5 April 1924.

Coulson Kernahan, 'W. H. Hudson as I knew him', *The Nature Lover*, May 1934.

Philip G. Brown, 'A Hampshire Village' (Silchester), *The Nature Lover*, June 1935.

Louis J. Halle, 'Hudson's Pampas Today', *Audubon Magazine*, July–August 1948.

'On Re-reading *Green Mansions*', *The Land*, Winter, 1947–8. Both reprinted in *Storm Petrel and the Owl of Athena*, Louis J. Halle, Princeton University Press and Oxford University Press, 1970.

Oliver Edwards, 'A Traveller in Big Things Also', *The Times*, 11 October 1956.

G. Bernard Berry, 'When Hudson Cycled Up The High Street', *The Times*, 26 November 1963. 'Hudson's Secret Village Among The Downs,' *ibid.*, 4 December 1965. 'In Search of W. H. Hudson's Old Thorn Tree', *ibid.*, 28 May 1966. 'W. H. Hudson's Wiltshire', *Country Life*, 2 March 1967.

Helen Thomas, 'A Memory of W. H. Hudson', *The Times*, 27 August 1965.

Dennis Shrubsall, 'Round and about Silchester with W. H. Hudson', *Hampshire: The County Magazine*, January 1980.

J. H. B. Peel, 'Village come true', *Daily Telegraph*, 3 November 1980.

Books containing references to W. H. Hudson

A Literary Pilgrim in England, Edward Thomas, Methuen, 1917.

Impromptus, Arnold, 1923. *Good Morning and Good Night*, Constable, 1934, Margaret Brooke, Ranee of Sarawak.

The Flurried Years, Violet Hunt, Hurst and Blackett, 1926.

Men and Memories 1900–1922, William Rothenstein, Faber and Faber, 1932.

Grey of Fallodon. The Life of Sir Edward Grey, Afterwards Viscount Grey of Fallodon. G. M. Trevelyan, Longmans Green, 1937.

Don Roberto. The Life and Works of R. B. Cunninghame Graham, 1852–1936, A. F. Tschiffely, Heinemann, 1937.

Return to Yesterday. Gollancz, 1932. *Mightier Than The Sword*, Allen and Unwin, 1938, Ford Madox Ford.

Pleasures and Speculations. 'Naturalists', Walter de la Mare, Faber and Faber, 1940.

The Last Pre-Raphaelite. A Record of the Life and Writings of Ford Madox Ford, Douglas Goldring, MacDonald, 1948.

The Golden Echo, David Garnett, Chatto and Windus, 1953.
Summer's Lease, John Rothenstein, Hamish Hamilton, 1965.
Gilbert White And His Selborne, Anthony Rye, Kimber, 1970.
Springtime in Britain, Edwin Way Teale, Cassell, 1971.
Letters from Edward Thomas to Gordon Bottomley, ed. R. George Thomas, Oxford, 1968.
Stand Fast, The Holy Ghost. An Autobiography, Rupert Grayson, Tom Stacey, 1973. Rupert Grayson was a director of the firm who published Roberts's *Portrait* and *Men, Books and Birds*.
The Nature Novel from Hardy to Lawrence, John Alcorn, Macmillan, 1977.
George Gissing. A Biography, Michael Collie, Dawson, 1977.
In Patagonia, Bruce Chatwin, Cape, 1977.
The Old Patagonian Express, Paul Theroux, Hamish Hamilton, 1979.
Talks with Thomas Hardy at Max Gate, 1920–1922, Vere H. Collins, Duckworth, 1928, 1978.
Great Friends, David Garnett, Macmillan, 1979.
Edward Garnett: A Life in Literature, George Jefferson, Cape, 1982.

Other sources

Annual Reports of the Smithsonian Institution of Washington, 1866–9.
Proceedings of the Zoological Society of London, 1869–76.
Charles Darwin, *Journal of Researches into the Geology and Natural History of the Various Countries visited by HMS 'Beagle'*, Henry Colburn, 1839.
The Origin of Species by Means of Natural Selection, or the Preservation of Favoured Races in the Struggle for Life, John Murray, 1859.
Imperial Calendars, 1834–50, Public Record Office.
Census Returns, 1841–1881, Public Record Office.
Registers of Births, Marriages and Deaths, General Registry.
Kelly's Directory, 1871–84.
London Weather, J. H. Brazell, HMSO.
The Naturalist In Britain, David Elliston Allen, Allen Lane, 1976.
Nature In Trust. The History of Nature Conservation in Britain, John Sheail, Blackie, 1976.

Index

309

MORE OXFORD PAPERBACKS

Afoot in England

W. H. Hudson

Whenever he could W. H. Hudson escaped from London to ramble through his beloved southern counties. In *Afoot in England* he describes their landscape and wildlife with an observant and affectionate eye.

'Hudson's strengths are clearly apparent: a marvellously readable and unforced style, a piercing clarity of perception, and a wonderful way with an anecdote, whether animal or human behaviour. The best moments of these essays are gloriously fresh.' *The Times*

Hampshire Days

W. H. Hudson

First published in 1903, this is a personal celebration of
the delights of Hampshire – its abundant wildlife,
mysterious barrows, impressive New Forest, and its
human 'characters'. Hudson shares with Gilbert White
the gift of making his observations in a vividly readable
style. The result is a sensuous kaleidoscope of the colours,
scents, and songs of the English countryside.

'A classic volume of natural history written in 1903;
whether noting the behaviour of a baby cuckoo in a
robin's nest or commenting on the mutual mistrust of
dark-eyed and fair country people, Hudson's observations of a nearly vanished world are superb.' *Sunday
Times*

The Life of the Fields

Richard Jefferies

Richard Jefferies — naturalist, ardent conservationist, philosopher, novelist, and reporter — wrote these essays, first published together in 1884, as articles for newspapers and magazines. They reveal the variety and depth of his interests, ranging from tips on poaching fish and advice on landscape painting, to a scathing description of Paris — 'stiff, wearisome, and feeble . . . the plainest city in Europe'. He writes not only of the countryside in all seasons — the south coast in January, March on the Sussex Downs, summer in Wiltshire — but also describes a summer day in Trafalgar Square: 'The sunlight and the winds enter London, and the life of the fields is there too, if you will but see it.'